Anti-Discriminatory Practice in Counselling and Psychotherapy

second edition

Professional Skills for Counsellors

The *Professional Skills for Counsellors* series, edited by Colin Feltham, covers the practical, technical and professional skills and knowledge which trainee and practising counsellors need to improve their competence in key areas of therapeutic practice.

Titles in the series include:

Counselling by Telephone
Maxine Rosenfield

Time-Limited Counselling
Colin Feltham

Personal and Professional Development for Counsellors
Paul Wilkins

Client Assessment
edited by Stephen Palmer and Gladeana McMahon

Counselling Difficult Clients
Kingsley Norton and Gill McGauley

Learning and Writing in Counselling
Mhairi MacMillan and Dot Clark

Long-Term Counselling
Geraldine Shipton and Eileen Smith

Referral and Termination Issues for Counsellors
Anne Leigh

Counselling and Psychotherapy in Private Practice
Roger Thistle

The Management of Counselling and Psychotherapy Agencies
Colin Lago and Duncan Kitchin

Group Counselling
Keith Tudor

Understanding the Counselling Relationship
edited by Colin Feltham

Practitioner Research in Counselling
John McLeod

Anti-discriminatory Counselling Practice
edited by Colin Lago and Barbara Smith

Counselling Through the Life-Course
Léonie Sugarman

Contracts in Counselling & Psychotherapy, second edition
edited by Charlotte Sills

Counselling, Psychotherapy and the Law, second edition
Peter Jenkins

Medical and Psychiatric Issues for Counsellors, second edition
Brian Daines, Linda Gask and Amanda Howe

Anti-Discriminatory Practice in Counselling and Psychotherapy

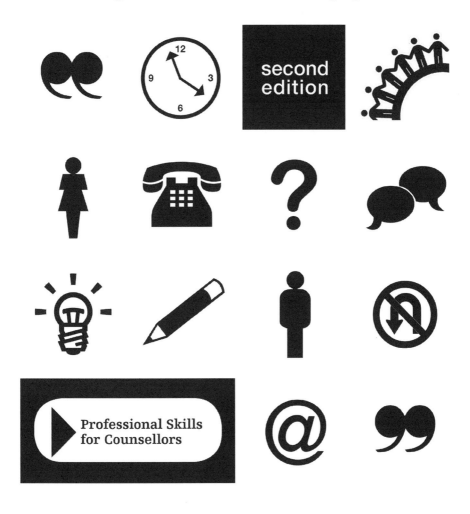

second edition

Professional Skills for Counsellors

Edited by **Colin Lago & Barbara Smith**

SAGE

os Angeles | London | New Delhi
Singapore | Washington DC

First edition published 2003
Reprinted 2004, 2006, 2007
This second edition published 2010

SAGE Publications Ltd
1 Oliver's Yard
55 City Road
London EC1Y 1SP

SAGE Publications Inc.
2455 Teller Road
Thousand Oaks, California 91320

SAGE Publications India Pvt Ltd
B 1/I 1 Mohan Cooperative Industrial Area
Mathura Road
New Delhi 110 044

SAGE Publications Asia-Pacific Pte Ltd
33 Pekin Street #02-01
Far East Square
Singapore 048763

Library of Congress Control Number: 2010925918

British Library Cataloguing in Publication data

A catalogue record for this book is available from the British Library

ISBN 978-1-84860-768-2
ISBN 978-1-84860-769-9 (pbk)

Typeset by C&M Digitals (P) Ltd., Chennai, India
Printed and bound in Great Britain by TJ International Ltd, Padstow, Cornwall
Printed on paper from sustainable resources

This book is dedicated to four little boys, Colin's grandsons
Luke and George and Barbara's grandsons Joel and Luc

Contents

List of Contributors

Aaron Balick is the director of the MA in Psychoanalytic Studies at the Centre for Psychoanalytic Studies at the University of Essex and a UKCP registered psychotherapist working in London. He has a special interest in relational psychoanalysis and psychotherapy and is a founding and executive member of The Relational School, UK. In addition to his academic and clinical work, Aaron is a media spokesperson for the UKCP and a mental health writer, consultant and media contributor for the BBC.

Saira Bains is a Director of Psychological Services for the NHS in South London. She is a Chartered Psychologist (BPS) and a UKCP Registered Integrative Psychotherapist. She also does consultancy work for organisations, training and is a supervisor. Her doctoral research reflected her passionate interest in narrative, autoethnography and issues connected to racism and its impact upon the self, families and communities. She is currently working on a book of narrative accounts of racist trauma.

Camila Batmanghelidjh is an award-winning social entrepreneur and psychotherapist who works with marginalised children. She is the founder of two British children's charities, Kids Company and The Place 2 Be. She is currently director of Kids Company, which supports over 13,500 children and advocates the rights of vulnerable children. She has pioneered innovative psychotherapy with 'hard to reach' children, successfully widening the sphere of counselling by delivering it at street level. She speaks regularly at conferences and has contributed to numerous publications, her book *Shattered Lives* was shorted listed for the Young Minds Book Award 2006.

Jude Boyles is a human rights counsellor who has been counselling refugees for the last ten years. Jude has practised as a counsellor for 17 years, the first 11 of which were for a statutory mental health crisis service in West Yorkshire. In 2003 Jude established the first Medical Foundation centre outside London and has managed the Medical Foundation for the Care of Victims of Torture North West centre for the last seven years. Prior to training as a counsellor, Jude worked in feminist organisations working around male violence against women. Jude remains active in a number of feminist campaigns against male violence. Jude is a national trainer around male violence against women and for the Medical Foundation.

Stephane Duckett obtained his PhD in clinical psychology in 1989 from Temple University. For the past eight years he has worked as part of the Psychology Service for Older Adults at the Royal Free Hospital in London (UK). He has had over 60 publications primarily in relation to his work with older adults in the areas of age discrimination and psychology more broadly.

Suzy Henry initially trained in fine art, before working in a bookshop for many years. For the past five years, she has worked for a mental health team in Sheffield as a support worker; supporting people in 'crisis' within their own homes. Suzy is at the beginning of her counselling career; she is a trainee counsellor in Sheffield where she is studying a BSc in counselling and psychotherapy at Temenos, which is a person-centred education and training facility. Her interests are in the dynamics of power in the therapeutic relationship and in the affects of trauma and abuses of power. Suzy has grown up with a facial disfigurement.

Anne Kearney is a freelance trainer, supervisor, counsellor and author working in Manchester having taught adults for many years. Her writing includes *Counselling, Class & Politics – Undeclared Influences in Therapy* (PCCS Books, 1996). Anne's interests are in politics and working with diversity. She is a founder member of The Counselling Collective.

Colin Lago was Director of the Counselling Service at the University of Sheffield from 1987 to 2003. He now works as an independent counsellor, trainer, supervisor and consultant. Trained initially as an engineer, Colin went on to become a full-time youth worker in London and then a teacher in Jamaica. He is a Fellow of BACP, an accredited counsellor and trainer. Deeply committed to 'transcultural concerns' he has had articles, videos and books published on the subject. He was recently awarded a DLitt in acknowledgement of his work within the field of Transcultural Therapy.

Roy Moodley is Associate Professor of Counseling Psychology at the Ontario Institute for Studies in Education, University of Toronto, Canada. He is also the Director of the Centre for Diversity in Counselling and Psychotherapy. His research interests include critical multicultural counselling/psychotherapy, race and culture in psychotherapy, traditional healing, culture and resilience, and gender and identity, with particular reference to masculinity. His recent publications include: *Carl Rogers Counsels a Black Client: Race and Culture in Person-Centred Counselling* (PCCS Books, 2004), *Integrating Traditional Healing Practices into Counseling and Psychotherapy* (Sage, 2005), and *Race, Culture and Psychotherapy* (Routledge, 2006).

Lee Murphy is a Master's candidate in the department of Adult Education and Counselling Psychology at OISE, University of Toronto, having completed her practical training in Family Practice Social Work at Women's College Hospital. She holds a BSc in Biological Sciences from University of Calgary (BEd OISE/UT) and has worked in publishing at the Canadian National Research Council in Ottawa. She currently teaches in Toronto, where she lives with her family.

Zenobia Nadirshaw is Head of Learning Disability Psychology Services at NHS Kensington & Chelsea and a Consultant Clinical Psychologist. She has worked in the NHS for 35 years as a clinician, service manager, consultant, supervisor and trainer. She has been active in the profession and practice of psychology involving diversity and equality issues. She has won several awards over the years from the British Medical Association and the British Psychological Society. Zenobia also sits on several

Gillian Proctor is a Clinical Psychologist working for Bradford and Airedale Community Health Services. She is an honorary research fellow at the University of Bradford and an honorary senior lecturer at the University of Leeds. She is the course lead of the MSc in person-centred psychotherapy at Temenos, Sheffield. Her particular interests are in ethics, politics and power. She is the author of *The Dynamics of Power in Psychotherapy and Counselling* (PCCS Books, 2002). She is co-editor of *Encountering Feminism: The Intersections of Feminism and the Person-Centred Approach* (PCCS Books, 2004) and *Politicising the Person-Centred Approach: An Agenda for Social Change* (PCCS Books, 2006). She is cynical about the benefits of psychotherapy for society and is more interested in self-help and encounter groups.

Gail Simon trained at the Kensington Consultation Centre in the early 1990s and has since undertaken a Professional Doctorate in Systemic Practice. She runs reflexive writing courses for counsellors and psychotherapists in London, Yorkshire and Manchester as a form of supervision or to encourage publication and teaches research on the post-qualification MSc Relationship Therapy at the Relate Institute and the systemic modules on their qualifying course, MA Relationship Therapy. She also facilitates monthly supervision groups in Manchester and London and supervises at Bradford Relate. The Pink Practice, which was 20 years old in 2010, is her home base for therapy work.

Barbara Smith is a UKCP registered and BACP accredited psychotherapist working as a Lecturer in Counselling in Liverpool. She is also an independent therapist specialising in Transactional Analysis with adults and children in individual and group therapy. She has a strong research interest in anti-oppression and cross-cultural counselling. She recently spent two years in the Maldives Islands designing and delivering a counsellor training, and her doctoral research relates to her international work. She works extensively with survivors of abuse and is a supervisor and trainer for counselling with children and adults. She has published in the areas of diversity, children's esteem and adventure therapy.

Brendan Stone is an academic based in the School of English at the University of Sheffield. His research and teaching interests centre on the relationship between narrative and human identity, with a specific focus on first-person narratives of distress and trauma. In both his research and teaching, he works across various disciplines including Medicine, Social Work, Psychology and Occupational Therapy. He is increasingly involved in working directly with users of mental health services. As a long-term mental health service user himself, he has a strong commitment to the rights and empowerment of individuals living with mental distress, and is committed to promoting service user-led research. He is a Senior

Fellow of the Institute of Mental Health, and a Service-User Governor to the Sheffield Health and Social Care Foundation Trust.

William West is a Reader in Counselling Studies at the University of Manchester in Britain where he is Director of the Counselling Studies Programme and where he delights in supervising doctoral students. He is a Fellow and accredited practitioner member of the British Association for Counselling and Psychotherapy. William's key areas of research and publication include counselling and spirituality, culture, traditional healing, supervision and qualitative research methods.

Foreword to the Second Edition
Mick Cooper

Within the world of counselling and counselling training, anti-discriminatory practice can sometimes be seen as an adjunct to the 'real' therapeutic work. We communicate our empathy, make our interpretations, learn about cognitive processes, and only after that, start to reflect on such issues as class, ethnicity or gender, and how they might impact upon our client's lives, the therapeutic relationship and our own being.

If the essence of counselling, however, is to help our clients actualise their potential, and if we strive to do this, most fundamentally, through a deep acceptance of them in all their 'otherness', then anti-discriminatory practice needs to be central to all our training and therapeutic work. For our clients, as well as for ourselves, aspects of our being like our sexuality, ethnicity and gender are all integral to who we are. And in a world in which there is so much hostility, judgement and discrimination towards people when these aspects take particular forms, we are unlikely to be able to help them (or ourselves) without addressing, and overcoming, issues and challenges in these areas. This is not just at the internal level. Our clients inhabit a real world with real discrimination and real barriers towards growth, and working with them to meet these external obstacles may need to be an important part of our work.

More than that, if we want our clients to feel proud of themselves, to prosper and to feel great about who they are, then we need to find ways of moving beyond anti-discriminatory practice to help them positively value and celebrate their difference. As counsellors, it is not enough for us to be able to tolerate otherness: whether a client's working-class background or their lesbian identity. We need to have the capacity to join with them in positively prizing and finding the strength and beauty in these elements of their being.

One of the themes that runs throughout this book is that this is by no means easy. It is one thing to talk about practising in anti-discriminatory ways and celebrating difference; quite another to actually do it. We are all deeply schooled in a myriad of prejudices, and in tolerating discrimination, from an early age. Hence, to challenge it, and not just in ourselves but in the society we live in, takes time, commitment and effort. More than that, as counsellors, we are challenged to find a way of owning our own prejudices without falling into self-blame, apathy or victimhood. In this respect, as a profession, we may be at the very cutting edge of developing constructive anti-discriminatory practices.

It is sometimes argued that we do not need to concern ourselves with practising in specifically anti-discriminatory ways, or with learning about different identities and forms of oppression, because we should treat each client as an 'individual'. Research, however, does not support this position. Again and again, studies of marginalised groups show that they do want therapists to know about the specific challenges and issues that they face and, more than that, they do not want to be the ones who have to school them in this.

In this brief foreword, I have tried to suggest that counselling and anti-discriminatory practice go hand-in-hand. To practice in a way that is not anti-discriminatory can hardly be called counselling (and, indeed, research shows that prejudice in the counselling relationship, whether intentional or unintentional, can be deeply damaging); and to engage with another in a way that supports them against prejudice and discrimination, in itself, may be highly therapeutic. In this respect, this second edition of *Anti-Discriminatory Practice in Counselling and Psychotherapy* demands a place on every counsellor's bookshelf. Through examining discrimination in such areas as sexuality, gender, race and class, and exploring how counsellors can face these challenges in constructive and effective ways, a major contribution is made to the advancement of counselling practice. And this is not just in work with clients who face specific forms of discrimination in these areas. As the editors make clear, this book is about articulating and developing a value base: one which strives to respect and prize otherness and difference; and, in as much as each one of our clients and every one of us is a multifaceted composite of identities, differences and othernesses, it contributes to the development of a philosophy of practice that is relevant to us all.

Foreword to the First Edition
Natalie Rogers

This book is a bold and much needed undertaking. It is timely, highly organized, extremely informative and practical, with many useful suggestions. Colin Lago and Barbara Smith have done the counselling and psychotherapy profession a great favour by gathering diverse authors to educate and stimulate those of us who are therapists. They encourage us to dig deep into our own blinkered spots of discriminatory practices.

I am honoured in being asked to write this foreword. Honoured, because a book on anti-discriminatory counselling practice is a pioneering contribution, asking therapists to examine their own beliefs and cultural stereotypes as they face their clients. Colin Lago and I met as participants of an intensive person-centred weekend where we were all exploring our personal issues in relation to diversity. We discovered it is not always easy to face one's own racist, sexist, or discriminatory behaviour. However, it is necessary and enlightening and brings us closer to the oneness of humanity.

I also feel humbled in being asked to write this piece because I am a white, upper-middle-class, heterosexual, elder American retired from my psychotherapy practice. There is a part of me that says a therapist who has experienced extreme discrimination should be writing this, perhaps a black, lesbian, disabled person. However, I have experienced my own second-class citizenship as a woman, which turned me into an active feminist aged 40. Also, my longing for social justice in a world full of discriminatory practices is deep. I believe, as the editors and authors of these chapters believe, that we must look into our personal attitudes and cultural history to become counsellors for those who have experienced discrimination. Although our intentions may be good, there is a great deal we need to learn from those who have led a life of oppression and discrimination. It is this openness to the experiences of others that I wish to address.

I proudly carry the philosophical legacy of my father, Carl Rogers, who was one of the founders of humanistic psychology and the author of *Client-Centered Therapy and the Person-Centered Approach*. It is his extensive research into the core conditions that foster the client's growth that is relevant here. The conditions of empathic listening, congruence and unconditional positive regard are key to the client–counsellor relationship. The client-centered approach emphasizes understanding the world as the client experiences it. As we create a safe, supportive, accepting climate and listen deeply to the experiences of our clients, they peel away their own layers of defence and self-doubt. By listening empathically to their rage and pain at experiences of exclusion, abuse, and discrimination and the deep scars these leave in their self-esteem, we enable them to go through the dark tunnel of despair into the light of self-care, self-esteem and personal empowerment.

Entering into the frame of reference of the client sounds easy. It is not. It means leaving aside our own need to be an authority figure or have the answers. It is also true that as we put aside our ego needs to understand the felt experience of the client, we open ourselves to our own personal change; something not all therapists are eager to do. One way to learn about discrimination and oppression is to listen in depth, without judgement to our clients, friends and colleagues. This, along with educating ourselves through literature, art, films, friends, continuing professional development and examining our internalised cultural beliefs, will help us to become better therapists.

It will also help us to review the ways in which we have felt personally discriminated against when we were clients. How well I remember the white male therapist who assumed I should stay in my role as supporter of my husband's work rather than step out into the professional world myself. In contrast, a person-centred, white, male therapist listened patiently to me as I explored my sense of having 'lost myself' in my marriage. At that time I no longer knew who I was, nor did I have any self-esteem. I was seriously considering ending my life. However, by being deeply heard (which is so healing in and of itself) and by being considered a person of worth by my therapist as well as reading some early feminist literature, I realized that as a female I had a 'right to be me'. Now as a teacher of therapists and a group facilitator, I am keenly aware of women in that same predicament of living a life determined by the culture of the times. I am able to hear their anger and internalized self-deprecation and help them learn about the society that has insisted they hide their strength and power.

I bring forth my own example to point out that as therapists we can learn by sharing our experiences of discrimination when we were clients. Telling our personal stories of feeling misunderstood, or oppressed, or abused as a client will help us learn from each other, regardless of race, age, religion, gender or sexual orientation. Unlike many books that discuss the particular symptoms and problems of the client, these authors put the emphasis where it belongs, on the beliefs, values, and practices of the therapist.

This second edition not only incorporates four completely new chapters on arenas of concern not considered in the first edition but also introduces seven new writers who have contributed new ideas on the themes featured in the first edition. It is clear that these new contributions are written with great commitment to the overall thrust and stance of this book – that of anti-discriminatory practice in counselling and psychotherapy.

This pioneering book insists that the training of counsellors and psychotherapists include their own self-analysis in the world of both subtle and not-so-subtle discriminatory practices. It challenges us to discover how we are racist, ageist, and sexist, homophobic or insensitive to those who are disabled or have religious beliefs other than our own. Yet, as a reader I never felt blamed, put-down or ignorant. Somehow these authors have written about very emotionally loaded subjects without putting the reader in a defensive stance. I found each chapter an invitation to open new doors to my mind and spirit. The final chapters give us concepts and training ideas to promote self-awareness and ways of making a difference to create a more just society.

Natalie Rogers PhD., author of: *Emerging Woman: A Decade of Midlife Transitions*, and *The Creative Connection: Expressive Art as Healing*.

The basis of this text appeared in the first edition and has been updated for this second edition.

Acknowledgements

This book came into being at a special moment involving two synchronous, coincidental events. First, the series editor, Colin Feltham, had proposed and discussed such a book to me over a sandwich lunch. Upon my return to the office that day I was asked to telephone a 'Barbara Smith from Liverpool' who had rung while I was out. Barbara had called to say she had enjoyed reading the book I had written with Joyce Thompson on *Race, Culture and Counselling* and that she thought another one needed doing on anti-discrimination and counselling. I explained that I had just that lunchtime been discussing such an idea and that we should talk further. My first and personal acknowledgement then is both to Colin Feltham who had the idea and to Barbara, the co-editor of this volume, who also had the idea! We are indebted to all the chapter writers for their contributions and commitment to the overall mission of this book. Indeed, we have to thank them also for forbearance during a period when editing work on the book had to take a back seat as both of us were simultaneously caring for our very sick mothers who passed away last summer. This book therefore is also dedicated to them. An important thank you to my family – Gill, Becky and James – who continue to tolerate a preoccupied dad, and to all colleagues and friends who have inspired and supported me in the aspirations towards social justice embedded in this book.

Update to this second edition: Since the publication of the first edition I have taken early retirement from the University of Sheffield but have continued to work as an independent practitioner, offering therapy, supervision and training. I continue to enjoy the wonderful opportunities I am given to meet fellow travellers on this journey towards social justice and anti-discriminatory practice. This new text is dedicated to my grandson, Luke.

Colin Lago, December 2009

Thanks to Colin Lago who, without even having met me, trusted me to take on this project with him. It has been an honour to work with someone who believes so deeply in social justice. I would like to acknowledge the wonderful support of my friends and colleagues Alison, Brian, Helen, Jane, Karen and Mary. Barbara Webster for her kindness and nurturing. Kaye Richards has been an inspiration and her enthusiasm for the book has been tireless. Thanks to Andrea Cropper for teaching me over many years about the nature of oppression and its impact on our world. To Ronnie Murphy for his invaluable perspective on children's rights. To my students who so bravely and openly discuss these issues in ways which help us all to grow and to my clients who teach me so much about surviving oppression. A special thanks to my children Wendy and Gary for their love and patience. And to you, reader, for caring enough to pick up this book.

Update to this second edition: For two years after the publication of the first edition of this book, I was teaching and researching in the Maldives Islands. I would like to acknowledge my friends and colleagues in the Islands for their wisdom and support, especially Aminath Ismail and Al Rasheed. In particular I would like to acknowledge my Maldivian students for their commitment to their counselling training and their courageous work in responding to the needs of their country after the tsunami.

This book is dedicated to my grandsons Joel and Luc who bring joy into my life.

Barbara Smith, December 2009

Ethical Practice and Best Practice

Colin Lago and Barbara Smith

> Counselling and psychotherapy have often been criticized for focusing on the psychology of the individual and on the internal life of the client while ignoring the impact of the social, economic and cultural environment in which people live. (Feltham and Horton, 2000: 24)

Over recent years there has been a critically growing concern that the counselling and psychotherapy profession has been broadly dominated by middle-class values and has been accessed mostly by those from privileged groups in society. People from marginalized groups (for example, people with physical or learning disabilities, black people, unwaged people, etc.) are less likely to have had access to, been able to afford, or been referred to therapeutic services. Notwithstanding the above trends in the use of available services, the British Association for Counselling and Psychotherapy (BACP) has increasingly moved towards the adoption of counsellor accreditation and ethical criteria that are broadly socially inclusive and anti-discriminatory in intention, requiring members to have considered and sought training in this complex arena.

We come from the perspective that anti-oppressive/anti-discriminatory practice is both ethical practice and best practice (Thompson, 1993; Smith, 1999). We have used two different umbrella terms: 'anti-discriminatory' and 'anti-oppressive' practice. Burke and Dalrymple (1996) draw the general distinction between these two terms as that of acknowledging the legal underpinning of anti-discrimination, supported by a range of government acts, laws, policies and practices, and the humane concerns embodied in anti-oppressive practice. Thompson describes the link between discrimination (the unequal distribution of power, rights and resources) and oppression (the experience of hardship and injustice): 'One of the main outcomes of discrimination is oppression' (1998: 78).

This book, then, hails from a deeply held value base: that of seeking to explore and challenge oppressive and discriminatory practices in (and outside of) the field of therapy, and to advocate theories and modes of therapeutic and political interaction which respect the autonomy, capacities and the social position of the client.

That stated, we want to acknowledge the complexity and challenge that faces the professional field and the individual practitioner who takes up this often painful, confusing and isolating quest. Ironically, the challenge here is for the counsellor to change, rather than the client, and our invitation to readers is to dare to really feel the consequences of assuming this deeply philosophic stance in their personal and professional transactions with others. Taking on the ideas contained within this book will inevitably cause a shift in one's comfort zones, the journey being one of moving from a position of safety to the unknown, where there are many more questions than answers, more uncertainties than certainties, and possibly more critics than supporters.

In an absorbing article on the values of independent thinking and radicalism, Christopher Hitchens quotes his grandmother who had given him a bible in which she had written her favourite texts, one being 'Thou shalt not follow a multitude to do evil' (Hitchens, 2001). Independent thinking is a courageous stance needed for this journey. It is easy to become tired, demoralized and de-motivated, resorting to received modes of thinking and practice. A return to the comfortable old ways! Experience has taught us, however, that meeting these challenges brings rewards in terms of our relationships with other people, including our clients and students, and indeed with ourselves.

Historical learnings from a sister profession

The psychotherapeutic field is somewhat advantaged here in that the social work profession has for a long time been concerned with anti-discriminatory (ADP) and anti-oppressive (AOP) practice. We may therefore learn from these developments and indeed errors that have been tested, researched, taught and criticized whilst also recognizing the important differences between the two professions.

Thompson (1993) traces some of the historical roots underlying this rationale for social work. The 1960s were a significant period, he argues, in a number of ways. First, feminist thought made leaps forward, gaining recognition as a 'liberation movement'. Issues of equal rights and equality of opportunity became firmly established on the political agenda. Also, during the 1960s, issues surrounding the oppression of 'ethnic minorities' and racial discrimination achieved more prominence politically, socially and in the mass media.

Thompson also notes the general popular tendency towards the raising of consciousness inspired by both the drug culture and political radicalism. The late 1960s saw the emergence of the student protest movement, a time, he notes, 'of idealism and anti-establishment challenge of the status quo' (1993: 3).

Within the field of mental health and illness, writers such as Thomas Szasz (1970) and R.D. Laing (1965, 1967) radically challenged the contemporary views of the time, forever influencing subsequent thought and practice in this field of human distress.

Formerly dominated by a psychoanalytic view, social work came under the newer influence of sociology, with its emphasis on social processes and institutions rather than the previous, tighter, individualized focus upon the person. A series of legislative developments by government supported these general tendencies of the time, including the Race Relations Acts (1965, 1968, 1976), the Equal Pay Act (1970) and the Sex Discrimination Act (1975).

The broader field of therapeutic endeavour (counselling, psychotherapy, clinical psychology) has similarly and inevitably been influenced by the social trends, events, debates, academic discourses and government legislation in recent decades, though given its powerful underlying value base, geared towards the assistance of the individual (predominantly), the major focus of much training and professional practice has remained within the individualized, psychologized perspectives of personal change and transformation. Despite this, there has been a wide range of published voices within the field urging therapists to become familiar with the differing arenas of discrimination and oppression in society, drawing therapists' attention to the socially, culturally and politically structured nature of human beings' existence (see D'Ardenne and Mahtani, 1989; Eleftheriadou, 1994; Lago and Thompson, 1989, 1996, 1997; and Pedersen et al., 1981 on matters of race and culture; Chaplin, 1989 on counselling and gender; Corker, 1994; Makin, 1995 and Segal, 1997 on disability issues; Davies and Neal, 1996 on gay and lesbian issues; Carolin, 1995 on working with children; Craig, 1998 on attitudes to ageing; Kearney, 1996 and Bromley, 1994 on class; and Thorne, 1998 on spirituality).

Each of these social arenas has distinct characteristics and multiple discourses, in addition to their similarities and interconnections. This will become clearer as the following chapters are examined. Any simple attempt, therefore, to assemble these various facets into an apparently over-arching homogenous system of AOP and ADP in therapy will be doomed from the start (Wilson and Beresford, 2000). It seems to us that, for many therapists, the issues that they develop a 'passion' for and sensitivity to often reflect their own previous histories and experiences. It is helpful to broaden this out, however, to develop this knowledge-base and sensitivity to the many areas of social life in which oppression occurs. This is a major challenge, particularly as this knowledge itself is specifically determined by the biases of background, training, readings and experiences, both personal and professional.

The client and the therapist in the context of 'society'

> Civilization as we know it is based on the violation and domination of subordinates by elites. Violation, domination and hegemony are common to all oppression. All oppression is heinous, dehumanizing and confusing. (Burstow, 1992: 63)

A central tenet of this book is that the individual and the society within which they are raised are inextricably intertwined. The power of the 'social context' to shape a person's sense of identity, esteem, values, beliefs, behaviours and perceptions is enormous, and some would argue total, as in the South African proverb 'I am because we are'. How and where we are raised, what stories and experiences we are exposed to – all are ingredients of the interconnectedness between the growing child, the immediate carers (most frequently the family) and key agents of socialization such as education, religion, health, politics, law and communicated messages embodied in the media. All have an (often unconscious) influence on our views of ourselves, of others and of the world. At the Institute for the Healing of Racism, there is a view (and one to which we subscribe) that discrimination and oppression damage *everyone*. We damage our boy children by teaching them that they are superior to girl children; we damage our white children by teaching them, however unintentionally and subtly, that they are superior to black children. The confusion and pathology which follows really belongs to the *oppressor,* but is projected onto others. Nelson Mandela suggests 'The oppressed and the oppressor alike are robbed of their humanity'. The healing of this begins with awareness.

Given the above, we recommend an examination of the impact of *ideology*, *hegemony* and *discourse,* and a context of how they operate within society and upon individuals.

Ideology

Thompson defines ideology as 'a set of ideas which are associated with a particular set of social arrangements' (1993: 24). A review of the concept will reveal that, despite its relative youth as a concept, the analysis and definitions of ideology itself are a cauldron of competing ideas and hypotheses (McLellan, 1995: 2).

Continuing his appraisal of the term, Thompson says: 'the ideas base safeguards the power base. In fact this is what characterises ideology: the power of ideas, operating in the interest of power relations' (1993: 24). Hall notes: 'ideology helps to sustain social order because it is part and parcel of the power relations in society – it influences how power works and how conflict is expressed and managed' (1986: 6).

Both Althusser (1971) and Berger (1996) have noted the process of internalization, of the taking in, by people, of the dominant ideologies so that these ideologies become internalized and believed and the relationship between that which has been internalized and the external source(s) from which it emanated may often remain unknown and concealed. We are all therefore subject to the influences of many ideologies to the extent we fully believe they represent our own view of things. To dig beneath the surface of these simplified belief structures is so important, yet so difficult to the discerning therapeutic practitioner.

Hegemony

Hegemony, the second mechanism to be considered, is described as 'political dominance of one power over others in a group in which all are supposedly equal' (Hutchinson, 1993). An example of this would be where one group or social collectivity gained power, status and position at the expense of other, less favoured groups.

Hegemony is therefore closely linked to the notion of exploitation, although not necessarily in any deliberate or intentional sense. It is also closely linked to the notion of ideology, for it is often through the vehicle of ideology that hegemony operates (Thompson, 1993). Part of the ideological base of hegemony is the idea of an 'out group', a group of people defined in negative terms and assigned an inferior status. This tendency is quite clearly, therefore, part of the process of discrimination and oppression.

Hegemony is especially important in societies in which electoral politics and public opinion are significant factors, and in which social practice is seen to depend on consent to certain dominant ideas that in fact express the needs of a dominant class (Williams, 1983).

Discourse

The Concise Oxford Dictionary (1974) describes discourse as a talk, conversation, dissertation, treatise or sermon – 'to hold forth in speech or writing on a subject', or 'a serious conversation between people on a particular subject' (Collins, 1991).

Discourse analysis has become a significant research area across the social sciences, in recognition of the fact that any interaction between two people is shaped and informed by the processes they both bring to it, these processes being both internal (to each) and external (the other) and relational (between them).

In attempting to draw together the implications of these three dynamic social processes we may observe the very profound, complex interweaving of thought, beliefs, values, influences and perspectives that perpetually surround and engage us in everyday life. In short, we, as editors of this text, also have to acknowledge our part in contributing to the shaping of an alternative hegemony within counselling and psychotherapy through the very writing and editing of this book.

The above dominant and dominating socio-cultural-political processes may be identified as significant contributors to oppressive and discriminatory beliefs and practices in society.

Identity development and the 'other'

Important research has been conducted (and much critiqued) in the last two decades on the consequences of such processes upon people's sense of identity, particularly in relation to those who are seen to be 'different'. Much of this research has been conducted within the field of racial and ethnic identity formation and, we believe, has much to inform those in the counselling/psychotherapy profession.

Carter quotes a personal communication from A.J. Franklin who notes that 'when writing about race one constantly struggles with the question of how much emphasis to give historical, socio-economic, socio-political, intrapsychic and contemporary events' (1995: 2). As authors, we are sensitive to Franklin's notion of the difficulties in knowing where to place the emphasis, though through the above descriptions of ideology, hegemony and discourse we more specifically wish to acknowledge the 'Gordian knot' of complexity that nevertheless systematically communicates different messages of worth, value and treatment to different people and groups within society.

Carter (1995) argues that race has been and continues to be the ultimate measure of social exclusion and inclusion (Carter is writing here of the American context, though there are some similarities in the UK) because it is a visible factor that historically and currently determines the rules and bounds of social and cultural interaction (Kovel, 1984; Smedley, 1993).

The following chapters refer to the experiences of people from a range of different groups within society, some of whom are visible and thus identifiable in some sense as 'other' than the dominant group. For the purpose of a clear example, however, let us return to the identity formation models referred to above which are also psychological models (specifically pertaining to the USA where this work was developed) and which offer within-racial-group variations as well. In Carter's view, race and racial identity are integral aspects of personality and human development (1995: 4). Yet, paradoxically, the personal meaning and significance of 'race' has not been extended to white Americans (1995: 11).

Taking this perspective as the stimulus, it seems that the categorization of 'otherness' is attributed to those not conforming or belonging to a dominant 'norm'. From Carter's quote above that notes white as a 'norm' we may also recognize other hegemonic/ideological positions relative to those occupying the position of the 'other' – those in the dominant group have little awareness of their position as being white, or able bodied, or heterosexual and so on. 'Norm' therefore, somehow, remains unquestionable, not worthy of exploration, indeed out of awareness. Rochlin (1992: 203–4) wryly challenges this in his 'Heterosexual Questionnaire' – asking heterosexuals to consider such questions as 'What do you think caused your heterosexuality?', 'Is it possible that your heterosexuality is just a phase you may grow out of?' and 'To whom have you disclosed your heterosexuality? How did they react?' Similar questions are all too common to gay men and lesbians.

The lived complexity of all these societal and social dynamics provides a somewhat clouded, dense, confused and contradictory picture, yet multiple waves of research continue to point to socially and professionally embedded interactions and behaviours that result in discrimination and oppression of those from marginalized groups. The various forms of oppression mediated through the dominant ideologies, hegemonies and discourses (which support discriminatory behaviours) impact greatly upon the identities of people from these marginalized groups, at the very least in terms of:

- alienation, isolation and marginality;
- economic position and life chances;
- confidence and self esteem; and
- social expectations, career opportunities etc. (Thompson, 1993: 151)

There are no simple, overarching assumptions that can be made in terms of the forms that oppression and discrimination take. Different groups experience complex patterns of oppression, and indeed (within the groupings considered in this text) individuals may experience multiple oppressions (see Chapter 14 for further discussion).

The power of language

> Sticks and stones may break my bones but words can never hurt me. (A children's saying)

Language, often the very tool through which we conduct our therapeutic processes, is a complex and ever changing 'minefield'. Any conversation with others, let alone that conducted between counsellor and client in the therapeutic situation, alerts us to the power of language to buoy us up or pull us down, to enhance self-esteem or to sabotage self-confidence, to inflict pain or to encourage, to influence positively or negatively, to manipulate or to understand (Lago, 1997). In this regard we are most concerned about the sensitivity of the therapist's use of language (and para-verbal behaviour) in relation to their clients.

'Words really are important', argues Will Hutton in an article critical of the political influences of the American Right that has sneered at ideas and ideals of political correctness (2001). In drawing attention to the politicized usage of words, Hutton demonstrates powerfully how (in this case) the American Right was quick to declare war on the cultural manifestations of liberalism by levelling the charge of political correctness against its exponents and in so doing, discrediting the whole political project. Setting out with the intention of sensitizing each other to the power and impact of language, 'political correctness' eventually became a term of some derision that subsequently evoked very strong reactions in people concerned not to be 'policed' in their use of language, however apparent the justice of the cause. One of the difficulties here is a tendency for people to take an oversimplified view of the issue of language use. For example, one of the authors has often been asked by students to tell them what they are 'allowed' to say and what they are 'not allowed' to say, fearful of being attacked or shamed for saying the 'wrong' things. We cannot ignore the power of language in maintaining oppressive power relations. Thompson (1998) explains that the question of language use is not 'a simple lexicon of taboo words that are to be avoided' but is a complex and powerful vehicle that contributes to the maintenance of oppression. He highlights the importance of power dynamics in interactions between workers and service users in the caring professions, identifying a number of key issues:

- *Jargon* – the use of specialized language, creating barriers, which reinforce power differences.
- *Stereotypes* – terms used to refer to people from different groups, i.e. older people as 'old dears'.
- *Stigma* – terms such as 'mental handicap' carry a damaging stigma.
- *Exclusion* – this might be inadvertently asking a Muslim what his 'Christian' name is, rather than his 'first' name.
- *Depersonalization* – this relates to terms such as 'the elderly' rather than 'older people' and 'the mentally ill' rather than 'people with mental distress'.

A common argument in discussions about the power of language is that language not only describes reality, it *determines* reality. Thompson quotes Spender:

> Through my language and socialization I did learn to see as *sensible* many arrangements in my society which an 'outsider' (who did not share my socialization) would find absurd. So at one stage I did learn, for example, that it was sensible to give the least educational experience to those who appeared to take longer to learn. I did learn that it was sensible to classify some forms of skin pigmentation as possessing mystical powers. I did learn that it was sensible that one half of the population should be paid for their work while the other half should not. I did learn that it was sensible to ensure the survival of the species by amassing a vast arsenal that could destroy the planet many times over. And I did learn that it was sensible to see men as superior. (1998: 66)

We believe it is critically important to explore our use of language as therapists. Mindful of some of the settings in which counsellors work and the specific difficulties clients struggle with, we need to be sensitive to some of the words in common use and which are, in effect, deeply offensive. Working with people who have dependency problems, for example, do we subscribe to terms like 'drug user', 'drug abuser', 'drug pusher' or 'recreational drug use'? Do we use terms like 'alcoholic', 'alcohol abuser/misuser'? It is only in recent years that we have developed a language to describe the phenomenon of child sexual abuse. Previously there was no discourse and children's distress went (as it often still does) unheeded. Burstow (1992: 202) refers to 'eating disorders' as 'troubled eating'. She says 'There is nothing more orderly than the precise regimen that women who are anorexic follow'. We hear of 'date rape' and somehow it is thought to be less traumatic or damaging than other rape, and which term most appropriately describes the reality of women who are intimidated, tortured, battered and sometimes murdered by their partners – 'domestic violence' or 'woman battering'? Burstow (1992) refers to 'psychiatric survivors' having been 'psychiatrized' by the system, and Wilson and Beresford (2000) use the term 'people with madness and distress' rather than the more sanitized 'mental health service users'. These are just some of the questions we invite readers to consider when contemplating their use of language with clients.

Though perhaps only as an adjunct to this specific aspect of the chapter, Lee (2000) draws our attention to the developing field of 'cyber counselling'. Given the reliance of cyber communication, at present, on being word based, the cyber counsellor will have to pay detailed attention to their use of language with cyber clients to avoid discrimination and disempowerment. In short, the therapist will need, even more, to become a 'wordsmith' (Lago, 1996).

A critique of the critique

The fields of knowledge, research and practice in relation to social justice and social inclusion are ever changing in approach, language and emphasis. Each shift of position, philosophy or policy may cause great anxiety, concern and disagreement. This is inevitable within the process of cultural and societal change, but at the personal level, individual practitioners may be sorely challenged to grapple with new and emerging ideas, particularly when they may have strongly held, earlier personal positions on these subjects.

An earlier section of this chapter took the example set by the sister profession of social work as a template for understanding the essential thrust of this book, that of aspiring to practices and policies in counselling which are anti-oppressive and anti-discriminatory. It is to the same profession, or indeed a critique of it, we now return in the hope that, as a body of practice, we may not repeat what Wilson and Beresford argue has happened to social work. They say of their critique:

> Whilst acknowledging the emancipatory aspirations of anti-oppressive practice, it also considers its regressive potential. ... This discussion highlights the failure, so far, to significantly involve service users and their organizations in the development of anti-oppressive theory and practice. It considers how the ideology and structures of anti-oppressive social work impact upon service users; the problems raised by expert appropriation of users knowledge and experiences ... (2000: 553)

A major concern they express is that of the silence of clients' voices (and clients' organizations) in a consultation process that takes their opinions and experiences into account in informing new practice and practitioners. The therapeutic profession does have the advantage that trainee counsellors experience their own therapy and are therefore, at least for a time, 'service users' – a somewhat different situation to that of most social workers. Readers will gather from the biographies of the authors of this book that most have experience of surviving some form(s) of discrimination or oppression either through being a woman, a gay man, a lesbian, black, working class, disabled or older. We each come from a place of commitment to and passion for promoting good ethical practice, which acknowledges the social and political nature of counselling and of clients' concerns.

We invite the reader to develop awareness of the social and political 'backdrop' to their clients' stories. Does this woman, for example, stay in a violent relationship because of her personal psychology, or do issues of poverty and powerlessness and lack of appropriate support services contribute to her problems? Is she a black woman? What would her (and her children's) experience be of a refuge where all the other women, including workers, were white? And if she were a lesbian, how might she be received or understood by her heterosexual peers?

Is this older gay man isolated and lonely because he is shy and lacking in confidence or is there a deep fear of homophobic abuse due to previous experiences; or is it because gay scenes are often exclusive, seemingly valuing only youth and 'beauty'? Is this black child's school refusal 'separation anxiety' or is it due to a fear of daily racist bullying, in a school that has no bullying policy and where the staff deny the existence of racism?

Wilson and Beresford pose very challenging questions to anti-oppressive social work practice from their perspective as both lecturers in and users of social work. In short they are led, from this standpoint, to pose the fundamental question, is the very concept or possibility of anti-oppressive social work theory or practice, at least as it is currently produced and practised, possible? Just what is it, they ask, that constitutes anti-oppressive social work? A complex contradiction is presented here, as anti-oppressive practice is generally offered as an unquestionable good. Yet there is little recognition of the possibility that such ideas or theories could, in themselves, be oppressive or reproduce social injustice.

As counsellors we might ask ourselves similar questions.

Summary

Within these chapters, we offer an opportunity to reflect (as counsellors and citizens) on our attitudes and received ideas about different social 'groupings' and their experiences of counselling and wider society. We have been cautious about not wanting to produce a 'how to' text, for instance lists of characteristics about communities and cultures, focusing on the client rather than our own need to be independent in our thinking and abandon ideas and practices which perpetuate discrimination and oppression. We invite readers to consider the concepts of *anti*-discrimination and *anti*-oppression in that these require a *proactive* approach. As therapists, our subtle and unintentional processes can support the broad social pattern of discrimination, and anti-oppressive practice (as distinct from non-oppressive) requires us to question our own practice and challenge individuals and institutions (in particular our own profession, however well intentioned) which maintain the oppression of our clients.

The only real 'how to' we offer is that of beginning to see that the pathology, and the need for healing and change, in this context, lies within the oppressor, *us,* and the oppressive structures which *create* and *exacerbate* our clients' distress.

Key points

We have found the following key issues helpful in developing our practice with all clients.

- As therapists we are often agents of change and can promote change on a political as well as an individual level.
- Acknowledge that racism and other oppressions are part of British society and as such we must recognize these in ourselves.
- Address our own denial and avoidance of these issues through effective supervision.
- Commit ourselves to ongoing reflective practice: the political climate is fluid and changing.
- Challenge oppression in all its forms, even when it feels uncomfortable.
- Examine the use of terms that may be degrading or hurtful.
- Affirm our client's cultural identity, acknowledging their survival skills and coping mechanisms.
- Be sensitive to issues of isolation, due to marginalization, and clients' need for outside support.
- Offer alternative views about distorted beliefs about self where the client has been misinformed about their own and other social groups.
- Be aware that black, gay, female or disabled clients, etc. may not be bringing issues of race, gender, sexuality or disability to therapy.
- Recommend reading (bibliotherapy) and films which address the issues the client may bring.
- Use consultation or referral if we feel inadequately equipped to help our clients.
- Take steps to become more knowledgeable about other cultures, lifestyles, values and histories.
- Broaden our range of helping styles to accommodate different cultural expectations and needs.
- Undertake to find out what community groups and resources are available for clients who want to contact people with a shared experience of oppression.
- Align ourselves with struggles against oppression outside the therapy room.
- Examine policy which might unintentionally exclude people.
- Make anti-oppressive practice integral to training courses rather than just add-on modules.
- Start now.

References

Althusser, L. (1971) 'Ideology and Ideological State Apparatuses', in B. Bruster (trans.), *Lenin and Philosophy*. London: New Left Books.

Berger, P.L. (1996) *Invitation to Sociology*. Harmondsworth: Penguin.

Bimrose, J. (1993) 'Counselling and Social Context', in R. Bayne and P. Nicholson (eds), *Counselling and Psychotherapy for Health Professionals*. London: Chapman and Hall.

Bromley, E. (1994) 'Social Class and Psychotherapy Revisited'. Paper presented at the Annual Conference of the British Psychological Society, Brighton.

Burke, B. and Dalrymple, J. (1996) *Anti-Oppressive Practice – Social Care and the Law*. Buckingham: Open University Press.

Burstow, B. (1992) *Radical Feminist Therapy – Working in the Context of Violence*. Thousand Oaks, CA: Sage.

Carolin, B. (1995) 'Working with Children in a Family and Divorce Centre'. *Counselling* (BAC). Vol. 6, No. 3, pp. 207–10.

Carter, R.T. (1995) *The Influence of Race and Racial Identity in Psychotherapy: Towards a Racially Inclusive Model*. New York: Wiley.

Chaplin, J. (1989) 'Counselling and Gender', in S. Palmer and G. McMahon (eds), *Handbook of Counselling*. London: Routledge and Rugby BAC.

Collins School Dictionary (1991) London: Harper Collins.

Concise Oxford Dictionary, The (1974) Oxford: Oxford University Press.

Corker, M. (1994) *Counselling – The Deaf Challenge*. London: Jessica Kingsley.

Craig, Y. (1998) 'Attitudes to Ageing: Its Social Constitution, Deconstitution and Reconstitution'. *Counselling* (BAC). Vol. 9, No. 1, pp. 49–53.

D'Ardenne, P. and Mahtani, A. (1989) *Transcultural Counselling in Action*. London: Sage.

Davies, N. and Neal, C. (1996) *Pink Therapy*. Buckingham: Open University Press.

Eleftheriadou, Z. (1994) *Transcultural Counselling*. London: Central Books.

Feltham, C. and Horton, I. (eds) (2000) *Handbook of Counselling and Psychotherapy*. London: Sage.

Hall, S. (1986) 'Managing Conflict, Producing Consent'. Open University Unit 21 of D102, Social Science: A Foundation Course.

Hitchens, C. (2001) 'Letters to a Young Contrarian'. *The Guardian, Saturday Review*. 10 November, p. 3.

Hutchinson Encyclopaedia (1993) *The 1994 Edition*. Norwich: Helicon.

Hutton, W. (2001) 'Words Really Are Important, Mr Blunkett'. *The Observer*. 16 December, p. 26.

Kearney, A. (1996) *Counselling, Class and Politics*. Manchester: PCCS Books.

Kovel, J. (1984) *White Racism*. New York: Columbia University Press.

Lago, C.O. (1996) 'Computer Therapeutics: A New Challenge for Counsellors and Psychotherapists'. *Counselling* (BAC). Vol. 17, No. 4, pp. 287–9.

Lago, C.O. (1997) 'Race, Culture and Language: A Redefinition of Terms'. *RACE Journal* (BAC). No. 12, Spring.

Lago, C.O. and Thompson, J. (1989) 'Counselling and Race', in W. Dryden et al., *Handbook of Counselling in Britain*. London: Tavistock-Routledge. (Also in S. Palmer (ed.) (2002) *Multicultural Counselling: A Reader*. London: Sage.)

Lago, C.O. in collaboration with Thompson, J. (1996) *Race, Culture and Counselling*. Buckingham: Open University Press.

Lago, C.O. and Thompson, J. (1997) 'The Triangle With Curved Sides: Sensitivity to Issues of Race and Culture in Supervision' in G. Shipton (ed.), *Supervision of Psychotherapy and Counselling*. Buckingham: Open University Press.

Laing, R.D. (1965) *The Divided Self*. Harmondsworth: Penguin.

Laing, R.D. (1967) *The Politics of Experience and the Bird of Paradise*. Harmondsworth: Penguin.

Lee, C.C. (2000) 'Cybercounselling and Empowerment: Bridging the Cultural Divide', in J.W. Bloom and G.R. Walz (eds), *Cybercounseling and Cyberlearning: Strategies for the Millennium*. American Counseling Association: Alexandria.

Makin, T. (1995) 'The Social Model of Disability'. *Counselling* (BAC). Vol. 6, No. 4, p. 275.

McLellan, D. (1995) *Ideology* (2nd edn). Buckingham: Open University Press.

Observer Special Report (2001) 'Race in Britain'. *The Observer*. 25 November.

Pedersen, P., Draguns, J.G., Lonner, W.J. and Trimble, J.E. (1981) *Counselling Across Cultures*. Hawaii: East–West Center.

Rochlin, M. (1992) 'Heterosexual Questionnaire', in W.J. Blumenfeld (ed.), *Homophobia: How We All Pay The Price*. Boston, MA: Beacon Press.

Segal, J. (1997) 'Counselling People with Disabilities/Chronic Illnesses', in S. Palmer and G. McMahon (eds), *Handbook of Counselling* (2nd edn). London: Routledge.

Smedley, A. (1993) *Race in North America: Origin and Evolution of a World View*. Boulder, CO: Westview Press.

Smith, B. (1999) 'Potency, Permission, Protection and Politics'. *ITA News*. No. 55, Autumn, pp. 17–20.

Spender, D. (1990) *Man Made Language*. London: Pandora.

Szasz, T. (1970) *The Manufacture of Madness: A Comparative Study of the Inquisition and the Mental Health Movement*. New York: Harper and Row.

Thompson, N. (1993) *Anti-Discriminatory Practice*. London: Macmillan.

Thompson, N. (1998) *Promoting Equality – Challenging Discrimination and Oppression in the Human Services*. London: Macmillan.

Thorne, B.J. (1998) *Person-Centred Counselling and Christian Spirituality*. London: Whurr.

Williams, R. (1983) *Keywords – A Vocabulary of Culture and Society*. London: Flamingo.

Wilson, A. and Beresford, P. (2000) 'Anti-Oppressive Practice: Emancipation and Appropriation'. *British Journal of Social Work*. Vol. 30, pp. 553–73.

Anti-Discriminatory Practice Revisited

'Like it or not, we live in interesting times ...' (1966, Robert F. Kennedy)

Colin Lago and Barbara Smith

Life is understood backwards but must be lived forwards. (Soren Kierkegaard)

So much has happened within society since the publication of the first edition of this book. In that time we have witnessed a trend of movement from that of 'Affluenza' – a term coined by Oliver James in his book of the same name (2007) to a world in which the major international financial institutions have 'lost' extraordinary amounts of investments causing macro political, economic and sociological upheavals worldwide having enormous material, psychological and emotional consequences for individuals. Increases in the incidence of unemployment and poverty continue to be considerable.

These diverging trends in societal economics have serious consequences for all citizens in society. A recent book by Wilkinson and Pickett (2009) provides overwhelming evidence that the more unequal a society, the greater will be its social malaise. Countries with the greatest income inequalities (e.g. the UK) – where the top 20 per cent have over seven times that of the bottom 20 per cent – have higher levels of addiction, homicide, prison populations, obesity, teenage pregnancy and mental illness and lower levels of trust. For example, 25 per cent of Britons experience mental health problems in any one year compared to fewer than 10 per cent in Japan, Germany, Sweden and Italy where there is much less differentiation between incomes.

Though this relationship between 'straightened' societal circumstances and personal experience and interpersonal relationships is not a simple or linear 'cause–effect' process, it seems reasonable to suggest that for many whose identity is linked to minority group status, life experiences may become harder. Patterns of discrimination may become more pronounced, thus adding to the hardship and strain, both physical and psychological, experienced by those occupying 'the big 7' stigmatized identities: race, gender, sexual orientation, class, disability, religion and age (Moodley and Lubin, 2008).

Unawareness in the dominant majority

At a societal level, a further implication for those in minority groups or occupying 'stigmatized identities' is that those in the dominant group seldom define their own position as relative to minorities. Most frequently the dominant group assumes and adopts a position of being the 'norm' against which others are compared. For example, Robert Carter noted that 'the personal meaning and significance of "race" has not been extended to White Americans' (1995: 7). This particular phenomenon, that of 'whiteness', has been developed a little in the UK in the last decade by writers such as Tuckwell (2002), Ryde (2009), Lago and Haugh (2006) and Lago (2006). Casting our vision into the future, it will be important to note how the worldwide symbolic effects of the appointment of Barack Obama to the US Presidency in 2009 will impact upon the majority and minority cultures in many countries.

Parallel to the relatively recent studies of 'whiteness' reported above, similar explorations, perhaps, need to be developed pursuing questions such as 'What does it mean to be able-bodied/male/employed/heterosexual?' and so on. The importance of such a study would be to relativize these societal positions in relation to all the other positions removing them, therefore, from the dominant assumed position of neutrality, the norm (but certainly not to re-enforce their assumed and actual power).

Certain issues of diversity are occasionally hard to hear and take note of, particularly when there is no visible evidence of the difference. At a recent conference of therapists dedicated to an exploration of these issues, several participants had to remind the whole group, several times,

- that they were 'hearing impaired' and therefore would appreciate people speaking clearly; and
- that the food ordered for certain participants, because of their dietary needs, was not openly available to all conference participants – however attractive it looked.

In short, the whole field of 'difference and diversity' would benefit from the inclusion and increased awareness, by the majority group, of its own relative power position to that of other groupings within society. Susan Tomes powerfully expressed this sentiment when she wrote 'there's a limit to how much can be achieved by women advocating change on their own. ... Real progress will only be made when men decide that their lives have to change' (2009: 35).

Continued societal discrimination

Since the first edition of this book was published, the Commission for Equality and Human Rights (CEHR) was launched on 1 October 2007. This is a new organization that inherited the responsibilities of the three previously existing equality commissions: the Commission for Racial Equality; the Disability Rights Commission; and the Equal Opportunities Commission. It also has responsibilities on rights in relation to age, sexual orientation, religion and belief, and aims to ensure that unions and organizations such as the Citizen Advice Bureau have the correct training and information to advise people on these rights.

In addition, a new Equality Bill was published in April 2009 that aims to:

- introduce a new public sector duty to consider reducing socio-economic inequalities;
- put a new 'equality duty' on public bodies;

- use public procurement to improve equality;
- ban age discrimination outside the workplace;
- introduce gender pay reports;
- extend the scope to use positive action;
- strengthen the powers of employment tribunals; and
- protect carers, breastfeeding mothers, disabled people and club members from discrimination.

In contrast to the above aspirations embodied in this new Commission and Equality Bill, evidence has continued to emerge, since the first publication, of society's widespread discrimination towards minority groups. For example:

- *Disabled people*: A recent article was published in the *Guardian* apologising, on behalf of the police and prosecutors, for the fact that disabled people were being failed by the criminal justice system (Hirsch, 2009). This followed on from the publication of a report, published by several national organizations concerned for the rights of disabled people, highlighting numerous cases where offences had escalated, mainly because police officers had failed to respond appropriately (Scope, 2009).
- *Young black males* are now eight times more likely to be 'stopped and searched' than their white counterparts (Ryder, 2009). The government accepts that the widespread use of 'stop and search' powers by the police can create harm. In 2008 the Home Affairs Select Committee Inquiry stated that: 'Young Black People and the Criminal Justice System' recommended that the use of 'stop and search' in any given case should be balanced against whatever limited benefits it may bring. Only 13 per cent of stops lead to an arrest. Unlike traditional measures, these powers do not require a police officer to have reasonable grounds for suspicion in making a stop (Section 44 of the Terrorism Act, 2000/Section 60 of the Criminal Justice and Public Order Act, 1994). 'Last week's statistics revealed that "stop and search" of African Caribbean people under counter-terrorism legislation rose by a staggering 325 per cent. Half of all Section 60 stops in London were of black males' (Ryder, 2009).
- *Age discrimination* 'is rife in Britain. Since it is silent, insidious and non-violent, it isn't until you cross some rubicon of yourself that you realise just how prevalent and nasty it is. The perpetrators (that could be you) are seemingly ignorant of their behaviour and perfectly comfortable with this prejudice. Indeed, I hope people don't realise how rude and dismissive they are' (Soames, 2009: 21). Soames continues with stories of ageism in the NHS. There is anecdotal evidence of doctors who refer to their work as 'market gardening-tending cabbages'; of research demonstrating that stroke units do not offer the same scans and rehabilitation as they offer to younger people. 'Our thinking about old age needs a serious overhaul, just as previous attitudes to sex and race needed a damn good slap in the face. Legislation can only go so far in introducing a cultural sea change' (Soames, 2009: 21).
- *Prejudice towards gay people:* A study carried out by the occupational psychology consultancy Shire Professional has found that homophobic attitudes are more common than racism (BACP News Editorial, 2009b). 'Similarly, despite legislation and a general perception of more tolerance in the 21st Century

toward sexual preference, homosexuals living in the European Union are subject to widespread discrimination and often have to make their sexual orientation "invisible", according to a report released by the EU Fundamental Rights Agency. The report, which was presented at the European Parliament in Brussels, called on EU countries to improve equality, and provide for better training to officials as well as better reporting of hate crimes and other incidents. Morten Kjaerum, the director of the Vienna-based agency, said that there had been physical violence and deadly assaults against gays, lesbians and transgender persons ...' (www.neurope.ec/articles/Discrimination, accessed 16 November 2009).

Sadly, this list could be extended very easily. A scan of the daily newspapers, let alone professional journals and research reports, will reveal a stream of evidences of ongoing discriminations in society.

Needless to say, for this is the central motivation of producing this book, the experience of being discriminated against is one that leads to loss of self-esteem, personal misery, depression, extensive self-questioning, a constant state of vigilance, stress related illnesses, social withdrawal, self-harming and mental illness. Such experience can adversely affect relations with others and put enormous stress on families. The consequences are therefore very considerable upon people's capacities to be creative, productive and relationally confident.

In direct contrast to the above discriminations, Brawn-Williams has noted that 'our' responsibility, as theorists, therapists and researchers, is to understand the socio-political context of theory building and practice and thus to be mindful of the biases underlying our work (Brawn-Williams, Forthcoming.) This position requires a considerable commitment on our behalf, to reflection, ongoing exploration and attention when working with and responding to those deemed as 'different and diverse'. Indeed, we also may be, and be deemed by others as being 'different and diverse'. Difference is relational, both ways, a point that is explored in the section immediately below.

Therapeutic practice and anti-discriminatory awareness

The nature of our therapeutic work can be extremely profound and have life-changing potential for our clients. Schmid (2006), working from within the person-centred theoretical framework, provided a concise and succinct description of psychotherapy. (Please note that we are deeply cognisant of the fact that practitioners from some psychotherapeutic orientations might find these essential points as challenging to their perspective. However, we have chosen to use them here as they capture, with clarity and simplicity, four major arenas of therapeutic practice and research that do and will impact upon the 'trans-difference' therapeutic relationship.)

Schmid postulated that, in therapy:

- there is a fundamental 'we';
- the client is expert;

- the therapist is present; and
- dialogue is the process.

The first point above is now substantially researched and practice substantiated. The quality of relationship and therapeutic alliance between therapist and client accounts for approximately 30 per cent of successful therapeutic outcome (Norcross, 2002). Impediments to the construction of good working relationships in counselling and psychotherapy emanating from practitioners towards their clients (e.g. negative attitudes, pejorative stereotypes, fear, anxiety, etc.) will therefore significantly impact upon the potential for good relationship building and thus satisfactory outcomes for the client. Indeed, from the first instance of contact, what we, as therapists, see in clients is a combination of our projections and their defences. This simplest form of critical analysis of the participants at the outset of the therapeutic relationship across difference already signals caution as to our capacity to assist the development of the relationship.

Cooper (2008) cites research by Gelso and Hayes (2002) who define 'counter-transference' as 'therapists' reactions to clients that are based on therapists' unresolved conflicts'. This latter phrase – 'therapists' unresolved conflicts' – inevitably includes the therapist's negative reactions to clients of difference and diversity. They suggest that counter-transferential reactions can be thought of as either 'acute' (irregular and uncharacteristic reactions to specific clients) or 'chronic (habitual needs and behavioural patterns of the therapist), and they can also be thought of as existing as an internal state or as an external expression (Cooper, 2008: 197).

Ligiero and Gelsom (2002) found that negative counter-transference was associated with lower scores on all three dimensions of the Working Alliance Inventory. This finding suggests that greater levels of counter-transference (particularly negative counter-transference) may be associated with poorer therapeutic outcomes. Hays et al. (1997) found that greater levels of such behaviour were associated with lower levels of client satisfaction and self-reported gain. This only seemed to be the case, however, in the least successful therapy cases. In other words, when therapy was going well, therapist's negative reactions did not seem to be a particular issue, but when therapy was otherwise going badly, high levels of therapist counter-transferential behaviour seemed to be highly predictive of even poorer outcomes (reported in Cooper, 2008). What the above research suggests is that the more therapists can manage their negative reactions to clients, the more they can reduce the likelihood of it adversely affecting the therapy.

Schmid's second point above states that the client is an expert on their life. As Rogers has so profoundly articulated, the client knows best where it hurts, and at a deep organismic level, what can be tolerated, modified, addressed and changed and in what time frame (Rogers, 1961). The client's expertise is also embodied in their capacity to sense the helpfulness (or not) of the therapist and to evaluate the outcome of the therapeutic work. Indeed, they are a much more reliable source of appraisal of the efficacy of the therapy than are therapists (Cooper, 2008). Clients from 'minority' backgrounds are likely to be highly attuned and sensitive to (dominant group) therapist behaviours and responses, and where these are experienced as non-accepting, judgemental, anxious, 'minority issue avoidant' and so on, they are likely to exit therapy early (Thompson and Jenal, 1994).

As Vontress has noted, 'it is in the interests of the oppressed to understand the oppressor' (Forthcoming).

Third, the quality of the therapist's presence (substantiated in part by their capacity to listen deeply and respond empathically) is fundamental to both the construction of the relationship and to enhance the self-exploration process by the client. The therapist has to be open to all aspects of the client's identity (even those which appear to be contradictory) and facilitate their exploration. Therapists, in their striving towards 'presence'/relationship with the client, have to somehow manage (or bracket off) their own assumptions and attitudes towards the client to be truly available to them.

Within the context of working with 'diversity and difference', there is a danger that therapists may identify clients as templates of a particular collectivity; for example, 'they are disabled' or 'they are gay'. Although clients may emerge from an identifiable 'minority' community, it is critical to remember that they will individually perceive the reality of that and other communities differently. They also might identify strongly with other aspects of their identity that the therapist could not even imagine. Indeed, there may be many aspects of 'client identities' invisible to the therapist, which, for example, may include sexuality, disability, class, spirituality, addiction, divorce and trauma. The therapist's task is to accept and receive the client's own experiences and descriptions of their reality/ies. A multiplicity of identities might exist and are to be welcomed into the therapy dialogue, not selectively erased out by the therapist's own preconceptions or negative evaluations. (For a further exposition of this topic, see Chapter 14.) Take, for instance the following quotation by a client:

> 'When I think about all the marks I have against me in this society, I am amazed that I haven't turned into some worthless lump of shit. Fatkikecripplecuntqueer. In a nutshell. But then I have to take into account the fact that I'm articulate, white, middle-class college kid, and that provides me with a hell of a lot of privilege and opportunity for dealing with my oppression that may not be available to other oppressed people. And since my personality/being isn't divided up into a privileged part and an oppressed part, I have to deal with the ways that these things interact, counterbalance and sometimes overshadow each other. For example, I was born with one leg. I guess it's a big deal, but its never worked into my body image in the same way that being fat has. And what does it mean to be a white woman as opposed to a woman of colour? A middle-class fat girl as opposed to a poor fat girl? What does it mean to be fat, physically disabled and bisexual? (Or fat, disabled and sexual at all?)' (Lamm, 1995: 7–8)

Included within these concepts of presence and openness is the therapist's capacity to hear deeply the client's experience, without defensiveness, retreat or change of subject. 'Rage needs to be heard. This does not mean that it simply needs to be listened to. It needs to be accepted, taken within and understood empathically … The truth about rage is that it only dissolves when it is really heard and understood without reservations' (Rogers, 1978: 183). The intensity and ferocity of a client's outpourings who has suffered considerable emotional abuse and social injustice can be so frightening to some therapists that they cannot truly hear and stay with these experiences. Interventions aimed at reassurance, quietening things down or psychological (and indeed physical) withdrawal are likely only to re-enforce the client's views of society, their roles within it or their own negative self-evaluations. To truly accept (and be seen to accept) the client's view of their reality opens up the possibility for movement and change of that perspective they have held previously.

Schmid's fourth point above, that dialogue is the process, is already introduced within the above sentences. The activity of dialogue introduces both the capacity of the therapist to understand and work with the client's language/s and also be able to respond to and communicate with the client in sensitive, supportive, anti-discriminatory language. Where the therapist's language fails to address the client's concerns, therapeutic potential is severely limited. (See, for example, the research on the avoidance by therapists of addressing issues of 'race' (Thompson and Jenal, 1994).)

Emerging themes in statutory regulation and employment of counsellors and psychotherapists[1]

A significant and unsettling element of the socio-political context in which therapists are currently working is that of the impending intentions to introduce government regulation of all counsellors and psychotherapists. This new government-led initiative is also accompanied by developments by the Health Professions Council to delineate the competences and standards required of qualified therapists within their different theoretical orientations.

The profession (of 'talking therapies') has developed a long way from when it was conducted in voluntary organizations (such as the Marriage Guidance Council) some decades ago. These historic origins were perhaps more akin to the practice of traditional healers in other cultures who frequently worked on the margins of society. These latest planned interventions by the government combined with the developing movement of counselling and psychotherapy (from the margins) into mainstream health, educational and employment provision are likely to result in:

- an increasing usage of therapy services by all sectors of the population (wonderful in terms of offering a wider treatment choice to persons in a society where over 20 per cent, annually, suffer mental health difficulties) (Wilkinson and Pickett, 2009);
- a wide range and increasing number of qualified therapists from 'different and diverse' groups (again, this development is a positive one, increasing the opportunity for clients to experience a wider choice of therapists);
- a wide range and increasing number of clients from 'different and diverse' groups, thus increasing access to this form of help for psychological, emotional and relationship difficulties for all sectors in society;
- potential restrictions on therapist creativity and modes of interaction by therapists fearful of the new regulation and legislation culture (Thorne, 2009; Rogers, 2009);
- a potential skew, caused by government intervention, of the types of therapy available to clients, despite the extensive research validating the equivalency of a broad range of therapeutic interventions (BACP News Editorial, 2009a; Stiles et al., 2006; Elliot and Freire, 2008); and

- potential discrimination of clients who are not literate or competent (English) language speakers because of the already increasing requirements in many agencies for multiple form-filling, including client assessment outcomes after every session. (Would you dare to say or report on a form at the end of a session that your therapist was not helpful – a form that is seen by the therapist – when you already feel so wretched that you are desperate for any help you can get? Would you dare to fill in a form after counselling if you were an asylum seeker and anxious how the 'authorities' might interpret anything you wrote, even if the therapist was reassuring you that these forms were not accessed by government agencies?)

It is to be hoped that this new wave of central government intervention does not lead to professional practice that merely reflects the insensitivity of clients' existing worlds instead of supporting the development of practice that offers a place of refuge and healing for clients in counselling services. This 'noble intention-contradictory outcome' paradox is developed here from the early work of Goffmann (1968), Vontress (Forthcoming) and many writers featured in the *Asylum* journal). Indeed, as editors of this book we have a similar concern: in drawing attention to the importance of anti-discriminatory practice might we also be contributing (however unintentionally) to practice in some therapists that becomes discriminatory? As in the Chinese philosophy of yin and yang, where one cannot exist without the other, we perhaps have to accept that there will be incidences of practice that could be deemed to be discriminatory, despite noble intentions to the contrary. Following Jung's ideas, in the context of light the 'shadow' also exists and requires bringing into consciousness to reduce its destructive power. The quotation by Kierkegaard at the commencement of this chapter – 'life is understood backwards but must be lived forwards' – constitutes the important step of striving to modify and improve previous practice into more benign, positive practice. The profession, fortunately, encourages such forward movement through the support of continuing professional development and supervision. It is perhaps inevitable that mistakes will be made in the practice of psychotherapy, but the ongoing professional task is to recognize them, address them and learn from them.

Note

1   This particular section of the chapter reflects nationally driven professional concerns at the time of writing. We appreciate, as authors, that within some years these particular statutory processes will have developed and may form the status quo in which all therapists will be working. However, it seems important to us to note these developments at this point, and we apologize to future readers if the following concerns are no longer of great moment when they read them. Please just skip this section if it's of no concern!

References

Asylum: An international magazine for democratic psychiatry, psychology, education and community development. Available at www.asylumonline.net.

BACP News Editorial (2009a) 'IAPT issues statement on counselling in the NHS'. *Therapy Today*. BACP. June. p. 4.

BACP News Editorial (2009b) 'Prejudice study finds gay is the new black'. *Therapy Today*. BACP. February. p. 6.

Brown Williams, C. (Forthcoming) 'African women, race and gender politics and the work of Clemmont Vontress', in R. Moodley & R. Walcott (eds), *Counselling Across and Beyond Cultures: Exploring the Work of Clemmont Vontress in Clinical Practice.* Toronto: University of Toronto Press.

Carter, R. (1995) *The Influence of Race and Racial Identity in Psychotherapy:Towards a Racially Inclusive Model*. New York: John Wiley and Sons.

Cooper, M. (2008) *The Facts are Friendly: An Introduction to Counselling and Psychotherapy Findings*. Rugby: BACP.

Elliot, R. & Freire, E. (2008) 'Meta research outcomes on the person-centred approach'. *Person Centred Quarterly*. Newsletter of the British Association for the Person-Centred Approach. Ross: PCCS Books. November. pp. 1–3.

Gelso, C.J. & Hayes, J.A. (2002) 'The management of counter transference', in Norcross, J.C. (ed.), *Psychotherapy Relationships that Work: Therapist Contributions and Responsiveness to Patients* (pp. 267–83). Oxford: Oxford University Press.

Goffmann, E. (1968) *Asylums: Essays on the Social Situation of Inmates*. New York: Doubleday.

Hays, J.A., Riker, J.R. & Ingram, M.I. (1997) 'Countertransference behaviour and management in brief counselling: a field study', *Psychotherapy Research*. 7 (2), 145–53.

Hirsch, A. (2009) 'Police and prosecutors apologise to disabled victims of crime'. *The Guardian*.10 May.

James, O. (2007) *Affluenza*. London: Vermillion.

Lago, C. (2006) 'Upon being a white therapist. Have you noticed?' in C. Lago (ed.), *Race, Culture and Counselling: The Ongoing Challenge*. Maidenhead: Open University Press.

Lago, C. & Haugh, S. (2006) 'White counsellor racial identity: the unacknowledged, unknown, unaware aspect of self in relationship', in M. Cooper, B. Malcolm, G. Proctor & P. Sanders (eds), *Politicising the Person Centred Approach – An Agenda for Social Change*. Ross: PCCS Books.

Lamm, N. (1995) 'It's a big fat revolution', in B. Findlen (ed.), *Listen Up: Voices from the Next Feminist Generation*. Emeryville, CA: Seal Press.

Ligiero, D.P. & Gelsom, C.H. (2002) 'Countertransference, attachment and the working alliance: the therapist's contribution', *Psychotherapy: Theory, Research, Practice, Training*. 39 (1), 3–11.

Moodley, R. & Lubin, D. (2008) 'Developing your career to working with multicultural and diversity clients', in S. Palmer & R. Bor (eds), *The Practitioner's Handbook*. London, Sage.

Norcross, J.C. (ed.) (2002) *Psychotherapy Relationships that Work: Therapists Contributions and Responsiveness to Patients*. New York: Oxford University Press.

Rogers, A. (2009) 'Dare we do away with professionalism?' *Therapy Today*. BACP. May. pp. 26–9.

Rogers, C.R. (1961) 'The process equation of psychotherapy'. *American Journal of Psychotherapy*. 15 (1), 27–45.

Rogers, C.R. (1978) *On Personal Power*. London: Constable.

Ryde, J. (2009) *Being White in the Helping Professions: Developing Effective Intercultural Awareness*. London & Philadelphia, PA: Jessica Kingsley.

Ryder, M. (2009) 'The police need to stop and think about stop and search'. *The Observer*. 3 May. p. 19.

Schmid, P. (2006) 'The person in the person-centred approach: being-with and being-counter in the therapeutic relationship'. A weekend seminar conducted for Temenos, Sheffield. April.

Scope (2009) www.scope.org.uk/cgi-bin/viewnews and www.timetogetequal.org.uk/page.asp?section

Soames, E. (2009) 'I'm not invisible, I'm only in my fifties'. *The Observer.* 3 May. p. 21.

Stiles, W., Barkham, M., Mellor-Clark, J. & Cooper, M. (2006) 'Effectiveness of cognitive, person-centred and psychodynamic therapies as practised in the UK National Health Service'. *Psychological Medicine.* 36, 555–66.

Thompson, C.E. & Jenal, S.T. (1994) 'Interracial and intraracial quasi counselling interactions. When counsellors avoid discussing race'. *Journal of Counseling Psychology.* 41 (4), 484–91.

Thorne, B. (2009) 'A collision of worlds'. *Therapy Today.* BACP. May. pp. 22–5.

Tomes, S. (2009) A letter printed in the letters page of *The Guardian.* Saturday, 16 May. p. 35.

Tuckwell, G. (2002) *Racial Identity, White Counsellors and Therapists.* Buckingham: Open University Press.

Vontress, C. (Forthcoming) 'A personal retrospective', in R. Moodley & R. Walcott (eds), *Counselling Across and Beyond Cultures: Exploring the Work of Clemmont Vontress in Clinical Practice.* Toronto: University of Toronto Press.

Wilkinson, R. & Pickett, K. (2009) *The Spirit Level: Why More Equal Societies Almost Always Do Better.* London: Allen Lane/Penguin.

Racism as a Trauma

3

Reflective Anti-Racist Practice in Action

Saira Bains

Who is the Other? Can we ever hope to speak authentically of the experience of the Other? (Denzin and Lincoln, 2003: 606)

The reality of living in a multi-ethnic and multi-faith Britain in all its complexities means there is a widening of the debate on race and racism. The movement towards ideas of integration and social community cohesion means there is a need to understand the effects of exclusion, the issues related to belonging and the trauma caused by racism.[1] There is a therapeutic need to address the felt impact of the widening inequality gap between white and non-white other. How do we understand the tensions and racist projections that emanate from temporalised historical positions of power that have become ratified in territorial space? How can we begin to address these complexities within therapy without assuming that difference does not always exemplify oppression or domination?

Particularly since contemporary racisms are indirect and subtle, there is a need to examine the social and psychological without the reductive and singular explanations of racisms and its effects. Psychotherapy has responded to racism and the needs of ethnic and cultural groups by the creation of transcultural psychiatry (Fernando, 2001), cross-cultural counselling, intercultural and multicultural practices (Pedersen, 1985; Lipsedge and Littlewood, 1997).

Multicultural practice in turning to more inclusive and cognisant ways of being with difference has encouraged therapists to challenge their underlying assumptions and to develop cultural knowledge, sensitivity and explore cultural encapsulation (Pederson, 1985). The ideological concerns of multiculturalism are useful, but it has been criticised for its failure in assuming that core cohesive values and cultural uniformity exist.

The harsh reality of racism reveals that 87,000 people from black or minority ethnic (BME) communities said they had been a victim of a racially motivated crime in the UK in 2004 (Easton, 2006). This ranges from taunts, insults, physical assaults, intimidation and threats. There is persecutory anxiety on all sides of the divide as well as increasing religious and ethnic intolerance in the world.

This means that anti-oppressive practices within therapy are required to explore the hatred, denigration and the internalisation of dominant oppressions, when racism and its effects breach the psyche. We are required to become more interested in capturing the essence of the felt and lived experience of racism by cultivating reflective practices that enable our clients (and ourselves) to express what has become indescribable and subjugated within the subjective effects of racism.

In making connections to otherness within territories of difference, it is useful for therapists to make connections to the contradictions and ambiguities by navigating through the webs of racism, culture and belief systems. This has meant illuminating the impact of 'black and white' thinking whilst trying to move beyond it and revealing the dynamics of racism not as a natural instinctive process but based in power relations. For these reasons, it seems important to find unique and meaningful ways to hear our clients' voices that do not deny them power and replicate discriminatory experiences.

This has meant examining how the therapist might develop the attributes of a storyteller and listener as we strive to listen and record stories with a heightened frequency (Back, 2004). This might provide a dynamic and compassionate connection to racist trauma for those impacted by it and for those who try to work towards the healing of this woundedness. The narrative account also defies the idea that traumatic experiences are too painful to be told (Frank, 1995). Such storied accounts can bring dignity, respect and empathetic understanding to unchartered territories of racism(s).

Racism as a trauma

Dalal argues that racism cannot simply be reduced to splitting and projection but is a 'complex psycho-social phenomena that is driven by the pragmatics of power relations in the world' (2002: 227). He argues that the psyche is structured in a colour-coded way and the act of 'othering' is a socially created process that is a way of distancing and denying similarity. He suggests the use of the terms 'race', 'ethnicity' and 'culture' are interchangeable, and the emphasis on difference is made in order to estrange and detach the 'we from them' (2002: 33). This results in projection becoming a way of generating difference.

Racism as a trauma, rather than being trivialised within therapy, is a disguised issue because of the fearful and defended nature of racism. This compounds the client's anxiety that racism may be unspeakable, enhancing the fear of misattunement and humiliation that leaves the victim terrified of the re-enactment in the therapeutic relationship. This can result in racism being overlooked, misdiagnosed and minimised, which this is oppressive and silencing in itself.

The lack of understanding of the internal psychic wound of racism as a trauma can act as a denial of humanity and compassionate understanding of the other. This in part could be related to the difficulty in describing the splits between the oppressed and the oppressor and accessing language to describe these representations. This impasse or 'stuckness' in language and communication can become enmeshed in power relations.

The psychological effects of trauma and the impact of the Holocaust, sexual violation and natural disasters have been well documented (Figley, 1986). Clearly not all racisms will be experienced traumatically, but the trauma model could be a useful framework applicable to understanding racism and its effects on those of colour. Comas-Diaz and Jacobsen (2001) define various degrees and levels of racist stress, such as episodic racism that is a result of implicit and explicit racist encounters. Acute racism stressors are associated with frequent and persistent racism and chronic racist stress that is culminative and transgenerational. Of these groups they suggest a proportion will develop post-traumatic stress disorder.

According to the DSM-IV (APA, 2000), trauma is defined as experiencing, witnessing and confronting an event(s) that threatens death or serious injury, and this may be a danger to the physical integrity of the self or others. The reaction to this involves intense fear, helplessness or horror. From this definition, trauma not only involves some type of danger, but it is also characterised by a sense of powerlessness that wounds the individual's psyche. It could be argued that the imprint of racist trauma is both different in some of its effects from other traumata whilst significantly overlapping other traumatic experiences.

In conceptualising trauma in this sense, as a product of the black experience this trauma has a particular aliveness and layering in its effects as an ongoing possibility for recurrence in any sphere of life. The experience of not feeling at home in one's inner and external world means being left with a sense of helplessness and loss of volition. The effect of racist trauma alters self-perception and self-esteem, and disturbs the structures of safety. This can result in mistrust, contemptuousness or ambivalence towards one's culture, ethnic identity and self. This in turn can result in profound alienation, loss and relational disconnection that can produce a need to defensively assert, deny or hide in one's cultural experience.

What is more specific to this trauma is that it can be experienced as an intentional act by another human being (even if unconsciously enacted), which can be most profoundly damaging to the self. Racist trauma acts as an interruption to personal existence and the embodiment of self. The 'why me' of this powerful experience is not just feeling hated and persecuted because of one's skin colour but the deeper personal implications of this rests in what is symbolic and core to what one seemingly represents. This acts as a kind of spirit killing and violence to one's soul (Bell and Singley, 2004).

This brings me to autoethnography, which in practice I have integrated with psychotherapy as a suitable and respectful method to interpret and understand the subjective traumatic effects of colour racism on the self. This method does overlap with narrative practices and thinking in its prizing of life stories and testimonials to co-construct coherent life narratives. Autoethnography is not a distinct form of therapy and as it is rarely used in psychotherapy it is necessary for me here to briefly outline its uses and practice.

Autoethnography describes the making and reforming of subjectivities that sit on a continuum between art and science and are usually creative and analytic first-person accounts (Ellis, 2004). Autoethnography focuses on reflexivity and how stories can be useful in expressing the felt meanings of an encounter. This appears as a type of critique and resistance in diverse forms such as novels, song, poetry, performance and memoir.

As a personalised research methodology, it can vary its emphasis on 'auto', the representations of self, 'graphy', which can represent research, and 'ethnos', related to culture and groups (Ellis, 2004). Autoethnography attempts to confront dominant forms of representation and power in an attempt to reclaim marginalised voices.

The best way to describe the method is to demonstrate it, and the following excerpt is taken from autoethnographic and psychotherapeutic research I undertook with my family group, who were immigrants to Britain from India and Pakistan. In this excerpt my brother and I are research collaborators constructing a narrative account to explore what becomes located in the physical representation of skin.

I wrote this story using my brother's words, collective images and photographs to aid emotional recall. My brother had final editorial control as we revised and adapted this narrative together. This meant seeking out what was conveyed and felt rather than theorised and giving voice to implicit, bodily felt and intuitive knowledge.

What you are about to read has emerged from lived experience and is reflective of how language both subverts and represents the tracks of trauma. It is a story that attempts to capture the symbolic and cultural imprint of racist trauma in a specific narrative account.

Racism as disconnection and loss

Although I have experienced racism, the primary scars I bear from racism are as a witness. It is as if I adopted these scars without knowing how they came to being. Yet I have carried the weight of terrible guilt in seeing those closest to me wounded more directly by something I escaped. I consciously did not know how profoundly it had shaped these key relationships. Racism, for me, was bound in the wrappings of humiliation and silence. It was so tightly swathed, I only heard it as a whisper. I have always been fearful of the quality of how it was spoken and heard.

I battle with the inadequacy of my words in describing the intensity and profoundness of the love I have for these present absent men – my Father, Uncle and Brother. It was as if they had gone out into the world, felt at war and returned home, dismembered and absent. I have struggled with tracing the roots of my estrangement and disconnection from them; it has always been such a mysterious ache. I know in a very real way now that disconnection and absence are the central features of trauma that sit amongst the ruins of repression and denial. I have mourned and grieved for what has been irrecoverable whilst feeling a burning need to reclaim these lost connections. Quite simply, I have wanted to bring them home.

My brother's story, interwoven with my own

He is my older brother but I felt like the older one. I wanted to shield him from the harshness of the world. How do I describe what it has been like to watch him carry the silent woundedness of racism? When it seems like these events were a tangle of insidious, intangible hurts that were shattering and lived as a heavy oppressive silence between us, until we embarked on this journey.

As I write this, I stare at his photo as a 4-year-old child and he is turning his face towards the sunlight: spirited and playful. To me, he was always so fiercely beautiful and fragile. We would wake at dawn in our excitement to play elaborate games and tell each other stories late into the night until my throat got scratchy. I long for my gentle playmate; a bringer of sugary sweets and stories that lit fires in my mind.

I agonised as to whether the research might harm him further. I had to ask, whom am I writing to and why? What would the implications be when the context moved to the public field? Which voices were suppressed? What are the ethics of taking this into the public world? Issues around confidentiality buzzed in my head. What would the research do to our relationship? Would I be derided and discounted by the 'therapeutic community' for revealing not just myself but, even worse, my family? Could we find the language, which sits beyond trauma, to describe what cannot be spoken?

There were and are no real answers to these questions and uncertainties, but I had a growing belief that this was a valuable and necessary journey.

As we grew up, I would notice my brother's face smeared with an unspoken trail of dirty tears when he got home. He never spoke of his terror; of the cruelty he endured every day, as a child and as an adult. Each day he wondered 'will I be safe today?' – a plea that persists today. He said there was little escape from the relentless battle that became his life at school in the 1970s. 'I took the name-calling, hits, the humiliation, it was relentless and I stopped feeling the pain, I remember once just standing there with the blows raining down on me, I only felt paralysis.' He faced similar racist hate outside school. The unflinching realities of perpetual violence and attack were prevalent as it was then fashionable to go 'paki bashing' (which was the violence perpetuated against the Asian community). The era of paki bashing meant the taunts followed me too. I internalised this and I would sing the chants of 'we are going paki bashing' at the top of my voice. That seemed to shut them up, at least for a while.

There was no safety net and no soft landing. There was no shelter from the violence and contempt. Perhaps nothing was done because those people in authority could not relate to it. There was a prevalent notion that he should stand up to his aggressors. This was not simply racist bullying, it was more complex. The journey home for him was potentially terrifying, his vulnerability and exposure made the journey feel longer than it should. After spending his bus fare on sweets for me, covered in lint from his deep pockets, he had to walk the treacherous route home. This revelation brings another ache of guilt and complicity.

Our parents could not offer the buffer; they were a visceral reminder of why he was so ashamed of his skin. He could not form the words to name this to our parents or me. We were the physical representation of skin that was hated, that he wanted to wipe away. With no way to speak of his trauma, his body became a voice for it. He became perpetually ill; these psychosomatic symptoms have followed him into his adult life. He was crippled by agoraphobia, anxiety and thoughts of suicide. 'I fell apart completely; I am like humpty dumpty, trying to put the pieces back together again.'

He made creative attempts to minimise the horror of it all. He instituted complacency and passivity as a strategy to survive, one, of many. He also attempted to fight back against the racist eruptions from black and white males alike. He fought one, but how could he fight them all? He sealed up the hood of his blue anorak, entombing him, where he could pretend to be invisible, but he looked like a walking spaceman, a clearer and more precise target. He describes the stale smell of spit on his cheeks and hears the echo of slaps on his head that somehow became painless and routine. The trauma of it all is fused, like newspaper print on skin, exposing his shame. He described his self as an unprotected shell and existing in an unnameable shame. He remembers feeling it was as if his skin was turning into plastic. It encased him in an artificial layer of protection that smelled vaguely of rubber and was unyielding. The humiliation had stripped him of himself. He disassociated and disconnected from his reality. He tried to make himself so unseen, all the daylight faded out of him.

(Continued)

(Continued)

As he recounts this, I feel physical pain in my body, a constriction in my chest and I want to go back in time and pull him back to me. Has this not always been my role, to try to shield him? Knowing, even though I was a little child and that I was destined to fail, feels like a truth that brings little solace; I feel only desperate sadness.

As he sat curled on the sofa revising the first draft of the narrative, he said, 'I think what I have been trying to find in my life for a long time is a reason to live. I have been unable to look after myself, see myself or be close to anyone. So, I remember making the decision to leave my old self behind. I had to leave you behind too.'

I am stunned to hear this named but I recognise its truth. I became lost to him and he could not recognise me. He would look through me and he could not register contact. I watched him peeling away and I did not understand what was corrupting our contact. I now understand the terrible aloneness I felt when I was with him. I have been the unknown witness to the quiet withering and emasculation he endured.

A missing piece of the picture is put in place and this brings recognition and under-standing, but it is followed by anger and guilt. I get lost in the bindings of the hierarchy of pain; is his pain not so much greater than mine? Do I have a right to this anger? Yet I am angry at being erased. Where do I let this loss sit? A part of me wants to recon-stitute this loss and repair it, offer it up to be fixed.

I feel less helpless now because I can see him. He looks at me as if he is seeing me again for the first time. I realise that racism took him away from me. It also helped me find a way back to him. Yet the effects of these traumatic absences have left empti-ness in my life, and we struggle with wondering how we might find each other. As I voiced my sadness in missing him whilst he was seemingly present, something began to change, something between us. I am able to love him just as he is, in the hope that there are moments when he is returned to me, which happens every now and then, sometimes in a moment of stillness with a kind word or a loving gaze. For now that is good enough.

Transformation and healing

What seemed most traumatic was the incomprehensibility of the racist experience. In its raw unconstructed state it had significant impact in structuring and framing behaviour, and the reclaiming of a less than conscious experience means accessing incoherent parts of ourselves through self-conscious inquiry.

There is no simple construction of victim and oppressor in this storied account. I have reframed it as a narrative of transgenerational and intergenerational racist trauma. This silencing bind has been dismantled and replaced by self-expression and a sense-making process, which has brought relief and empathy that acts as an antidote and balm to the shame. With renewed hope and a place to speak from we have begun to weave a new pattern.

This process has been transformational for me and for those I have collaborated with, and is best illustrated by the following vignette.

At the beginning of my research, I had an ordinary encounter when getting a taxi. I slide into the taxi as I register the racist hate in the taxi driver's eyes. I am surprised and uncomfortable as I inhabit his confined territory, his taxi seems like a closed-off taut world of hate and revulsion that leaves me unsettled and unsafe but reminds me that I have to be able to dwell in this place. I grapple with describing the vibrations and static in the air as no words were used, but it was a felt experience. I begin to wonder if the narrative experience can act as a vehicle for meaning for others and myself? At the time, I imagined how it would be to not feel just the wrench and pain of racism but the textures and colours of the experience in a more integrated and less fracturing way.

It is almost four years later. I have been cooking rice with my mother, the aromatic Indian herbs and spices envelop me and I feel a mixture of self-consciousness and pride about this as I journey home. As I get into the taxi preoccupied with these very thoughts, I slowly recognise the same taxi driver. He recoils from me, as if I am able to pollute and invade his being. I look at him steadily, filled with curiosity. Where does this contempt come from? What does it do to him? I experience what I can only describe as warm expansiveness and loving compassion for him. I happily beam at him because he is representative of the journey that has reshaped me. I do not experience his hate as a terrible wound. I do not hurt. I feel no fear. I am not ashamed. In that moment and for a long while afterwards, I feel completely free.

The integration of autoethnography and psychotherapy

I have developed a more direct and specific integration of psychotherapy and autoethnography as such authoring has the potential to blur the boundaries between subject, object and otherness. This is not bound up in a conceptually rigid framework as a set of explicit tools. Rather it is an approach in itself that embodies a way of being that facilitates an internal bridging and connection with the other. This involves a deeper conscious awareness, the development of an attitude and a way of life that can be helped by the therapist being autoethnographic with self. This becomes part of their reflection and their reflexivity when thinking about clients. The interaction between autoethnography and psychotherapy is a journey of personal discovery and a self-reflective process. It is a relational and collaborative process that seeks psychological interpretations and illuminations that enhance our understanding of areas of heightened sensitivity that can transform and enhance one's capacity to be more accessible and present in relationships.

The approach is multi-method in emphasis and can include narratives, art, plays and performance to arrive at an in-depth understanding of the area being studied. It demands that one challenges representation, language, psychological and cultural constructions with heightened awareness and forming a critical subjectivity that may sit outside dominant psychological knowledge and theory. This is an attempt to create new ways of thinking about the familiar without resolving ambiguities but being able to reside in and around them. This develops the capacity to tolerate uncertainty and develop greater awareness and insight. This can also extend forms of empathy and an internal connection to the other that can be indirectly experienced, even if the narrative account is dissimilar to our own.

The taboo for therapists in naming their experiences openly and publicly can feel like contravening therapeutic boundaries as it demands we use our vulnerability (and possibly that of others), therefore we are required to consider carefully the ethics and implications of this. However, it allows for self-disclosure in the form of storytelling that can accelerate meaning through it ethical use. The audience (or reader) becomes a witness to the testimony of author and through this they themselves become implicated in what they are witnessing.

Therapist reflection on anti-racist practice

As therapists we can begin to reflect and become more available to disentangle the contradictions within our stories and develop an increased awareness of our own unconscious racisms, fears and guilt. This means exploring the complexity of racism and race and dismantling its construction into smaller, digestible parts to identify how one becomes raced. The racial and cultural stereotypes that we have about each other are a starting point that requires deconstruction. The inhibitors to therapeutic contact in working with racism means questioning what does otherness evoke in us? How do our own narratives interrupt the client's possibilities?

The therapist needs to explore these issues when sufficient trust and safety have been established and the acknowledgement of the external reality of racism before entering the client's internal space, as Hamer suggests: 'traumatic experiences of racism obliterate the individual's ability to hold onto transitional space, where the subjective cannot be experienced as such because the external reality feels so compelling' (2002: 64).

The language of racism can define and oppress subjectivity and make this trauma difficult to demarcate and describe. This means finding a way of speaking the emotional language of the client. Hall (1992) recognises that those of colour speak 'from a particular space, out of a particular history and out of a particular experience' (1992: 258). The interplay between this and specific individual narratives must be recognised and heard with the therapist listening in a particular way.

For instance, the therapist might become interested in how the client's skin colour might point to a history of racist projections. Skin colour does not just imply that we are required to be cognisant of difference; we also are required to explore the effects of possible trauma (without assuming it) and identity abrasions that come from this. This insight means accessing memories of racism and its accompanying trauma that may contribute to current and ongoing psychological distress, social maladjustment and disconnection.

It appeared to me the hallmark of racist trauma is this disconnection, as one's humanness has been lessened in worth. I think this compromised self seems to mark one as an outcast within the wider society and the community to which the individual belongs. This has implications for our understanding of racist trauma in which internalised shame becomes a source of identity and results in cognitive and psychosomatic disorders and identity abrasions. These factors result in an altered self that impacts upon object relatedness and produces an increased sensitivity to loss. The internalisation of negative projections and dominant oppressions compounds this loss of self-structure.

Conclusions

In summary, perhaps dominant narratives of psychotherapy can be challenged by storied methods to help the 'outsider' better understand this ruptured experience upon the self. Writing as a mode of inquiry, testimony and survivorship becomes another lens through which to view racist trauma. This means bringing to life methods that could possibly bypass subjective prejudice by connecting individual stories to the universality of experience. It is important to reveal the personal as the political and to evoke a resonance and vibration within the reader. This alternative narrative habitat can enhance understanding as these stories migrate beyond the teller to acquire new contextual meanings. The embodiment of this can become a source of awareness and wisdom that attempts to validate and humanize trauma experiences.

Advice for good practice

Racist trauma is a largely silenced discourse that requires interpretation, definition and reintegration. The therapist needs to do more than just engage in discourse around the importance of respect and tolerance for difference. There is a need to examine how we can displace language from the things that cannot be said into things we can find a more compassionate way to name as we begin to problematise racism.

As therapists, we are required to find a way to live with the ambiguous nature of racism, as messy and complex; as it interrupts a sense of being and thinking about racism in an arena where powerful feelings are enacted, conflicted and entangled resisting simple understandings. I have tried to demonstrate that it is possible to live with tensions and diversity between the multiplicities of voices in racism and the multiplicity of difference in which sameness is located. Where the therapist feels less constrained by having developed the capacity to be more available to enter into the webs of racialised discourse.

Note

1   I have been interested in how concepts of black and white are 'experienced' and internalised. I should emphasise that skin colour is disposed to some disparity and is often used to define racial groupings. Due to this and the spurious nature of race and skin colour, I recognise that there is no representative black or white person (Tuckwell, 2002). Racism is not just restricted to being of colour. In actuality racist treatment differs, and is vastly dependent on class, gender, sexual orientation, nation, skin pigmentation and age. Within contemporary socio-economic and political dynamics, people of colour experience the more negative effects of racism

(Miles, 2003). The fundamental principles of hate and violence on the basis of physical characteristics are linked to a sense of threat to personal and group survival is a recurrent concept (Bhui, 2002).

References

APA (2000) *Diagnostic and Statistical Manual of Mental Disorders* (4th edn). Arlington, VA: American Psychiatric Publishing.

Back, L. (2004) Writing in and against time. In Twine, F. and Warren, J. (ed.), *Racing Research, Researching Race: Methodological Dilemmas in Critical Race Studies* (p. 210). New York: University Press.

Bell, D. and Singley, B. (eds) (2004) *When Race Becomes Real: Black and White Writers Confront Their Personal Histories.* New York: Lawrence Hill.

Bhui, K. (2002) *Racism and Mental Health: Prejudice and Suffering.* London: Jessica Kingsley.

Comas-Diaz, I. and Jacobsen F.M. (2001) 'Ethnocultural Allodynia', *Journal of Psychotherapy Practice Research,* 10 (4), 246–51.

Dalal, F. (2002) *Race, Colour and the Processes of Racialization: New Perspectives from Group Analysis, Psychoanalysis, and Sociology.* London: Brunner, Routledge.

Denzin, N.K. & Lincoln, Y.S. (eds) (2003) *The Landscape of Qualitative Research Theories and Issues.* London: Sage.

Easton, M. (2006) 'Racism and race crime redefined', BBC News, 8 November. Available at: http://news.bbc.co.uk/1/hi/uk/6128466.stm (accessed May 2010).

Ellis, C. (2004) *The Ethnographic I, A Methodological Novel about Autoethnography.* Walnut Creek, CA: Altamira.

Ellis, C. and Bochner, A. (eds) (2002) *Ethnographically Speaking: Autoethnography, Literature and Aesthetics.* Oxford: Altamira.

Fernando, S. (2001) *Mental Health, Race and Culture* (2nd edn). Basingstoke. Palgrave Macmillan.

Figley, C. (1986) *Trauma and Its Wake: Autobiographic Essays by Pioneering Trauma Scholars* (Psychosocial Stress Series, No 8). London: Routledge.

Frank, A. (1995) *The Wounded Storyteller.* Boston, MA: Houghton Mifflin.

Hall, S. (1992) *Representations: Cultural Representation and Signifying Practices.* London: Sage.

Hamer, F. (2002) 'Racial transference reactions in psychoanalytic treatment'. In Moody, R. and Palmer, S. (eds), *Race, Culture and Psychotherapy: Critical Perspectives in Multicultural Practice* (p. 64). London, New York: Routledge.

Lipsedge, M. & Littlewood, R. (1997) *Aliens and Alienists: Ethnic Minorities and Psychiatry.* London: Routledge.

Miles, R. (2003) *Racism* (2nd edn) (Key Ideas series). London: Routledge.

Pederson, P. (1985) *The Handbook of Cross-Cultural Counselling and Therapy.* Westport, CT: Greenwood.

Shaw, R. (2003) *The Embodied Psychotherapist: The Therapist's Story.* Hove and New York: Brunner-Routledge.

Tuckwell, G.M. (2002) *Racial Identity, White Counsellors and Therapists.* Buckingham: Open University Press.

Saira Bains is currently writing a book on autoethnography and racist narratives. She would welcome any interested parties contacting her.

4

Child-Centred Practice

Looking for the sandwich in the therapy room

Camila Batmanghelidjh

In the service of writing this chapter I am going to attempt an explanation to place the significance of culture and ethnicity in the context of therapeutic work with children. All explanations are somewhat limited because they emerge from an individual's thinking maps, so whilst I hope my intellectual narrative offers you some organisation of the relevant central themes, I urge you to take it with a pinch of salt; anyone claiming to be able to explain culture and ethnicity risks 'hubris'.

The origins of therapeutic thinking has historically emanated from the psychology of the individual. Western thinkers who had access to written communication dominate the therapeutic narrative. The forefathers who set the intellectual discourse in motion were Freud, Klein, Jung and their students and colleagues.

Freud predominantly conceptualised a human being as a 'layered individual' whose most visible presence in the public space revealed the 'conscious' self, and whose invisible expression was the 'unconscious' self (Freud, 1933). The process of therapeutic success was formulated as the unconscious becoming evident to conscious, so that the individual had greater control and was less impulsively driven by drivers. The emphasis was clearly on the dynamics within the individual. If one looks at Freudian thinking, it could be argued that it's culturally specific, i.e. inclusive of cultural latitudes because it predominantly described the psychology of Viennese middle class neurotics. Or one could argue that it is culturally excluding because the theory didn't conceptualise individuals from other cultures and backgrounds. The point of this example is that any one theory of human definition could either be culture specific or culture deprived at any given time.

Alongside Freud and his focus on individual psychology, the 'object relations' (Fairbairn, 1952) school of thought placed the emphasis on a dyad between mother and baby, which was thought to create imprints of ways of relating in individual children. This influenced how these children defined and related to others. So, mother–child object relations created the framework for other object relations.

In the context of this theory, the intensity of exchanges are often biologically driven, emanating from baby to breast contact and progressing to other human interactions, with barely any acknowledgment of culturally or ethnic variations. For example, in some cultures babies are breast-fed by several lactating mothers, whereas in others, due to overcrowding or polygamous marriages, children develop different notions of attachments which are not based on a dyadic imprint.

The notion of 'individuation' also throws a challenge to the impact of culture on psychology. The narrative of personal development in Western culture has a baby defined as symbiotically dependent on the mother, and the process of maturation is conceptualised as a journey towards self-sufficiency and separation from parental carers, as individual competencies acted upon the cultural environment. Psychological health in this context is seen as how independent, self-sufficient and personally achieving the individual becomes. Often notions of subservience, forgoing personal needs in order to meet the needs of the collective, are seen as psychological failures. However, in some cultures excessive individualisation, the dominance of ego-psychology, is seen as failure. Excellence in developmental milestones is measured by making the ego subservient: making the self invisible in the service of the collective.

Perhaps archetypal psychology, articulated by Jung (1981), gives us the greatest possibility for grappling with the tension between individual and collective psychology. Jung believed that human beings negotiate at all times a tension between individual experience and collective experience. Collective experiences were considered by him to be expressed in archetypes: universal constructs which in some ways elevate above cultural differentiations and operate in the realm of essential psychology, for example fundamentals, such as mother archetype, father archetype, hero, villain, and so on. Jungian archetypes can best be described as universal manifestations of humanity shared across cultures. For Jung, a human being demonstrates personal growth when they moved from individual ego-psychology to the humility of universal archetypes, that is, the ego was sublimated to the universal.

It is in the act of sublimation that the beginnings of spiritual psychology also emerge. The difference between negating the self to contribute to a community in the context of a culture which demands service to the collective and spirituality is that spirituality begins with a concept of the individual, whereas negation does not. Spirituality acknowledges the individual and the understanding of the self as an entity, and then diminishes it in the service of the collective. Cultural selflessness begins with, and expects you to develop no ego-psychology. Spirituality on the other hand has ego-psychology subservient to the service of something greater than the self, sometimes defined as God.

The reason I am using such broad brushstrokes through psychological and cultural thinking is to illustrate that the narratives of personal psychology reside in a polarity between individual development excluding cultural influences, or individual negation in the service of the collective as defined by the culture.

In the context of such a tension, culture could be defined as a community's conceptualisation of the value of a human being and their duty to themselves and others, a space of collective meaning making. Ethnicity, on the other hand, is biologically determined, a genetic heritage that is not influenced by culture but will be altered by mergers of people from different cultural backgrounds.

However, it would be wrong to differentiate absolutely between culture and ethnicity. Our understanding of modern genetics and neuroscience makes it evident that cultural drivers can make aspects of a human gene expression more dominantly expressed. For example, if you live in an environment with a social structure which is very violent, then those aspects of your gene which are programmed for violence management are required to be more activated. We also know that the human brain is an ongoing construction job; human relationship sculpts our brain's capacities. Therefore the cultural environment into which we are born is likely to impact our neurochemical functioning.

I hope in this short space I have cautioned you against a rigid cultural or ethnic theoretical framework. It is best to leave the space fluid, but understand the influences that play into it.

The humility of not knowing

The essence of diversity is the individual's experience of it. Diversity is about personalised shades of experience emanating from universal colours of humanity, but each person takes from the universal what is relevant to them and alters it by their own interpersonal experiences. This chapter illustrates how diversity manifests itself in a therapeutic contract. My intention is to show how one experience has many layers. The more layers denied, the more aspects of the child's experience is left outside the therapeutic door. Denial of diversity leads to loneliness because not all of the child is embraced, welcomed and accepted, but only those aspects which the therapeutic worker has capacity for registering. Culturally sensitive therapeutic work and child-centred practice is about widening the lens of perception so that the welcome is huge and all embracing.

The learning presented here stems from the two children's charities I founded over the last 17 years. In 1991 when I founded The Place2Be, offering counselling to children in schools, a 7-year-old was trying to kill herself. She was putting a plastic reading folder over her neck and wrapping a towel round it, waiting to suffocate herself to death. She taught me one of the most important lessons of work with children: she challenged the assumption that behind every child is a responsible carer who will take that child to therapeutic appointments. In excess of 90 per cent of abused children are abused by their carers, who are unlikely to take them to an appointment for help. Since the age of 5 years, this girl was sexually abused by three men who lived in a tower block opposite. For two years, this child could not find anyone to help her evade the abuse.

I realised that if a service was going to be sensitive to children's needs it had to be based on facilitating self-referrals by children, so that is why I set up a counselling service in schools where the presence of a permanent team leader who built relationships with the children would allow a child to ask for help directly. Once the Place2Be began to be nationally disseminated, I became interested in adolescents who were not in school and, in 1996, founded Kids Company by creating a street-level centre where children and young people could access psycho-social programmes of care, again without being dependent on adult referrals.

In 2009, as I write, the University of London has completed a comprehensive three-year evaluation on Kids Company. The statistics demonstrate that 84 per cent of the children who self-refer to our street-level centres arrive homeless; 87 per cent suffer from psychiatric and significant emotional difficulties; 81 per cent are addicted to substances, of whom in excess of 90 per cent were introduced to drugs by their parents or carers; and 82 per cent of the children are surviving through crime. In the sixth richest country in the world, where scientific and cultural developments are cutting edge, why has life for some children reduced itself to mere survival? Flicking through the pages of newspapers and media channels I notice that adults are frightened *of* children rather than frightened *for* them. Kids Company is a street-level project delivering psychosocial interventions in 37 schools and three street-level centres across London. In excess of 97 per cent of our children self-refer. What they all have in common is the absence of a functioning adult in their lives, with the role of child and carer often reversed. Without a responsible parental figure, the child becomes invisible, unable to communicate their needs or hold service providers accountable. The first rule of child-centred therapeutic work is to see the child, but the question becomes what do you see, and once you have seen it, what do you do about it?

Seeing the child

To illustrate the complex layers of seeing children I would like to explore the case of Zeinab (not her real value)

Zeinab is an 11-year-old girl whose father is a major drug dealer and extremely violent. He is black and from an Islamic background. Her mother is Irish and suffers from schizophrenia. Zeinab has been exposed to a great deal of violence within the family home. Initially, it presented itself in domestic violence. Subsequently, Zeinab was sexually abused by one of the father's drug-abusing acquaintances. The abuse involved genital penetration. Zeinab heard about us from other children on the estate. Her primary request was for food. Her father had been absent due to imprisonment and her mother was too unwell and chaotic with the household money. As staff began home visits they realised that Zeinab was sleeping on the floor and lacking in basic clothing. Once food and clothing were provided for her, her trust in the key workers increased. One of the workers noticed that Zeinab was washing her hands excessively and the skin was peeling away to reveal sores. Within ten days Zeinab disclosed sexual abuse. Alongside reporting of this abuse to statutory agencies, her worker began helping Zeinab look at the impact of this experience. If trauma for this little girl could be illustrated through the symbolism of a sandwich, the layers would be described as follows:

- Poor and disrupted attachment provided by the mother as the primary carer impoverished Zeinab's ability to soothe herself and calm her own distress because no-one had provided her with the experience of being comforted. In fact, Zeinab struggled against experiencing her own existence in a vacuous way. It is through the love and attachment of a 'mother'[1] that the baby knows they exist because the mother says so, and behaves as if someone is there at the receiving end of her love and concern. Zeinab struggled to evidence her own experience; often she experienced herself spinning in infinity ungrounded, without boundaries. Zeinab was not afforded resilience through alternative attachment experiences – that is other potential maternal figures like aunts, neighbours and so on – because the family was very isolated and secretive. Poor attachment and its impact represents the top piece of bread of the sandwich. The more robust the attachment, the more the individual is contained, like a substantial piece of bread holding the sandwich contents together.

- The bottom piece of bread of this symbolic sandwich is quality of paternal attachment. Her father brought risk into the household. His interpretation of Islam meant that he forced Zeinab to wear a hijab scarf covering her hair and neck. She had to wear trousers under her dress and long sleeves so that her flesh would not be visible to men. Zeinab had to pray five times a day, not play with dogs, or eat pork, or watch movies where there was possibility of a naked body. The rituals of Islam were forced upon her without the spirit of a religion which takes duty of care to one's children immensely seriously. In the context of her father's care, Zeinab's body had to be rendered invisible. This notion of 'individual invisibility' in the service of the collective is culturally driven because of Zeinab's Islamic influences. With her poor maternal attachment it fed into Zeinab's disturbed sense of self.
- In between the traumatic attachments created by mother and father, Zeinab's other experiences create her life narratives. This is the 'filling' of the sandwich. For her, being sexually abused was catastrophic. First, it was the sense of being powerless as the man pinned her against a wall. Her fright hormones sealed the intricate details capturing the smell of his breath, the repetitive pace of his movements, the pain, his insulting words, and sealed the catastrophic moment into the emotional centres of her brain in the form of a shocking unresolved memory. Years later Zeinab recalled the event as if its terrifying characteristics reappeared, making 'then' 'now', unmediated through the passage of time. She has flashbacks and night terrors. This is a symptom of post-traumatic stress reaction, to which individuals with poor maternal attachment are more prone (Perry and Azad, 1999). However, in the context of Zeinab's Islamic cultural influences, she is interpreting these night-terrors as God's punishment for her failing to remain sexually 'pure'.
- Another layer of the trauma is Zeinab's inability to deliver revenge. She was too small and weak to harm the man and regain some kind of power equilibrium. She became the 'unwilling container' of his aggression as he physically forced himself into her, but also psychologically invaded her with his adult desire and aggression. This primary experience of unwilling sexual penetration for a child is immensely difficult to negotiate, but added to the psychological assault is the cultural implication presented by the Islamic influences in her life. Zeinab feels she has been defiled through 'sin', upsetting Allah (God). The unbearable and catastrophic impact of feeling so contaminated is making Zeinab chronically wash her hands, hoping to make 'the dirt' go away.
- A further layer is the impact which presents itself at street level. Zeinab lives on an estate in South London where children learn very early the rules of power. Chronically abused children often define life in the context of 'top-dog' and 'under-dog'. Initially as the victimised, they fantasise escape and a compulsion to experience their own potency, which sadly can result in them becoming the aggressor. The rules at street level make it clear that anyone who is a victim without the capacity to avenge or cause significant harm will become further victimised: Zeinab carries a knife and torments younger children. 'Legitimate' power structures such as social care agencies or the police did not protect her from neglect and abuse, and she sees them as ineffectual. From Zeinab's perspective, power is exercised by the violent.

There are two cultural influences intensely mediating the sexual abuse of this girl. One influence is from her Islamic background, the other from the inner-city culture of violence. Each exerts a different kind of pressure on Zeinab's coping mechanism and meaning-making in relation to being abused. She will also have to negotiate the key worker's cultural influences in processing the abuse. The worker will bring to the relationship not only his or her familial culture but also a therapeutic, intellectual culture.

Zeinab has not told her mother or father that she was sexually assaulted; she is worried about not being a virgin and how she is going to explain her lack of 'purity' to the husband her father is likely to choose for her. Zeinab perceives being rejected by Islam for not being a virgin, but she also feels rejected by her mother for not being protected against the abuse. Both these experiences create for her a rationale that she is not worthy of being saved or loved, hence feeding into her sense of worthlessness. She is also confused about where the man's penis went, i.e. has it created a big hole in her? Does it mean she has a baby? All the confusions of a young child about her own biology are tangled up with the trauma.

The intense management of her feelings is distorting Zeinab's ability to concentrate in school. She is falling behind, being told off, and experiencing the taking in of teachers instructions as the taking in of an 'unwanted penis'. So many experiences are now being tainted by the traumatic event. She can't obey the simplest rules or stand in the lunch queue because any form of control exercised over her feels as catastrophic as being overpowered by the abuser. A tension develops around the required submissiveness of her individuality in the service of a cultural need for obedience: Islamic girls are to be understated and 'publicly subservient'. However, Zeinab is experiencing obedience as being equivalent to being overpowered by the abuser.

Feeling unsure of what really happened has left Zeinab with a secret compulsion to repeat the experience so that somehow she can assimilate the event having more control over its happening. So whilst intensely washing to 'get rid of the dirt', Zeinab places herself in situations of risk by inviting men to touch her sexually and then retreats. By doing this she almost redefines the trauma by managing the escape so that full penetration does not happen because she prevented it.

One traumatic event in Zeinab's life could be looked at in the context of only one isolated incident, or the combined implications could be captured across religion, street culture and psychological consequences. The more layers to Zeinab's 'trauma sandwich' are identified, the more Zeinab gets to be visible. With her visibility comes a potentially catastrophic moment. Will the therapeutic worker cherish her, choose her, and afford her loving care or will she be left exposed, un-embraced in that cold space of neutrality? When therapeutic workers see children and their pain it is imperative that the child does not feel rejected. Intellect and counselling skills void of emotional warmth are assaults to the dignity of a child. Alone, devastated, depleted and terrorised, Zeinab fears being excluded from collective acceptance.

Embracing diversity is not just about recognising it. It is about embracing into the collective all human beings because they share humanity, irrespective of differences created by cultural divide or trauma. So when speaking about the need for diversity and cultural competencies in therapeutic work with children, there are some experiences which have commonality no matter what the religious or cultural difference. Every human being needs nurturing attachments in order for their personal existence to be affirmed and for them to develop the appropriate neuro-physiological ability to manage emotion and energy. Our frontal lobe, the centre of personal management, is equipped to care for us and others because of the love and care it has received. No culture compromises on this fundamental requirement. It is imperative that the child feels cherished and chosen in the therapeutic space. Not seeing the child is worse than seeing and making mistakes. As long as you can love and cherish the child, and have the humility to ask when you don't know, then knowledge about ethnicity, cultural and religious issues becomes secondary to the universal meeting point of humanity.

Exercise: The trauma sandwich

Carefully read the case study below then identify the layers of impact a trauma is likely to have in the child's life. The purpose of the exercise is to make the child's experience visible in order to see the child and give them your all-encompassing, unconditional positive regard.

Omar: Omar is 15 years old. He was found at Victoria station without any legal papers. He describes himself as being trafficked from Sierra Leone and dropped off in England. The man who brought him over said he was coming back but never returned, leaving Omar to ask for help from strangers. Eventually the police at the station noticed Omar and delivered him to social services. Omar was placed in a bed and breakfast hotel and given £30 per week to live on. Others in the hotel with similarly devastated backgrounds began introducing him to mechanisms of street survival in England. Omar began participating in the drug trade; his immense capacity for violence meant that he became a respected criminal and feared on the street. Omar takes street drugs. He struggles to sleep, negotiating night terrors and flashbacks; in his own country Omar had been kidnapped by soldiers, drugged, forced to rape women, kill and maim others. Omar, misses his mother whom he describes as incredibly loving. His father, however, used to beat him with sticks and was prone to unpredictable rages. Can you make Omar and his needs visible?

Answer to the exercise

The themes that can be considered as 'filling for your sandwich' are listed below. See how many of these you captured:

- attachments and the consequent self-calming resources
- survivor's guilt
- behaviour as a perpetrator
- managing visual horrors of war

(Continued)

(Continued)

- the ease with which people can be killed and harmed and therefore the frailty of human life and implications about Omar's own life
- altered perceptions and personality as a result of drug use
- being harmed by his father and the army leaders who forced him into the war
- separation from his mother and siblings, and not knowing their fate
- the harm he would have caused to other mothers and their children
- arriving in a new country and culture not being able to speak the language
- interrupted education
- negotiating street violence and street culture in the new country
- being abandoned and isolated because of a lack of relatives or acquaintances
- being at the mercy of handouts and constant change of social workers
- inadequate living conditions
- feeling separated because of his culture and because he has killed and harmed others
- no ability to build his future because he has no legal status or papers
- unable to return to his country because relatives of those he has harmed would want to harm him and he is unsure if he has relatives to return to
- terrified of human relationships in case he loses them or harms them
- complicated feelings about being expected to experience gratitude for the help the state is giving versus the inadequacy and often disrespect with which the help is delivered
- preoccupations about 'karma' and whether he will go to hell because of the harm he has caused
- struggling against meaninglessness as he has an intrinsic understanding of how everything one builds up can be suddenly taken away, and an inability to aspire for his future
- worrying whether he will beat his own child like his father beat him and the continuing cycles of violence
- at times not being able to differentiate the girlfriend he has sex with from the women he raped
- the indignity of not feeling worthwhile enough or feeling he has enough legitimacy to be at the receiving end of help
- fear that people will look at him and think of him as a murderer
- the high he might have experienced from causing harm and killing
- tension between his African cultural background and the British cultural background in which he now finds himself.

The list is not exhaustive but these are some of the possible main themes.

Conclusion

As we struggle to attribute influence – biological, psychological and cultural – in a human being's life, we should be reassured by current neuropsychiatric developments. Somehow, modern science and its understanding of the human mind is closing the circle and taking us back to the origins of psychotherapeutic healing, before Freud, which began with shamanism. Shamanistic rituals were based on grappling with the spirit, which at times was thought to be placed within the individual or influencing individual functioning outside the individual. There was a sense that the spirit, in whatever manifestation, was both internal and external, influencing the psychology and functioning of a person. Through a process of rituals, exorcisms and the drama of healing, the shaman mediates, moderating the influences of the spirit and in the process endeavours to restore equilibrium to the individual who had sought help. If we substitute the word 'spirit' with 'emotion and energy', then we have the modern equivalent of spirit seen through the investigative tools of neuroscience.

Current understanding of psychological functioning in human beings is being redefined. Good health is thought to reside in an individual's ability to self-regulate, that is, manage personal emotions and energy. The frontal lobe is thought to be the seat of pro-social rationality, through the cognition of which the limbic system, the emotional centres of the brain deep inside the skull, is thought to be moderated and regulated. An appropriately functioning individual is one who can achieve personal balance using the inter-relationship between emotion and cognition in the service of moderating personal expression. A well cared for individual whose attachments have been robust will internalise the ability to calm down, supported by a network of other carers who can give resilience to this personal task of self-management. Challenges to the 'self-regulation' will be personal and cultural.

Depending on cultural differences there will be a bias between how much the individual takes responsibility for self-soothing and how much the collective will do it for them. But the fundamental task is to achieve a sense of belonging, being valued, feeling loved and being able to reciprocate it. No matter what, the cultural or ethnic background of an individual the archetypal need – of any human being – is to feel a sense of belonging and to be cherished in the generosity of which the ability to cherish others will emerge as altruism.

A therapeutic worker becomes like the shaman, a facilitator of appropriate emotional and energetic management. Initially, like a carer for a baby or like the collective for the individual, the therapeutic worker needs to be alongside the patient as a compassionate witness helping them facilitate their journey through emotional and spiritual turbulence towards equilibrium. It is a journey from fragmentation, devastation and isolation to cohesion, connectedness and being embraced. Cultural, ethnic and psychological frameworks are part of the meaning-making mechanism an individual requires to make sense of their existence in the world and in the context of others. Individuals from varied backgrounds will have differing significances in the bias they place on the influence culture and ethnicity plays on their sense of identity in the world.

The job of a therapeutic worker is to be informed enough to ask the questions and humble enough to wait for the answers. Cultures and ethnicities carry universal principles, but the uptake of every individual is different. The primary rule of culturally informed psychotherapy with children is to welcome as much of the child and their experience as is possible, so that they feel cherished once more.

Note

1 'Mother' acknowledges any maternal influence, not exclusively the birth mother.

References

Fairbairn, R. (1952) *An Object-Relations Theory of the Personality.* New York: Basic Books

Freud, S. (1933) 'New Introductory Lectures on Psychoanalysis'; *The Standard Edition of the Complete Psychological Works of Sigmund Freud,* 22 (ed. and trans. J. Strachey, A. Freud, A Strachey and A. Tyson). London: Hogarth Press and The Institute of Psycho-Analysis, pp. 1953–75

Jung, C.G. (1981) 'The Archetypes and the Collective Unconscious' 2nd edn. *Collected Works Vol.9 Part 1).* Princeton, NJ: Bollingen, pp. 1934–54

Perry, B. and Azad, I. (1999) 'Post-traumatic stress disorders in children and adolescents'; *Current Opinions in Pediatrics,* 11: 4, 121–32

5 Sexualities, Sexual Identities and Gender
An anti-discriminatory approach

Aaron Balick

> Gina sits across from her client Andy who is a gay man, in a sexless relationship with his long-term partner Eddie; however, Andy and Eddie have agreed to open their relationship to other sexual partners. While this keeps their sexual appetites sated, Andy also notes that his relationship feels too 'comfortable' and wonders if they are making the right choices. Gina notices her desire to 'coach' Andy back towards monogamy to achieve a better balance of the sensual and the emotional in his relationship; she feels reluctance and sometimes repugnance at Andy's sexual tales. However, she is not aware of her own envy of his sexual experiences, and the grief for the lack of a sexual life in her own marriage. Still, she is a good counsellor. She manages to 'bracket' her feelings providing a 'safe non-judgemental place' to 'contain' Andy's experience, actively resisting any impulses to be directive.

This chapter, which is an addition to the second edition of this book, replaces the chapter from the first edition entitled 'Gay affirmative practice' (Perlman, 2003). The reader will notice a substantial title change. While Perlman's chapter was inclusive of many sexualities (he refers to lesbian, gay, bisexual, non-straight and transgendered clients), the title itself draws from the tradition of gay affirmative therapy (GAT) that originated in the United States with Maylon's (1993) ground-breaking work on internalised homophobia (first published in 1982), and was popularised in the UK through the work of Davies and Neal (1996). While these insights from affirmative therapy will be maintained, it is necessary to include gender and sexual identities as they affect *everyone*, while retaining the awareness that those who lie further from the social notion of 'convention' are more likely to be psychologically and emotionally affected by their non-conventional identities than others (Friedman and Downey, 2002). How the contemporary counsellor integrates an anti-discriminatory position with regard to their clients of *any* sexuality or gendered position[1] will be the aim of this chapter.

A short history of therapy and counselling practice with non-conventional sexualities

> Andy knows that Gina accepts his gay identity – they have been working together for some time, and he feels comfortable with her. However, whenever he allows himself to speak explicitly about the sexual relations he is having outside his relationship he
>
> *(Continued)*

(Continued)

notices a strange feeling inside – akin to shame. He can't work it out. Gina smiles, nods, asks clarifying questions – but something is not right. As time goes on, Andy feels more and more uncomfortable. The feeling is familiar. He unconsciously starts to talk less about his sex life, and concentrates more on other things. The old familiarity and safety of their sessions resume.

Until the development of humanistic counselling in the 1960s, the thrust of psychotherapeutic practice and theory was anti-homosexual in nature, encouraging a practice that aimed to 'turn' homosexuals into heterosexuals (whether through the use of psychoanalysis or behavioural methods). Starting in the 1970s, one could see the beginnings of the pendulum swinging towards a 'gay affirmative' position in which gay and lesbian behaviours and identities were seen as non-pathological; these identities are consciously and actively affirmed, aiming to counter culturally produced internalised homophobia. In 1973, homosexuality was officially removed from the Diagnostic and Statistical Manual (DSM) (APA, 2000) in the United States (Lewes, 1995); this saw the development of strategies to treat individuals who identified as gay or lesbian from a non-pathology point of view, a process that became known as gay affirmative therapy (GAT). Today, the experience of individuals with non-conventional sexualities or genders may no longer attempt to be 'cured' nor 'affirmed', but rather non-judgmentally approached as an identity construct like any other. However, while individuals may overcome judgements received through messages absorbed from a public that is still often wary and uncomfortable with non-conventional sexualities and genders, it is a greater task for individual counsellors to work through their own unconscious identifications in a way that allows them to work freely with such individuals. However, the notion of 'conventional' itself is challenged as Freud reminds us: 'The sexual life of each one of us extends to a slight degree – now in one direction, now in that – beyond the narrow lines imposed as the standard of normality. The perversions are neither bestial nor degenerate in the emotional sense of the word' (1905: 50). By speaking about 'the emotional sense of the word'. Freud is referring to 'conventional thinking' and he is arguing that there is no such thing, *really,* as 'conventional being'.

Contrary to popular belief, Freud did not set the tone for the grievously anti-homosexual stance taken by psychoanalysis from the 1940s right up until the present (Lewes, 1995). According to Lewes, while Freud does at times theorise homosexuality as a developmental arrest, he also maintains that homosexuals are not sick; that psychoanalysis should not seek to 'cure' them; and that homosexuals should not be prevented from training as analysts. Freud famously responded to a letter from an American mother who wrote to him, concerned about her homosexual son: 'Homosexuality is assuredly no advantage but it is nothing to be ashamed of, no vice, no degradation, it cannot be classified as an illness; we consider it to be a variation of the sexual function produced by the certain arrest of sexual development' (1995: 20). The use of the word 'variation' here is important as it denotes a non-pathological claim on a sexuality that is different, though not 'sick'. Despite this, it was largely the movement of psychoanalysis to the United States that shifted theorising about homosexuality towards a pathological model with a moralistic tone (Abelove, 1993). The removal of homosexuality from the DSM was a great step for both the mental health professions' treatment of individuals with non-conventional behaviours and identifications, but it was also a great political step for the social liberation of 'non-straight' individuals.

The humanistic counselling movement developed as a reaction to the dominance of psychoanalytic and behavioural practices that it saw as using a medical model that put the 'disease' and the symptom before the actual person. In many ways, humanistic psychology in many of its forms 'got there' long before psychoanalysis did, especially with Carl Rogers' 'core conditions' in which Rogers 'came to believe that the quality of the relationship – specifically the therapists' congruence, uncon- ditional positive regard and empathy – were more important factors in the thera- peutic change than the specific techniques the therapist employed' (1990: 62). While some of these core conditions may be difficult to achieve authentically all of the time, their aim is noble; one can hardly achieve the core conditions while main- taining a pathologising view of their clients. However, by looking at these phenom- ena from a different angle, by critically examining *the very way in which we understand identities to be constituted*, we can begin to open up the experience of marginal sexual and gender identities to greater understanding and change; the influence of postmodern and queer theory has done a great deal to shake up thinking in this area.

For the past 25 years or so, the advance of postmodernism has become a major plank in academic thinking. 'Postmodernism' is a term that covers a difficult and hotly disputed location in contemporary philosophy, and furthermore, its influ- ence on psychotherapy and counselling. Loewenthal and Snell's description is necessarily reductive, but useful for our purposes; they describe the postmodern perspective as one that attacks modernist ideas, opposes 'over-arching visions of "rational" or late Enlightenment modernism' and favours 'diversity, multiplicity and uncertainty, over system, ideology and generalisation' (2003: 4–5). In other words, postmodernism challenges what we think we know about the 'truth' of things, and implores us to 'deconstruct' how such truths are created (i.e. seeing 'truths' as socially constructed rather than essential). Queer theory is a branch of postmodernism, and is generally understood to subvert 'modern' and 'binary,'[2] conceptions of sex and gender. Alsop et al. describe queer theory's goal to 'render it evident that neither gender nor sex is a natural category – indeed, the very idea of a "natural" category is simply an effect of discourse' (2002: 106). In this quote you can see how notions of the essential 'truths' of gender and sex as 'natural' is criticised under the rubric of queer theory. Queer theory takes classical psychoa- nalysis and other modernist perspectives to task for their close association to binary notions of sex and gender, patriarchy, misogyny, heteronormative practice, and the social production of identities. The appropriation of postmodern and queer theory was naturally seized upon by the psychotherapies; after all, counsellors and psychotherapists are in the business of working through notions of 'identity' every day of their working lives: any contemporary discussion of sexual or gender identi- ties would necessarily have to engage with queer theory, whether one agrees with its premises or not. Since anti-discriminatory practice is concerned with ensuring that marginalised *identities* are managed appropriately in counselling practice, we might come to find that queer theory and postmodern perspectives run somewhat askew of these aims. With queer theory and postmodernism being the current locus of contemporary theorising of gender and sexual identity, some serious thinking needs to be set up on working through how these notions may be integrated into anti-discriminatory counselling practice. However, postmodernism is no panacea: it was not created with regard to clinical application, therefore much thought should be given to the application of its principles.

Relational perspectives (see Dimen and Goldner, 2002, and Aron, 1996 for example), in my opinion, have the most theoretically cohesive conception of the integration of postmodern theory and the practice of psychotherapy. Relational thinking is applicable across the board of therapeutic models and can be seen to resonate with many principles of humanistic practice and theory in its radical positions with regard to mutuality, power-relations, and the co-construction of experience between therapist and client.

Towards a contemporary anti-discriminatory practice

While humanistic and psychoanalytic perspectives are both broadly 'non-directive' in nature, GAT, in acknowledging the importance of internalised homophobia, does seek a more active approach to repair that damage. The objectives of affirmative therapy is 'to provide corrective experiences to ameliorate the consequences of biased socialization … this is not a prescription for how to do psychotherapy. Instead, it is a frame of reference for the accomplished clinician' (Maylon, 1993: 81–2). In an earlier work (Balick, 2009) I critically evaluated GAT in the context of relational theory and the influence of postmodernism. I concluded that while GAT laudably aims to repair the damage of internalised homophobia, it does not adequately interrogate the less fixed aspects of identity, nor the relational aspects of identity that are co-created *in-vivo*. Identities are hard won and frequently provide individuals with a sense of safety and belonging: especially those individuals who find themselves closer to the margins than to the centre. However, the clinician must also keep in mind that identities are not necessarily fixed and taking them as so may limit the complexity and depth of the therapeutic endeavour. At the same time, clinicians must not be seduced by the ideological imperatives within queer theory that insist on identity fluidity. Replacing a heterosexist outcome with a postmodern or queer one simply replicates the prizing of a given sexual or gender identity over another. When we ask the practitioner to consider the unconscious aspects of the co-created relationship we can begin to work directly with the co-constructions of such identities as they exist in the room *between* therapist and client. This approach removes the dialectical notion of fixed *or* fluid identities and replaces it with one that is multiple and co-created: it removes the need for a political and radical 'challenge' and replaces it with an open co-creation.

The consulting room as relational re-play, repair and moving on

Gina notes that the content of the sessions with Andy has changed. He seems more comfortable: to have moved on from his preoccupation with sex outside his relationship. Gina even has a feeling of relief about this. Yet despite this change, there is a sense of something undone – something unspoken and broken – sessions feel superficial. Things with Andy's partner have not improved, yet the relationship no longer comes into the therapy sessions. Gina decides to inquire about this in the next session.

The theoretical foundation of GAT is crucial to retain because it foregrounds the damage done to a marginalised sexual identity over time. However, moving beyond affirmative therapy we come to understand that these experiences are not limited to individuals on the 'margins' of convention, but are universally applicable since we *all* have aspects of ourselves that lie outside convention. Furthermore, while we can see the protective nature of identity categories like 'gay', 'straight' or 'transgendered', we can also see how such identities can be limiting and resistant to the flexibility. What is fundamental here is that a series of relational ruptures can be traced back to an individual's sexual or gendered subjectivity. These ruptures can be seen to begin in early family life; they are then repeated, echoed and replayed through relationships with siblings, extended family, and social groups as time moves on.[3] A survey of research studies carried out by Friedman and Downey (2002) indicate that both gay men and lesbians may be more at risk for mental health issues such as depression, drug and alcohol dependency and suicide than heterosexuals, while Fish and Harvey (2005) draw particular attention to the difficulties stigma causes in queer youth. The fact that gay and lesbian youth (alongside the panoply of other possible sexual and gendered constellations) are growing up in a 'toxic environment' (2005: 58) comprised of social stigma and verbal and emotional assault. These sorts of 'assaults' are likely to occur throughout an individual's life, and it is perhaps for these reasons that lesbian, gay and black individuals are more likely to access psychotherapeutic services, and to stay longer (King et al., 2007).

The counselling encounter has the capacity to echo the feelings of rupture that may have been key components of previous relationships. When speaking of the multiplicity of gender and sexual identities as lived in both counsellor and client, it is crucial that psychic space is created for such identities to express themselves freely. Aspects of gender and sexual identity that fall outside convention are likely to be encumbered with negative associations if they are conscious, or at the unconscious level, foreclosed altogether. Having had such aspects of the self rejected by parents and early social groups, such individuals are likely to be hyper-vigilant of rejection within their counsellors; such perceptions of rejection may be purely transferential (i.e. projected onto the therapist and assumed to be real) or the rejection may emanate out of the counsellor's actual judgement, or indeed out of the therapist's own defensiveness about his or her own unconventional sexual or gender identity. As Cornett describes:

> If the psychotherapist is subtly or blatantly rejecting, this expectation of rejection can grow into a transference phenomenon that tends to become the entire experience of psychotherapy for both the patient and the clinician – an experience that neither invites the patient to explore his authentic identity nor encourages him in this endeavor if he chooses to do so. (1995: 140)

It is important to take a short digression here in order to draw a distinction between transference phenomena and what might be called enactment.[4] Clarkson (2003) describes a number of 'modalities' of therapeutic relationships including the transferential/countertransferential relationship and the person-to-person or 'real' relationship. While these relational dynamics dip in and out of each other and often overlap, the terminology is useful in theoretical discussion. From the context of relational psychoanalysis, the person-to-person relationship is the object of greatest interest – this does not preclude transference phenomena. Taking a classical view of transference, I understand it, like Laplanche and Pontalis, as the re-emergence of infantile experiences transferred upon the analyst 'with a strong sensation to immediacy' (2004: 455). Hence, I would argue that the notion of rejection as an experience within the therapy could very well saturate the transferential relationship, whether or not the therapist is indeed rejecting. This may be dealt with in the usual way by working through and exploring the nature of the transference, interpreting it if necessary. However, what if the counsellor *is indeed* experiencing feelings of rejection towards their client? This *can* be understood as an enactment. The term 'enactment' comes from psychoanalysis (Jacobs, 1986) to describe events, feelings or memories that are evoked (acted out) within the therapeutic situation. Aron (2003) develops this concept further, maintaining that it is complex and sometimes paradoxical; he is wary of the term as it has historically been used because it brings with it the assumption that enactments can be seen as '"events" [that] happen from time to time ... but it denies that the patient and analyst are always enacting ... from beginning to end' (Aron, 1996: 212). He argues that the therapeutic encounter itself is *in a constant state of enacting*: recognising this enables counsellors to identify enactments as they occur (or usually, shortly after) and help to make sense of them. To come back to Cornett's discussion of the potential for rejection in the therapeutic dyad (in his case the rejection of the homosexual identity, but in a larger sense, the rejection of any gender or sexual identity), I think it is important to make the distinction between enactment and transference. While transference and enactment may overlap a great deal, there is most certainly a difference between *perceived* rejection and *actual* rejection. Both events can be dealt with in a broadly relational way. Despite being a projection, the perceived rejection will no doubt still inhibit relational functioning and will need to be dealt with actively – perhaps by drawing attention to the repeated nature of the expected rejection. If there is actual rejection occurring, then the relational work is likely to be much more subtle and complex. Such a rejection will be experienced by the counsellor who will then have to make some judgements about how such a rejection is functioning within him/herself, and take their intervention from there.

Feelings of rejection are a common enactment when it comes to therapeutic relations in relation to sexual or gender identities. Counsellors should be vigilant to the ways in which enactments occur within the co-created relationship with regard to sexual and gender identities and try, alongside their clients, to become conscious of and make sense of them.

Exercises for trainees

'I know it's silly,' says Andy in response to Gina's inquiry, 'but it felt weird talking to you about it. I would sit there looking at you, and it felt like talking to my mother about sex!' He laughed, and so did Gina. 'I know you won't judge me,' he continued, 'but I felt judged anyway – like you didn't want me to be having sex outside my relationship.' Gina looked at Andy, and had a sense that he had really got the measure of her. She could see that she did want this of him, despite her professional bracketing of her desires. She was able to identify this as an enactment and decided to take responsibility for her part in it.

After some grounding in the theoretical models above, experiential work in this area is essential in assimilating this information for use in practice. The thrust of the experiential component lay in an enquiry into how one 'grew up' as a gendered and sexualised being throughout one's life. The following questions are a good starting point, and these questions can be answered in relation to the age groupings below. Depending on the nature of the training organisation, such inquiry can be conducted through assignments, learning journals, dyad work, small groups or large groups. Good starting out questions include:

- How do I understand myself as a sexed person (female, male, intersex, etc.)?
- How do I understand myself as a gendered person (masculine, feminine, in-between, etc.)?
- How do I understand myself as a sexual being (including sexual identity, desire, fantasy, behaviour, etc.)?
- How have my important relationships contributed to this understanding of myself?

These questions should be asked for each age grouping with an emphasis on what aspects of the self were *particularly affected at certain times*; what started at one stage and was enhanced or deconstructed during others; what remained the same and what changed? Trainers should ensure that age-appropriate milestones are included in the discussion:

- *First two years*: Expectations before birth, early influence of primary caregivers, early language development, etc.
- *Ages 3–6*: Early family life, acculturation, symbolisation, etc.
- *Ages 7–11*: Influences outside the family, culture, pre-adolescence.
- *Ages 11–16*: Influence of peers, adolescence and puberty, sexual experimentation, etc.
- *Ages 16–21*: Growth of independence from family, influence of friends and lovers, etc.
- *Adulthood*: Changes in perspectives acquired along the way.

The aim of this experiential work is to encourage psychological and emotional thinking about gender and sexual identifications of the individual. It has clinical significance in that it prepares the trainee with a language and insight into their own process, encouraging an open-mindedness around the psychological and emotional possibilities inherent in their own identities. Sharing their experiences with others further opens up the field by encouraging understanding and acceptance of other identities and experiences. Once this 'insight' programme has been completed, trainees are then asked to think about applying these insights into clinical work:

- What are the power relationships inherent in the mix of genders and sexualities of the dyad?
- How might I apply the theories described above to my practice?
- What is the relevance of MY gender, sexuality, fantasy life, sex-life in the counselling relationship?
- How have I felt in my own counselling sessions as client with regard to sex, sexual identity, etc?
- How has the gender or sexual identity of my counsellor or therapist affected me? Consider how my own sexual self, sexual/gender identity, or sex/gender may play out in my role as a counsellor.

It should of course be made clear that such questions, both with regard to personal insight *and* clinical application, should be asked throughout one's work and throughout one's career. People's identities may shift over time, and perspectives, especially, change. Hence, this is not the sort of material that is trained in once and then left behind as 'done' – it should be a continued part of professional inquiry and personal therapy.

Conclusion

> 'Andy, you're right. I did think that. Every time you brought up sex with other people, I noticed a resistance on my part. I probably feel a bit protective over you and Eddie, and have worried that you two would louse things up. I think it's important I acknowledge this to you – but I also would like to get back to it and see if you can help me understand it from your perspective.' Andy sat with this for a moment, and then looked at Gina, 'I'm glad you said that. I was beginning to think I was going a bit mad. Like when my parents accepted me coming out, but never REALLY wanted to hear about what I was getting up to. They made all the right noises, but they were uncomfortable, I could tell; whenever I asked about it they said, "Don't be silly! We're fine with it!" The thing is, Gina, I'm not sure if I AM fine with what's going on with me and Eddie, and I really want to work this one out.'[5]

All individuals have a relationship (both conscious and unconscious) with their own sense of difference, and this is a fundamental aspect of an individual's identity. However complex identity is; it is tied together in a personal narrative that coheres under the auspices of the self. Its complexity frequently leads individuals to feel outside the 'in group'. It has been a contention throughout this chapter that in the same sense that the 'in group' is a myth, so is the notion of conventionality.

The relational perspective requires that the counsellor become as aware as possible of their own multiple identifications, and where this is not possible that they learn to accept such aspects of themselves about which they are less clear. Trainers can enable their trainees to work more effectively with this material by requiring that trainees engage in experiential work to get to know their own processes with regard to such identities. Bringing trainees up to speed on a minority of sexual identities/experiences, though potentially helpful, is not enough: rather, encouraging discovery and providing a safe space through which to explore the identifications of self and others in a facilitative environment is key.

Individual counsellors cannot be expected to know the ins and outs of every client's culture with regard to gender, sexual identity or behaviour. While some degree of sensitivity training may be necessary to encourage that individuals have some familiarity with a particular set of circumstances, there will always be lacunae in knowledge and experience. This can be okay so long as the counsellor is authentic about their ignorance, seeks to address it, and, crucially, remains attuned to their client and always actively seeking to recognise their client's uniqueness as an individual sexual and gendered human being. If there is one key to this entire perspective, it is that the counsellor should seek, as best as they can, to *recognise* their client, and resist as far as possible the continued set of *misrecognitions* that are likely to be present, and association with their notions of self. Continued vigilance to the co-created mutual nature of the therapeutic dyad will also be necessary.

Notes

1 In an effort to be completely inclusive, I understand 'sexuality and gender position' to include more than just identities, but also sexual behaviours, fantasies, or gender constructions (experienced with the body or not) that resonate outside socially sanctioned expressions or conventional ideas.

2 Sex and gender have historically been seen as a simple binary (i.e. two things in opposition). Male/female, homosexual/heterosexual, normal/perverse, single/married, are all examples of binary conceptions. Queer theory seeks to subvert and complicate this binary, or as Judith Butler puts it, to make trouble with gender (see Butler's seminal 1990 text *Gender Trouble*, the text commonly referred to as the progenitor of the queer theory approach).

3 Social science research like that of Cass (1979), Coleman (1987) and Troiden (1988) draw out developmental models of this process.

4 Such distinctions about the 'pureness' of a transference or of an enactment are made here for theoretical clarity. It is understood that these distinctions are often impossible to make in actual settings, and the difficulty of such distinctions are discussed below.

5 This vignette is fictional and is meant to be illustrative of theory, so it is necessarily compact and reductive. Whether or not to make a self-disclosure is a personal judgement of individual counsellors; however, it is crucial that practitioners disclose to themselves (and their supervisors) how they are responding to their clients, especially if it brings up difficult feelings. While it is necessary to take a non-judgemental approach to the choices of clients (in this case Andy and Eddie's choice to open up their relationship), this does not preclude exploring these choices in the face of challenging and uncomfortable feelings. When therapists and counsellors shut down aspects of their own internal dialogues, this is communicated unconsciously to their clients, and can re-play older foreclosures that the client has previously experienced with regard to their identities. The goal is to approach this old dynamic from a new perspective, releasing ossified dynamics and providing the opportunity for new ones.

References

Abelove, Henry. 1993. 'Freud, male homosexuality, and the Americans', in *The Lesbian and Gay Studies Reader*, ed. Henry Abelove, Michele Aina Barale, and David M. Halperin, 381–96. New York and London: Routledge.

Alsop, Rachel, A. Fitzsimons, and K. Lennon. 2002. *Theorizing Gender*. Cambridge, UK: Polity Press.

APA. 2000. *Diagnostic and Statistical Manual of Mental Disorders*, 4th edition. Arlington, VA: American Psychiatric Publishing.

Aron, Lewis. 1996. *A Meeting of Minds: mutuality in psychoanalysis*. Hilsdale, NJ and London: The Analytic Press.

Aron, Lewis. 2003. 'The Paradoxical Place of Enactment in Psychoanalysis: Introduction'. *Psychoanal. Dial.* 13: 623–31.

Balick, Aaron. 2009. 'Relational ethics beyond the sex and gender binary', in *Relational Ethics in Practice: narratives from counselling and psychotherapy*, eds. Lynne Gabriel and Roger Casemore. London: Routledge.

Butler, Judith. 1990. *Gender Trouble: feminism and the subversion of identity*. New York and London: Routledge.

Cass, V.C. 1979. 'Homosexual identity formation: a theoretical model'. *Journal of Homosexuality*. 4: 219–35.

Clarkson, Petruska. 2003. *The Therapeutic Relationship*, 2nd edition. London and Philadelphia, PA: Whurr.

Coleman, E. 1987. 'Assessment of Sexual Orientation.' *Journal of Homosexuality*. 14: 1/2. 9–14.

Cornett, Carlton. 1995. *Reclaiming the Authentic Self: dynamic psychotherapy with gay men*. Northvale, NJ: Jason Aronson.

Davies, D., and Neal, C. (eds). 1996. *Pink Therapy: a guide for counsellors and therapists working with lesbian, gay and bisexual clients*. Buckingham: Open University Press.

Dimen, Muriel and Goldner, Viginia. eds. 2002. *Gender and Psychoanalytic Space: between clinic and culture*. New York: Other Press.

Fish, Linda Stone and Harvey, Rebecca, G. 2005. *Nurturing Queer Youth: family therapy transformed*. New York and London: Norton.

Friedman, Robert and Downey, Jennifer. 2002. *Sexual Orientation and Psychoanalysis: sexual science and clinical practice*. New York: Columbia University Press.

Freud, S. 1905. 'Three Essays on the Theory of Sexuality.' *SE* 7: 123–245. London: Hogarth Press. 1953.

Jacobs, T.J. 1986. 'On Countertransference Enactments'. *J. Amer. Psychoanal. Assn.*, 34: 289–307.

King, M., Semylen, J., Killaspy, H., Nazareth, I., and Osborn, D. 2007. *A Systematic Review of Research on Counselling and Psychotherapy for Lesbian, Gay, Bisexual and Transgender People*. Rugby: BACP.

Laplanche, Jean and Pontalis, Jean-Betrand. 2004. *The Language of Psychoanalysis*. London: Karnac.

Lewes, Kenneth. 1995. *Psychoanalysis and Male Homosexuality*. Northvale, NJ: Jason Aronson.

Loewenthal, Del and Snell, Robert. 2003. *Post-Modernism for Psychotherapists: a critical reader*. Hove and New York: Taylor and Francis.

Maylon, A. 1993. 'Psychotherapeutic implications of internalized homophobia in gay men.' In *Affirmative Dynamic Psychotherapy with Gay Men*, ed. Carlton Cornett, 77–92. Northvale, NJ and London: Jason Aronson.

Perlman, Graham. 2003. 'Gay affirmative practice.' In *Anti-Discriminatory Counselling Practice*, eds. Colin Lago and Barbara Smith. 50–61. London: Sage.

Rogers, Carl. 1990. *The Carl Rogers Reader*. London: Constable.

Troiden, R. 1988. *Gay and Lesbian Identity: a sociological analysis*. Dix Hills, NY: General Hall.

Working with Women

Gillian Proctor

Women clients

> **Farzana** was referred to counselling by her GP because he had diagnosed her with depression; she struggled to get out of bed and face the day, since leaving her marriage to her violent husband. She was just managing to look after her four children. The GP had prescribed anti-depressants but Farzana reported that they weren't helping.

> **Sue** was referred to a counsellor because she couldn't explain why she kept bursting into tears. This was getting in the way of her caring for her partner, mother and partner's mother. The crying had begun when she had discovered that her partner's friend, who he socialised with whilst Sue was busy with her mother, had asked him to leave Sue. 'He's a good husband,' Sue explained, 'he says he doesn't want to leave me and he sometimes helps with his mother when my mother needs me, but he doesn't want to stop seeing his friend as that's his only fun in life.'

> **Deborah** explained at her first counselling session that this was the first time she had been somewhere other than her local shop for years and that she had got up at 5am to complete the full daily clean of her house before leaving. She wondered whether the sexual abuse she experienced as a child could be relevant, as her anxiety had increased enormously since hearing that her abuser had moved back to her local area.

I will use these three fictional women to illustrate the rest of the chapter.

Women in society

To suggest that women are still second-class citizens these days often provokes a defensive reaction. People point out how much has changed in recent history. Rife inequalities are obscured or blamed on women's choices or women are blamed for 'wanting everything'. Men often feel criticised when inequalities are pointed out and are keen to point out how their lives are made hard by women too, and women then often fulfil their socialised role of defending and caring for men who feel blamed. Women who bring a feminist agenda are often silenced, attacked or made the subject of humour. In settings of counselling training, conferences or groups, responses vary from outright hostility and dismissing of concerns from men and women to others desperately wanting to be able to talk about gender issues. The backlash against feminism is alive and well and has many strategies at its disposal.

Gender role expectations restrict both men and women but often discussion about this turns to blame and defence. This chapter focuses on how gender role expectations and the patriarchal structure of society causes women distress and lead to women being labelled 'mad'. Increasingly, attention is being drawn to the effects on men of changing gender role expectations given the challenge of feminism. This consideration is needed, at the same time as examining the continuing effects on women of the way our society is structured. I want to be clear that I believe we all (men and women) have responsibility for perpetuating or changing the status quo; this is not about exclusively blaming all men. But at the same time, due to the position of women in the patriarchal structure of society, often women have less access to the power needed to challenge these structures and expectations.

On what basis do I claim that women are still second-class citizens? In the Western world, women are overwhelmingly in low-paid, low-status or part-time work and are massively under-represented in positions of authority. Women are still largely responsible for childcare and housework, with 'good' men being those who 'help' their female partners with such tasks (such as Sue's husband who 'helps' with her caring responsibilities). We continue to be sexually objectified in the media and the prolific pornography industry and are told how our appearances should match up to a feminine norm and labelled if we 'fail'. The media celebrity culture constantly reinforces the images of what constitutes a beautiful and successful woman. Men's control of women in heterosexual relationships, the workplace and in education continues through violence, rape, sexual harassment and the perpetuation of gender stereotypes. Often these behaviours are subtler now and harder to challenge, but effectively control women in more insidious ways.

Globally, statistics for violence against women are frightening. In many countries, women are victims of 'honour' killings, where women are killed for their actual or perceived 'immoral behaviour'. Such behaviour may include marital infidelity, refusing an arranged marriage, failing to serve a meal on time or even 'allowing herself' to be raped. Hundreds of millions of women worldwide have suffered female genital mutilation (UNFPA, 2007). Millions of girls age 5 to 15 are introduced to the commercial sex market annually. Rape and domestic violence are highly prevalent in all countries where the questions are examined, with rape of women having long been used as a weapon of war.

Crime statistics in the UK show that 95 per cent of perpetrators of domestic violence (DV) are men and 90 per cent of victims are women (see www.womensaid.org. uk). Women's Aid begin to show how power and gender are related by pointing to DV as one of the consequences of the inequalities between men and women in patriarchal traditions where men have a 'sense of entitlement' to power and control over women and children (see Women's Aid, 2009). Mullender et al. (2002: 219), cited in Harne and Radford (2008: 148), surveyed 1,400 children between the ages of 8 and 16. They found that one-third of teenage boys and one-fifth of teenage girls believed that women 'deserved to be hit' in some circumstances. Harne and Radford suggest that 'domestic violence can be explained through hierarchical and gendered relations of power ... [it] can be seen as a social problem which does not occur in a vacuum but is a common feature of male-dominating societies' (2008: 147). Farzana's family believed she should expect the violence from her husband as this was a consequence of her not fulfilling her duties appropriately. Indeed, Farzana believed she was probably at fault for provoking the violence whenever she questioned her husband. She did not leave her marriage because of violence; she left, despite being disowned by her family, when she discovered her husband was having an affair with her sister.

Sex, gender and gender-role socialisation

The idea of *sex* in Western cultures is defined biologically in an essentialist way, although the idea of sex being so clear-cut and categorical as the definitions of male and female suggest has been clearly contested. Following a social constructionist perspective, I use *gender* to mean the socially and culturally defined practices, which generate frameworks of femininities and masculinities, within which gender differences emerge and are reproduced and challenged (Bilton et al., 2002). Gender appears to be one of the most critical aspects of our identity that we use to make sense of one another, for example, being the usual first question asked about a new-born baby. Despite gender being such an important defining concept of the kinds of experiences we have in society and how we see each other, it is little considered in counselling or therapy (see Proctor, 2008).

Giddens (2006: 465) describes various masculinities and femininities and labels the dominant Western discourses as *hegemonic masculinity* and *emphasised femininity*. Hegemonic masculinity (Connel and Messerschmidt, 2005: 832, 'the most honoured way of being a man') includes expectations of heterosexuality, fertility, authority, paid work, strength and physical toughness, whereas emphasised femininity includes compliance, nurturance, empathy, fertility and wanting to be a mother.

For Connell (1987), power or men's dominance over women is the central premise around which various types of masculinity and femininity are arranged, from the individual to the institutional level. This dominance–submission dynamic of power between men and women is a template for all relationships. So the dominant messages given to us all about men and women in relationships are:

- Compulsory heterosexuality – the most valid intimate relationship is between a man and a woman; to not be heterosexual questions expectations of one's gender.
- Men in intimate relationships with women are expected to be strong, tough and in authority.
- Women in intimate relationships with men are expected to be caring, understanding, compliant and desiring motherhood.
- Men's ambivalence towards femininity – hegemonic masculinity allows a need for nurturance and care from women but tolerates the ambivalence raised by this need by the sexualisation and objectification of women and femininity (Garde, 2003).

Gender and power: structural and post-structural approaches

We are all socialised to expect men to be powerful and strong. Arendt (1986) suggests that violence arises for the purpose of gaining or regaining power. To apply this to DV: men use violence to gain or regain a position of feeling powerful in relation to women. This fits with the Women's Aid assertion that men have a sense of entitlement to power over women, and violence is one of the potential strategies used by men to exert this power. For men who may feel inadequate or weak, violence can be a way to try to establish their sense of strength and authority expected by hegemonic masculinity. Farzana's husband felt humiliated when she questioned him about how he believed they should treat their sons, based on how he was brought up. He tried to regain his sense of power as a man in authority by demeaning her in public and with violence.

There are difficulties and limitations with this structural view of power that fixes people according to their structural positions or identities (such as gender) as either perpetrators of power and control or victims of it. This model sees these structures as fixed and has no place for individual agency. So within this model, men are always powerful perpetrators of violence or abuse and women always victims; there is no room for women to become survivors, or to have their own independent voice. It also doesn't explain the circumstances where the perpetrator of violence is a woman or the victim a man.

These problems with structural views of power have been pointed out in academic sociology or politics for several decades, and the post-structural view of power has been put forward as an alternative (e.g. Foucault, 1980). Post-structural approaches to power remind us how we are all agents in resisting the powerful messages, and furthermore, that resisting messages or alternative ways of being masculine/feminine are also available (see Proctor, 2002 for more on post-structural approaches to power). For Foucault, power is not a possession held by a person or group of people and wielded over a victim as in the structural view; instead, power is relational, between people in relationships. Power is inevitable, ever-changing and inescapable; dynamics of power are in all relationships. For Foucault, everyone has agency and uses different tactics or strategies to participate in the dynamics of power in relationships. He doesn't dismiss the power of structures, in fact his earlier works are very much about how these structures control us, but in his later works he concentrates on how we respond to these structures, or 'resist' attempts to disempower us. In a sense, his focus is political or even revolutionary; rather than focussing on the dominant messages and structures of power, his interest is in how marginalised people resist, however much their voices are ignored or minoritised. This post-structural understanding of power gives us a way for women to move from the position of victim to survivor in society and regain agency. It also helps women to understand both the strategies and tactics used by men in controlling them, and their own tactics or strategies in resisting this control, whilst leaving the option of deciding how these dynamics could be different in the future. Foucault's approach also helps us to understand how sometimes perpetrators are women and victims are men, as either gender can use strategies of power or resistance, but men have far more access to strategies of power and control in terms of their gender socialisation than women do.

I suggest in understanding gender and power that both structural and post-structural models are useful in understanding the importance of both structure and agency. For Farzana and her husband, he had the structural power and authority mandated by her family and societal expectations, such that Farzana was often blamed for provoking his violence. However, she was not just a victim. Her strategies of resistance included her insistence on how she believed their children should be brought up and her strategies to escape his violence, which included putting sleeping tablets into his drinks at night and, ultimately, leaving him. However, her agency was still limited by his greater authority in public life to make his voice heard blaming her for their divorce and encouraging her family to disown her.

Women and madness

Women's place in the history of madness further underlines our status as second-class citizens, at risk of being labelled, diagnosed and locked away from society if our behaviour does not fit with feminine norms. Chesler (1972) first exposed the gendered nature of madness. Szasz (1972) demonstrates how women who transgressed societal norms used to be labelled 'witches' in the Middle Ages and killed. Later, in Freud's time, women were labelled 'hysterics' if they failed to accept the roles allotted them without complaint. Showalter (1985) defines hysteria as 'the essence of the feminine'. She argues that 'hysteria' is a response to powerlessness, a reaction to expectations of passivity and an attempt to establish a self-identity.

I have argued (see Shaw and Proctor, 2005; Proctor and Shaw, 2005; and Proctor, 2007) that the diagnosis of borderline personality disorder (predominantly given to women) is the latest manifestation of diagnosing and stigmatising women who refuse to fit gender norms. I suggest that women's experiences in our society drive us mad, and then our responses to these experiences are labelled 'mad'. Women are in an impossible situation here, being devalued and stigmatised both for conforming to norms and for refusing to conform: the classic double-bind situation for women (Chesler, 1972: 93). Farzana was judged both for not leaving her violent husband and then for leaving him. Sue was judged both for spending all her time caring for her mother and her partner's mother and for not spending enough time looking after her husband. Deborah was judged for not 'standing up to' her abuser, by leaving the house and risking seeing him, and for not leaving the abuse behind her and 'getting herself a nice husband'.

Women are not just labelled mad, we are driven mad by our experiences in society. I shall use the example of DV to illustrate the association between this experience and distress. Victims of DV, such as Farzana, often end up in the mental health system due to the effects of this experience. It is hardly surprising that women who have experienced systematic emotional, physical and sexual abuse are left distressed, with little self-esteem or confidence, in fear or anxious, with traumatic memories of the abuse and with little hope for the future. Women who experience DV report more symptoms of mental distress, are at greater risk of suicide (DV is a factor in at least one in four suicide attempts by women) and are four times more likely to suffer from post-traumatic stress than women in the general population. Of women who have experienced DV, 64 per cent are diagnosed with post-traumatic stress disorder, 48 per cent with depression, and 18 per cent attempt or commit suicide (see www.womensaid.org.uk).

Chesler (1972) argued that psychiatry perpetuated gendered expectations by taking the central role in pathologising women in this way. Today the institutions of psychiatry continue to take a back seat against the oppression of women, often remaining oblivious to and disinterested in the experiences of violence and oppression causing distress for women, and diagnosing, controlling and blaming women for our resulting distress. Psychiatric and psychological models position the individual as someone who is disordered, ill or distressed; the problem is located in the individual rather than society. The power of medicalisation or psychologisation serves to divert attention from the environmental causes of distress.

Farzana's diagnosis of depression leaves the GP focussing on her not eating and sleeping and struggling to care for herself, rather than on the violence she has suffered. Sue was also diagnosed as suffering from depression and prescribed anti-depressants. Her life as a permanent carer was untouched. Deborah was diagnosed with obsessive compulsive disorder and agorophobia; the reasons for her fears and her experiences of abuse remained unacknowledged.

Counselling and therapy: perpetuating inequalities?

Are counselling and therapy any better? Surely it must be helpful for Sue to have someone listening to her story and encouraging her sense of agency and thinking about her own needs? However, Miller and Rose emphasise that 'we should be wary of celebrating psychological approaches as alternatives to psychiatry' (1986: 42). Psychological approaches can also be used as part of the armoury of power and control over the population, as Foucault particularly explains (see Proctor, 2002). Heyward, talking about therapy, states that 'sexual and power abuse are *inevitable* in a system so steeped in unquestioned assumptions of hierarchy and power' (1994: 204). Hence, I use the term 'therapy relationship' in all my writing instead of the more usual 'therapeutic relationship', as we really can't assume that this relationship is necessarily therapeutic at all.

Feminist authors also help us to understand the power in the institution of therapy. Chesler (1972) reminds us that the therapeutic encounter needs to be understood as an institution beyond how individual therapists are with individual clients and how this *institution* re-enacts the relationship of girls to their father figure in a patriarchal society. She suggests that the institutions of marriage and therapy support each other by isolating women from each other, encouraging dependence on an authority figure and talk and defusing emotions rather than action.

Although individual therapists may challenge this hierarchical expert-based idea of therapy, therapy itself as an institution remains unnoticed, which is likely to be a major factor in clients not perceiving the therapy relationship as equal however the therapist behaves. The role power of the therapist is not removed by any kind of therapist behaviour as a person. Deborah was very relieved to see a woman counsellor, but had strong expectations of being told what she should do and was scared she would be unable to follow these orders. Even when the counsellor explained that her job was not to advise, Deborah continued to believe that the counsellor would suggest she should get out of the house and she knew she would be unable to do so.

Person-centred therapists and many relational therapists aim for a mutual therapy relationship, believing that a therapist having power over a client is unhelpful and unethical. Cognitive behavioural therapists talk about 'collaborative' relationships, also not wanting to have power over clients. But how possible are truly mutual or collaborative relationships in therapy given the inevitable inequality in therapy relationships due to role power? I argue (Proctor, 2002) that person-centred therapists are in danger of obscuring this role power by focusing on a 'person-to-person' relationship. Similarly, I argue that the cognitive behaviour therapy terminology of 'collaboration' would more accurately be termed 'compliance', and this misleading terminology again obscures the power held by the therapist over the client (Proctor, 2009). Is mutuality possible in therapy, especially in the increasingly fear and risk-based climate (see Proctor, 2010)? Does the necessarily unequal relationship in therapy perpetuate relationships based on dominance and submission and consequently traditional unequal gender roles? Are we in danger of comforting ourselves with the principle of mutuality and thus buying into an institution of therapy that is more harmful than potentially good (see Proctor, 2006)?

One outcome of Sue being referred to counselling was that her husband and her mother believed that her bursting into tears was her problem, a result of something inside her, and that she needed to 'pull herself together'. Deborah's family used the knowledge that she was seeing a counsellor to put more pressure on her to stop cleaning and leave the house, as 'counselling should be helping you put all that behind you'.

What do women want?

To be able to move from the position of victim to survivor, a woman needs to be in a place where rather than being undermined, she is supported to find her agency and strength and authority to define her own life and relationships, fundamentally to challenge many of the expectations of emphasised femininity. At the same time, there needs to be an awareness of the whole context of a woman's life and the probable limitations of her agency to challenge expectations, and the potential condemning responses to her challenging these expectations. At different points, distressed women will need different kinds of support, ranging from advocacy, practical help with accommodation and finances, legal advice, medical treatment and counselling or therapy. Various responses from all the systems involved with women can help or hinder this process. I suggest that the difference between helping and hindering women to move from victims to survivors rests mainly on the issue of power. Any relationship that reinforces the woman's position as victim, takes control and power over her and undermines her agency, will hinder her recovery. Any relationship that fosters the woman's agency and ability to survive and resist and redefine her own life can be helpful. But aiming for a mutual counselling relationship may not be enough when Farzana needs legal help to challenge her ex-husband who is trying to take away their children. Counselling may not be enough to help Sue claim the carers' benefits to which she is entitled. Counselling may not be enough to advise Deborah when she does bump into her abuser and wonders if she is still able to take him to court for what he did. In all these scenarios, a counsellor with knowledge of other services that could provide this help can be invaluable.

Government legislation on mental health and women gives useful pointers for all mental health workers, and is also relevant to counsellors and therapists. The legislation recognises the link between experiences of violence and distress. The Department of Health (2002) states that one of the biggest risk factors in mental health for women is the experience of violence and abuse, and that over 50 per cent of women service users of mental health services have experienced violence or abuse.

This document (Department of Health, 2002) reports that women service users say they want services that:

- promote empowerment, choice and self-determination;
- place importance on the underlying causes and context of distress in addition to symptoms;
- address important issues related to women's role as mothers, the need for safe accommodation and access to education, training and work opportunities; and
- value their strengths and abilities and potential for recovery.

What can a counsellor or therapist do?

Self-awareness

Gender is an important consideration in counselling and therapy. As therapists, how much do we attend to the impact of gender on our clients? In Proctor (2002) I suggest that it may be helpful for therapists to have a checklist of considerations for the dynamics of power in therapy. This also applies specifically to the consideration of gender in particular within the dynamics of power. Therapists can think about their own positions and how their gender impacts on their attitude towards their role as therapists and how female and male clients may see them due to this gender. Women counsellors may need to question how much being a counsellor fulfils gendered expectations of women to be caring, and ensure that our own needs are not missed in the service of others.

To challenge the inevitability of the messages we are surrounded by, we can inform ourselves about other potential gender relations in the world, both within different cultures but probably mainly in science fiction, where alternative worlds are imagined (such as Piercy, 1976).

Reflective exercise

Area of consideration	Fitting expectations	Resisting expectations
Self as woman/man	How do you fit with gender expectations?	How do you challenge/resist gender expectations?
Others' perceptions of your gender	How do others respond to how you fit your gender expectations?	How do others respond to how you challenge/resist gender expectations?
Your views of others' gender	How do you view other women and men who fit gendered expectations?	How do you view other women and men who resist or challenge gendered expectations?
Personal history	What messages encouraged you to fit with gender expectations?	What messages encouraged you to challenge/resist gender expectations?
Structural identity	How does your gender interact with your other structural identities (such as ethnicity, age, class, sexuality, etc.) in terms of the messages you have received about yourself?	How may others see you, or what may others expect of you, given your structural identities, especially potential clients?
Therapist as woman/man	How does your role as therapist fit with gendered expectations?	How does your role as therapist challenge or resist gendered expectations?

Power and agency

To be of most help to a distressed woman, a counsellor or therapist needs to be respectful and encouraging of her agency and have an understanding of the context and social causes of their distress. The therapist must have an awareness of the social context of the woman's life during the process of therapy, to be alert to needs for other practical help and facilitate access to these services as appropriate.

The counsellor needs to give as much information as possible about counselling and the approach used to really ensure informed consent. The approach used needs to prioritise the woman's perspective and perceptions of her life with awareness of how undermining any challenge to her perspective could be, given the devaluing of women in society. Counsellors need to be aware of the messages surrounding us all about gender without assuming how any one woman may react to, internalise or resist these messages. Often these messages are so pervasive and taken for granted that these reactions are rarely articulated directly, being more implicit in the way we talk about ourselves.

Another potentially even more liberating option is group work, particularly following the model of self-help groups, where clients are there to learn from each others' similar experiences, with facilitators not taking the role of experts but putting themselves at the service of the group, if needed or wanted at all.

Counsellors may also want to consider whether clients can be offered a choice of gender of therapist, and consider if we seek therapy what would influence our choice of gender of therapist to check how much this may be reinforcing ideas from gender role socialisation of seeking women for nurturance. What does all this mean for the institution of therapy? Could it be that in professionalising emotional nurturance this relieves women from their traditional role as care givers? Or does the necessarily unequal relationship in therapy perpetuate traditional unequal gender roles and relationships based on dominance and submission? It is the responsibility of each counsellor and therapist to consider how they contribute to this or whether they can contribute to challenging these roles, and how far it is possible to work towards therapy relationships based on mutual recognition of equal persons.

References

Arendt, H. (1986) Communicative power. In S. Lukes (ed.), *Power* (pp. 61–74). Oxford: Basil Blackwell.

Bilton, T., Bonnett, K., Jones, P., Lawson, T., Skinner, D., Stanworth, M. and Webster, A. (2002) *Introductory Sociology* (4th edn). Basingstoke: Palgrave Macmillan.

Chesler, P. (1972) *Women and Madness*. New York: Doubleday.

Connell, R.W. (1987) *Gender and Power*. Cambridge: Polity Press.

Connell, R.W. and Messerschmidt, J.W. (2005) Hegemonic masculinity: rethinking the concept. *Gender and Society*, 19(6), 829–59.

Department of Health (2002) *Into the Mainstream: women and mental health*. London: DoH.

Foucault, M. (1980) *Power and Knowledge: Selected interviews and other writings 1972–1977*. Brighton: Harvester.

Garde, J. (2003) Masculinity and madness. *Counselling and Psychotherapy Research*, 3(1), 6–15.

Giddens, A. (2006). *Sociology* (5th edn). Cambridge: Polity Press.

Harne, L. and Radford, J. (2008) *Tackling Domestic Violence: Theories, policies and practice*. Berkshire: OUP.

Heyward, C. (1994) *When Boundaries Betray Us: Beyond illusions of what is ethical in therapy and life*. New York: HarperCollins.

Miller, P. and Rose, N. (1986) *The Power of Psychiatry*. Cambridge: Polity Press.

Mullender, A., Hague, G., Imam, U., Kelly, L., Malos, E. and Regan, L. (2002) *Children's Perspectives on Domestic Violence*. London: Sage.

Piercy, M. (1976) *Woman on the Edge of Time*. London: Knopf.

Proctor, G. (2002) *The Dynamics of Power in Counselling and Psychotherapy: Ethics, politics and practice*. Ross-on-Wye: PCCS Books.

Proctor, G. (2007) Disordered boundaries? A critique of 'Borderline Personality Disorder'. In H. Spandler and S. Warner (eds). *Beyond Fear and Control: Working with young people who self-harm* (pp. 105–20). Ross-on-Wye: PCCS Books.

Proctor, G. (2008) Gendered dynamics in person-centered therapy: does gender matter? *Person-Centered and Experiential Psychotherapies*, 7(2), 82–94.

Proctor, G. (2009) CBT: the obscuring of power in the name of science. In R. House and D. Loewenthal (eds). *Against and For CBT: Towards a constructive dialogue*. Ross-on-Wye: PCCS Books.

Proctor, G. (2010) Boundaries of mutuality in therapy: is mutuality really possible or is therapy doomed from the start? *Psychotherapy and Politics International*, 8(1), 44–58.

Proctor, G. and Shaw, C. (2005) Hidden agenda. *Open Mind*, 133, 12–13.

Proctor, G. (2006) Therapy: opium for the masses or help for those who least need it? In G. Proctor, M. Cooper, P. Sanders and B. Malcolm. *Politicising the Person Centred Approach: An agenda for social change* (pp. 66–79). Ross-on-Wye: PCCS Books.

Shaw, C. and Proctor, G. (2005) Women at the margins: a critique of borderline personality disorder. *Feminism and Psychology*, 15(4), 483–90.

Showalter, E. (1985) *The Female Malady: Women, madness and English culture, 1830–1890*. London: Virago.

Szasz, T. (1972) *The Myth of Mental Illness*. London: Paladin.

UNFPA (2007) Available at www.unfpa.org/webdav/site/global/shared/documents/publications/2007/726_filename_fgm.pdf, accessed 1 April 2010.

Women's Aid (2009) *Domestic Violence: Frequently Asked Questions Fact Sheet*. Bristol: Women's Aid. Available at www.womensaid.org.uk/core/core_picker/download.asp?id=1636, accessed 1 April 2010.

Disfigurement and Visible Difference

7

Suzy Henry

There can't be anyone, I am sure, who doesn't know what it feels like to be disliked, even rejected, momentarily or for sustained periods of time. Perhaps the feeling is merely indifference, mild annoyance, but it may also be hurt. It may be that some of us know what it is like to be actually hated – hated for things we have no control over and cannot change. When this happens, it is some consolation to know that the dislike or hatred is unjustified – that you don't deserve it. (Foreword, *The Bluest Eye* by Toni Morrison, 1970, published by Chatto and Windus. Reprinted by permission of The Random House Group Ltd)

Let us consider the luxury of having our worst fears about ourselves safely hidden from the critical scrutiny of the external world.

Now consider how you would be affected if you believed that your appearance exposed all that is most deplorable about you. You look unnatural, all of your grotesqueries betrayed in your face. Your appearance is shocking: 'I am shocking!' I grew up believing the way I looked revealed my abnormalities; my face elicited distress, mistrust and even hatred from those 'forced' to look at me. As a child I spent long days thinking 'There is something terribly wrong with me and the way I look. I am ugly and repulsive. I look absurd …'

In our practice we are likely to work with clients who perceive themselves to look unacceptable; their appearance is not only a disappointment, but they consider themselves, as I did, to look strange and unusual; even believing that their actual existence is hurtful to others and harmful to those they come into contact with. This may well be mirrored in the expressions and behaviour of people they encounter. Confronting looks of horror and disgust. Many people who are affected by visible difference will have experienced exclusion, victimisation, and even rejection and blame for the way they look.

This chapter is concerned with counselling people who are visibly different. Needless to say, not all clients who have negative attitudes towards the way they look will be, or will have ever been, 'disfigured' in any way. Their distress is no less potent and destructive to their fragile sense of self and, whilst writing, I am mindful of *all* people who perceive their appearance as damaging.

I was born with a cleft ('hare') lip and a cleft palate. This affected the appearance of my nose, which was flat or 'squashed' until my mid-teens, when a thin slice of my rib cartilage was used to 'repair it'; to give it more length and shape. Indeed, I have had in the region of 15 operations to look the way I do today. For example, the cleft in the roof of my mouth was restored using bone chiselled from my hip and my chin, providing the structure needed to implant two porcelain teeth. As you might expect, my changing appearance has had a considerable effect on my life;

much of this experience, especially when growing up, has been psychologically and physically painful.

Historical, social and cultural attitudes towards appearance: the politics of being visibly different

Our appearance plays a dominant part in our self-concept and if that appearance has been judged and evaluated negatively, then this will have a detrimental impact on our overall levels of self-esteem. Furthermore, the inability to recognise ourselves due to an enforced change to our appearance (such as a traumatic injury) represents a profound disruption to a person's self-concept and can constitute a major challenge:

> The sight of our familiar appearance does much to reassure us about our identity; however, we are taken aback when our appearance does not conform to our own internalised self image ... Physical changes to the body, and in particular the face, powerfully affect the way we experience ourselves and takes some time to assimilate into our self-view. (Rumsey and Harcourt, 2005: 1–2)

It is equally important to state that people can feel enhanced by their changed appearance, expressing feelings of 'post traumatic growth': living successful, fulfilling and rich lives (Millstone, 2008).

Notions of beauty are not exclusively a contemporary phenomenon; prejudice towards people's appearance does not exist within a vacuum, 'evidence for the fascination humans have with physical appearance comes from a rich variety of sources, including mythology and legends, anecdotes from history, fairy tales and a variety of contemporary sources' (Rumsey and Harcourt, 2005: 1).

However, whilst attitudes towards appearance and disfigurement are long established, a culture may exert its influence through a process of 'values attribution':

> If we take the concept of Self as an example, a culture might give a message on the 'right' kind of Self to possess. The messages might be consistent and pervasive in declaring the kind of Self which is to be valued. In this culture, exceptions would exist but they would be dishonoured and even pathologised.
>
> A different kind of cultural influence exists where the 'symbolisation parameters' of a culture dictate the *only* kind of Self which is possible. This represents a much greater level of cultural construction and constriction. Here the 'right' kind of Self is so embedded in the culture that there can be no exceptions. At this level of embeddedness it is not only seen as a value and a choice – the nature of Self is defined by that which can be symbolised ... Some cultures are 'theoretically bounded' by their symbolisation parameters. (Mearns and Thorne, 2000: 188)

Distorted views about disfigurement are deeply embedded in Western culture and the social impact is reinforced by negative portrayals of disfigurement in literature, film and other popular media. Visible difference is regularly aligned with having a 'damaged personality'. This myth is perpetuated where disfigured people are represented as malign by their *repellent* appearance; for example, the 'psychopathic' serial killer in the Robert Harris' book *Red Dragon* has a cleft lip; and in Wes Craven's horror film *The Hills Have Eyes* (1977, 2006) the 'mutants' who live in the isolated desert of New Mexico, who are disfigured and/or disabled, are malevolent outsiders targeting their benevolent, 'beautiful' victims by sexually assaulting, torturing and murdering them. Sensitive and tender depictions exist but are exceptional; for instance, Joseph Merrick *The Elephant Man* and Quasimodo *The Hunchback of Notre Dame* (Victor Hugo, 1831). The Falklands veteran Simon Weston has done much to challenge negative attitudes towards disfigurement.

Philosophy, science and medicine have been consistently mobilised over the ages to provide a framework of explanation of how the inner is expressed in the outer. The Western tradition of *physiognomy* provides a basic idea that the face serves as a field of 'signs' which, read rightly, could be used to determine the nature of the soul behind the facade. We are irredeemably programmed to work from appearance at the deepest biological level. It is widely accepted that we make stereotypical (especially 'snap') judgements of people on the basis of their outward appearance (Rumsey and Harcourt, 2005).

The current television documentary series 'Body Shock' (2003 onwards), with inflammatory titles such as *The Girl with Two Faces*, *The Curse of the Mermaid* and *I am the Elephant Man*, is cruelly insensitive: sustaining and exacerbating voyeuristic attitudes, promoting difference as 'spectacle' – evoking comparisons with the negative side of 'freak' or 'side' shows.

Diane Arbus (1972), known as 'the photographer of freaks', was inspired by (and a fan of) these shows and romanticised performers (Adams, 2001). In 1972 she described the term 'freak' as having become a metaphor for estrangement, alienation and marginality; 'the dark side of the human experience'. The shows, which seemed poised on the edge of extinction by the mid-1960s as public demands that 'freaks' be given dignity (Bodan, 1988), are currently experiencing a renaissance in popular culture and performance art, in an empowered climate, reclaiming terms which would be derogatory from outsiders' lips.

According to research published in 2009 by Cardiff University and the Healing Foundation, Wardle and Boyce found that people with a disfigurement are rarely shown on British TV. Analysis of 8,650 hours of prime time television – one year's output – found only 293 representations – and on these rare occasions, they were usually presented only in fictional programming as plot devices and in stereotypically negative ways, such as gangsters with scars and people with burns living as recluses.

What constitutes 'visible difference'?

It is difficult to define a 'disfigurement' precisely. Not everyone would describe their scar, facial marking, birthmark or other 'condition' that affects their appearance as a disfigurement. Broadly speaking, the word describes a visible malformation which is the consequence of a physical condition; it is not a condition in itself

(Bradbury, 1996). *Changing Faces* (a UK-based charity that counsels, supports, represents and gives information to people with disfigurements to the face, hands and/or body, and their families) clarifies the word 'disfigurement' from a clinical perspective to describe the aesthetic effects of a mark, rash, scar or skin graft on a person's skin or an asymmetry or paralysis to their face or body. As practitioners, we must not make assumptions; culture and individual bias play a significant part in the subjectivity behind determining what physical appearance is considered 'normal' and in whom we perceive 'disfigurement'. A definition adopted by several researchers is that a disfigurement is a 'difference from a culturally defined norm which is visible to others' (Rumsey and Harcourt, 2005).

> [T]here are two distinct opinions on what constitutes a visibly different appearance: that of the person whose appearance is under consideration and that of others who observe it ... 'Visible differentness' may be regarded as a highly individual concept, which is derived both from self-comparison with the 'normal' appearances of others and from others' expressed opinions. The relevance of observers' judgements lies in how they behave towards people who have visibly different appearances. (Harris, 1997: 79)

Issues arising from difference may belong to the perceiver, not the perceived (Lago, 2007). 'It would seem that the therapist's comfort in recognizing and responding directly to the client's particular identity or circumstances is a key ingredient towards successful therapeutic outcomes' (2007: 261).

The language of visible difference

> Definition of Disfigure •v (disfigures, disfiguring, disfigured) spoil the appearance of. •DERIVATIVES disfigurement n. (*Oxford English Dictionary*)

The word 'disfigurement' carries an emotional impact and is *not* ideal. How then do we begin to find an adequate language to explore visual difference with clients (people facing repudiation and objectification because of the way they look) without replicating intolerant, judgemental or devaluing attitudes? It is challenging not to be co-conspiratorial. The word 'disfigurement' relates to a defect. However:

> [T]he stigma lies in the meaning attached to the word by the user ... any other word would soon develop the same stigma; it is not the word that is at fault, but the meaning it has for people ... there are no satisfactory substitutes, but *words which hurt should always be used with care, and with an understanding of their potential impact.* (my italics: Bradbury, 1996: 1)

Growing up I thought of myself as 'deformed'. Some words resonate more with me than the word 'disfigurement'. People may well use words such as 'abnormal' and 'intolerable' or similar to describe their appearance and I would *not* advocate avoiding their use. However, it goes without saying that 'the distress and anger which often accompany these words are an indication of their power to hurt' (Bradbury, 1996). Language should be used tentatively and with awareness, reflecting the content with which they are used by clients. We need to modify our skills and language appropriately (Lago, 2007).

The language of (dis)appearance

There currently exists a lack of recognition of issues that surround visible difference; this absence provides an opportunity for people who are disfigured (many of whom are socially isolated and excluded) to feel an ongoing traumatisation and sense of marginalisation. If we as counsellors fail to recognise people who are affected by disfigurement as a discriminated group (ignoring disfigured people's existence by omission), we run the risk of propagating the belief that people who are visibly different remain unacceptable to 'the majority', or 'social norm'; thus, sustaining the pejorative consensus that people with a visible difference are 'inferior' and that disfigurement represents 'otherness'; fostering acquiescence and vulnerability to judgemental external and introjected opinions and attitudes.

> The fundamental denial of responsibility by society further damages victims, who subsequently internalise responsibility and self blame. (Lago, 2007: 258)

Of the literature that does exist about counselling people who are visibly different, the language used is often objective; suggesting challenge; creating an unnecessary power dynamic, i.e. my appearance remains a problem to those around me. As people 'managing' or 'coping with' a disfigurement, we may feel obliged to concede that *'unless I am willing to accept that my unfortunate attitude towards the way I look is "wrong", I will be unable to cope with the way I am perceived by others. Therefore, it is not only the way "they" see me that hurts, but the way I see myself. My feelings are wrong. I am wrong. I must change.'*

Should the onus be on me to change when society could equally address its attitudes towards what constitutes 'normal' and 'abnormal'?

Possible causes of disfigurement

As therapists we endeavour to avoid the categorisation of our clients, seeing people as individuals. 'The client cannot and should not be reduced to his or her visible identity' (Lago, 2007). However, it may be helpful to look at the causes of disfigurement in an attempt to move beyond categorisation and classification and towards the individual.

Visible differences result from a variety of causes. There are three broad categories of disfigurement: congenital, acquired and disease process.

Congenital disfigurement

Some types of conditions causing visible differences are fully manifested at birth (for example, a cleft of the lip), whereas others become more evident over time (for example, neurofibromatosis). Harris (1997) proposed that the classification of a 'congenital disfigurement' should be those that exist 'pre-memory', that is to say that the person has no memory of life without the disfigurement. (Rumsey and Harcourt, 2005: 89)

For people born with a disfigurement, psychological effects may occur at many stages throughout their lives, but early experiences will generally be affected by disfigurement (Bradbury, 1996). Children who are visibly different usually grow up with an awareness of their difference, and this may lead to a sense of being too visible to others. I grew up with a real sense of being invisible yet highly visible.

Acquired disfigurement

Acquired disfigurements can be the result of trauma, such as: injuries caused during conflict; scars from road traffic accidents and industrial injuries; burn injuries; scalding, leaving discoloured and deforming scars; assault and torture; surgical interventions, for example, the aftermath of cosmetic surgery. For people disfigured by traumatic injuries, seeing their scars (and experiencing the reactions of others towards them) can bring back memories of the trauma. Acquired or traumatic disfigurement can also be the result of self-harm; scars may not only result in, but can also be the result of self-hatred.

Disease process

People of all ages can suffer from diseases which leave them with temporary or permanent disfigurement … Disfigurement as a result of disease is usually progressive, and it may be a long time before the permanent disfigurement can be seen. Disfigurement can also result from surgery to treat the disease. This is most obvious in head and neck cancers, where life-saving surgery can lead to the removal of areas of the face. The success of reconstruction depends on the site of surgery and on the amount of tissue and bone removed. (Bradbury, 1996: 3)

Scars are the result of the biologic process of wound repair in the skin and other tissues of the body. Thus, scars can represent healing for someone *and* can be a permanent reminder.

A changing appearance: surgery and its psychological impact

Following reconstructive surgery, it can take time to accept oneself when witnessing an unexpected or unfamiliar self-image. People's own reflection can leave them feeling re-traumatised and shaken, taking time to adjust to their changed appearance. Mirrors can be alluring *and* arduous. There may be a (long) period of time when our appearance is merely tolerated, both by ourselves and others. What is more, it is not the case that surgery is a 'cure' that will 'fix' someone's appearance.

As a result, this can lead to false expectations, not only on the part of those who are disfigured, but also on the part of strangers and society at large. Strangers may feel that they have permission to comment and to ask questions about our appearance; others may express a gamut of feelings ranging from embarrassment to expressing anger and genuine hostility.

Modern reconstructive surgery can be effective in reducing conspicuousness; however, a disfigurement can rarely be removed completely, and scarring, asymmetry or changes of complexion usually remain. During the reconstructive process, which can last years (in my case my entire adolescence consisted of yearly, invasive surgery), the 'abnormalities' in our appearance can become more prominent. My changing appearance was an awkward, embarrassing and often frightening process – for all to see.

'Minor' or 'severe'?

It is well documented (Bradbury, 1996; Rumsey and Harcourt, 2005; Millstone, 2008) that the severity of a disfigurement does not correlate with the amount of distress experienced.

For people who have a so-called 'minor' disfigurement the effects can remain potent, impactful and (re)current, and can have a major affect on someone's confidence and self-worth, especially if the disfigurement appears in the communication triangle – eyes, mouth and nose area – as this is the area where people focus their attention (Millstone, 2008):

- influencing the way someone lives their life;
- how they relate to others, shaping their view of themselves in the world;
- remaining distressed and considering themselves disturbing to others; and
- feeling extremely self-conscious, 'on duty' and having to maintain near constant vigilance, resulting in an increased sense of responsibility.

I think it can be unhelpful to employ terms such as 'severely disfigured' and 'less severe' or 'minor' disfigurements, as this language fails to capture the emotional impact that the disfigurement is having on someone's life and its frequently painful significance.

Looking for identity: beyond shame and recrimination

People who are affected by disfigurement may be mourning the existential loss of their identity. People who have an acquired disfigurement may be mourning the 'loss of not being who I was', and for people who are affected congenitally by disfigurement (having had numerous corrective operations) they may be mourning the 'loss of no longer being what I was not'. When I was born my parents made the decision not to photograph me, so for a long time I had no idea what I looked like when I was born; the only photograph of me pre-operations is a clinical hospital photograph, taken when I was 6 months old; when I was 20 years old I went through litigation to see it for the first time. Hence, I grew up with a phantasm of a baby, a monster, whom I cherished and who I did *not* want to be.

Studies have found that the general population respond to people with disfigurement with less trust and less respect, often avoiding having to look at or make contact with people who have a disfigurement (Millstone, 2008). The assumptions others form about what it means to live with a disfigurement may influence how they themselves deal with their own emotions when they, a member of their family or someone they meet is personally affected by a disfigurement. Many people feel the social pressure associated with stereotyping.

There is often shame and guilt associated with disfigurement. The way we feel about our appearance is synonymous with the way we exist in the world. The reality is that social norms change when someone perceives themselves, or others perceive them, to look or sound different. *People with a disfigurement are extremely vulnerable to prejudice.*

I was born in 1973,[1] there was very little advice given or support provided for my parents having given birth to a child with a cleft lip and palate, worrying about whether they might have been able to do something to prevent their baby's disfigurement, feeling responsible and trying to understand the long-term implications. People with a disfigurement were discouraged from meeting or socialising with one another, and peer support groups were not available. Counselling was not offered to my parents. The only situation where I met others who were visibly different was when I was in hospital having 'corrective' surgery. I did not grow up feeling that I was part of a 'diverse group' of people, I grew up feeling very isolated yet recognised that I *was* part of a group – of [disfigured] children who were equally disturbing to others and in need of repair.

As people who are visibly different, we are often secretive and reluctant to seek help because we fear what others will think of us and/or because we consider ourselves deserving of ridicule and/or because we are too self-conscious to speak out.

A therapeutic response: towards warmth and (self-)acceptance

It may help to identify any potential bias if I articulate that my particular core theoretical model is person-centred psychotherapy. I am attracted to therapies that come from a position that emphasise the uniqueness of each individual, with an emphasis on egalitarian relationships. I concur that there is no one 'best' therapy for everyone, and I encourage you to think and generate your own ideas about working with visible difference. However, because I find the following relevant to my development growing up with a cleft, I wish to share briefly some observations that Carl Rogers researched and wrote about throughout his life and career.

Rogers considered the infant to be born with an inherent motivational system, which he called the *actualising tendency* and which has been reified as 'the organism's innate tendency to actualise' (Embelton Tudor et al., 2004: 27). As we grow from infancy to adulthood an internal schism gradually develops, a split that separates our immediate awareness from our own deeper 'experiencing'.

> Our need to be loved and accepted can impair our ability to be 'congruent' and genuine. As infants the 'locus of evaluation' is firmly embedded within us, but as we grow physically, emotionally, and intellectually, we learn to 'introject' the evaluations that come from the external world until, for many of us, it is no longer possible to recognize the difference between what is internal and what is external, to know who we really are. (Kirschenbaum and Henderson, 1990: 155)

Frequently present in childhood, and at other times in life, *conditions of worth* emerge when a person experiences their worth as conditional on their doing something or behaving in a certain way. This is usually to satisfy someone else's needs, and can be contrary to our own sense of what would be a satisfying experience. The values of others become a feature of the individual's self structure – the person moves away from being true to themselves, learning instead to remain 'true' to their conditioned sense of worth (see Rogers, 1951: 59).

'Who puked on your face?' (A boy on Rickmansworth Station, my 14th birthday, 1987)

I lost confidence in myself at a young age; I experienced real estrangement (*disintegration*) between my 'self' and my feelings before the age of 5. Gradually losing faith in myself when I was still a child, I believed that only the experience of others could be trusted. For as long as I could remember my appearance had been judged harshly; I had been bullied emotionally, verbally and physically; laughed at, spat at, called names, hit or ignored. By the time I reached the age of 13 I hated myself and thought I deserved to be despised by others. Increasingly, I felt the need to live my life in terms of the expectations of others, since my own impulses and sensations were deemed by me as unreasonable and unreliable. I felt terribly ashamed. I could barely stand to look my own reflection. In public I walked looking at the ground.

In my final year school report my form teacher wrote: 'Suzy has much potential yet absences and illness seem to be plaguing her and hindering progress. Suzy must adopt a more positive and confident attitude towards herself to do herself justice.' It seems I needed further modification.

People who are affected by disfigurement may feel an increased need of unconditional reassurance from others. They may feel angry towards themselves and others, with chronically low self-esteem and depression, incredibly sensitive to criticism and rejection – anticipating and expecting it. Being numb may be preferable to feeling pain, anxiety and sadness, so people shut down quickly when confronted with the distressing experience of [social] rejection (see Forgas and Williams, 2002).

Negative attributions from others may become introjected into the 'diverse person's' psyche so that part of them also internalizes and identifies with societies' negative attributions ... In extreme forms this may lead to self-hate or a wish to radically change that part of self which has attracted negative assertions. (Lago, 2007: 258)

In the case of people affected by a disfigurement this 'radical change' is anticipated and [corrective] surgery is free of charge.

In the final report from my plastic surgeon, he wrote: 'Suzy is now content with her appearance, or as her mother says, is as content as she will ever be.' In the same year my GP wrote to my surgeon that 'numerous operations for her appearance have undoubtedly had psychological effects.'

Basic trust in the person may be something which has felt absent from the lives of those affected by disfigurement. Thus, it may be unhelpful for therapists to exhibit expertise; this involves the letting go of authoritarian power in the counselling relationship.

People who are affected by disfigurement may feel violated and misunderstood a great deal of the time, believing that there is something toxic about their existence.

> Clients may be asking if their way of experiencing themselves at that moment has the right to exist in the world. Any misnaming of the experience or suggestion that they look at the experience in a different way is experienced as an answer 'no' to the question ...
>
> Even slight misnaming or misunderstanding of the experience is likely to make the client feel violated ... Interpretive comments or advice are likely to be experienced as invalidating the experience altogether ... If distracted or contradicted they are likely to give up on the idea that such experiences have any significance. (Warner, 2000: 151)

An ongoing soothing, empathic presence may be essential to the disfigured person's ability to stay connected without feeling overwhelmed. Empathic understanding responses are often the only sorts of responses people can receive without feeling traumatised or disconnected from their existence (Warner, 2000).

In my experience as a client, the therapeutic relationship has been central. Psychotherapist Peggy Natiello considers 'a deep personal connection between therapist and client plays a major role in growth and healing' (2001: 26) and on the development of a truly authentic relationship '(t)he therapeutic relationship is unique in each situation, and grows out of the unanticipated and unrehearsed interactions between two particular people' (2001: 26).

Out of the cold: towards affirmation and concurrence

I keep returning to the following questions and I invite you to engage with them:

- Where does self-loathing come from?
- Who enables it?
- How does it become infectious and what are its consequences?
- To what extent do appearance issues influence me?

- How can I use supervision to explore my own attitudes to disfigurement?
- How can I find ways of challenging the current status quo in regard to others' attitudes towards visible difference?
- What do I need to do to equip myself to be more fully prepared for my clients?

When working with people who feel emotionally vulnerable and visibly different, we need to be able to reflect subjectively as much as possible; actively challenging our attitudes in order to dismantle discrimination and prejudice in our practise; working together with our clients, as equal partners, sharing expertise rather than dominating and attempting to control.

In an understanding climate, people who are affected adversely by their appearance will talk about their underlying impulses when this is relevant to them. Once clients gain a sense of security in their ability to hold experiences, the ability to hold good and bad images of themselves and others develops on its own (Warner, 2000).

My appearance affects who I am, as it does us all, but I am no longer ashamed of the way I look. Personal therapy has contributed greatly to this shift, away from self-loathing to self-acceptance. I passionately believe that whichever 'core model' we choose to work from, when working with people who are affected by disfigurement the relationship is the therapy.

Note

1 The Cleft Lip and Palate Association, also known as CLAPA, was established in 1979 as a partnership between health professionals and parents of children with cleft lip and palate. They provide support for new parents, for people with the condition and their families.

References

Adams, R. (2001). *Sideshow USA: freaks and the American cultural imagination.* Chicago: University of Chicago Press.

Arbus, D. (1972). *Diane Arbus.* Millerton, NY: Aperture Foundation.

Bogdan, R. (1988). *Freak Show: presenting human oddities of amusement and profit.* Chicago: University of Chicago Press.

Bradbury, E. (1996). *Counselling People with Disfigurement.* Leicester: BPS Books.

Embleton Tudor, L., Keemar, K., Tudor, K., Valentine, J. and Worrall, M. (2004). *The Person-Centred Approach: a contemporary introduction.* Basingstoke: Palgrave Macmillan.

Forgas, J.P. and Williams, K.D. (2002). *The Social Self: cognitive, interpersonal and intergroup perspectives.* Hove: Psychology Press.

Harris, D. (1997). 'Types, causes and physical treatment of visible differences'. In R. Lansdown, N. Rumsey, E. Bradbury, T. Carr and J. Partridge (eds). *Visibly Different: coping with disfigurement* (pp. 79–90). Oxford: Butterworth Heinemann.

Kirschenbaum, H. and Henderson, V.L. (eds) (1990). *The Carl Rogers Reader.* London: Constable.

Lago, C. (2007). 'Counselling across difference and diversity'. In M. Cooper, M. O'Hara, P.F. Schmid and G. Wyatt (eds). *The Handbook of Person-Centred Psychotherapy and Counselling* (pp. 251–65). Basingstoke: Palgrave Macmillan.

Mearns, D. and Thorne, B. (2000). *Person-Centred Therapy Today: new frontiers in theory and practice.* London: Sage.

Millstone, S. (2008). 'Changing Faces: living with disfigurement', *Therapy Today: the magazine for counselling and psychotherapy professionals*, 19(9).

Morrison, T. (1979). *The Bluest Eye.* London: Vintage. (Originally published in the USA in 1970 by Penguin.)

Natiello, P. (2001). *The Person-Centred Approach: a passionate presence.* Ross-on-Wye: PCCS Books.

Rogers, C.R. (1951). *Client-Centered Therapy.* London: Constable.

Rogers, C.R. (1959). 'A theory of therapy, personality and interpersonal relationships, as *developed* in client-centred framework'. In S. Koch (ed.). *Psychology: a study of science, Vol.3: Formulation of the Person and Social Context* (pp. 184–256). New York: McGraw Hill.

Rumsey, N. and Harcourt, D. (2005). *The Psychology of Appearance.* Maidenhead: Open University Press.

Wardle, C. and Boyce, T. (2009). *Coverage and Audience Reception of Disfigurement on Television.* Research funded by the Healing Foundation and the Wales Office of Research and Development.

Warner, M.S. (2000). 'Person-centred therapy at the difficult edge: a developmentally based model of fragile and dissociative process'. In D. Mearns and B. Thorne (eds). *Person-Centred Therapy Today: new frontiers in theory and practice* (pp. 144–71). London: Sage.

8 | Therapy with Seriously Distressed Clients

Brendan Stone

For the purposes of this discussion, I will define 'seriously distressed' clients (SDCs) as individuals experiencing unmanageable and disabling levels of distress which seriously interfere with their ability to lead a meaningful, peaceful and productive life. Most are likely to have received psychiatric diagnoses such as 'schizophrenia', 'borderline personality disorder', or 'bipolar disorder'. SDCs will include individuals who are voice-hearers, although it is important to note that many voice-hearers are *not* seriously distressed (Romme et al., 2009). However, the chief argument in this chapter is that what distinguishes SDCs from non-SDCs is not the nature of their distress but rather the ways in which their experience has been framed in cultural and medical discourse, and the resultant discrimination and prejudice with which they have to contend.

SDCs, including but not exclusively people diagnosed as 'mentally ill' (PDMIs), form one of the most stigmatised and socially excluded groups in Western societies (Leff and Warner, 2006; Thornicroft 2006a, 2006b). Most SDCs will have experience of discriminatory, oppressive behaviours and attitudes, predicated on perceived difference from socio-cultural norms (Byrne, 2000). The stigmatisation of those who, for example, have been diagnosed as 'schizophrenic' is of such a measure that they are frequently spoken of and treated as in some way less than human (Goffmann, 1961, 1968; Warner, 1985; O'Hagan, 1992, 1994; Read and Baker, 1996). The basis of my argument here is that prejudice against SDCs remains more pervasive and culturally acceptable than other forms of discriminatory behaviours because powerful discourses, including biomedical constructions of 'mental illness', tacitly and sometimes explicitly sanction oppression, which in turn exacerbates SDCs' distress (Thornicroft, 2006b: 4). Therapists, therefore, need to understand the nature of SDCs' oppression so as not to perpetuate it.

The medical model and discrimination

A wide variety of research demonstrates that stigma and discrimination do not simply emerge from ignorance but are produced by socio-cultural structures and discourses, including the medical model of 'mental illness' – the position that mental illness is rooted in malfunctioning biology (Hill and Bale, 1981; Mehta and Farina, 1997; Walker and Read, 2002; Dietrich, 2004; Read et al., 2004a, 2006; Baumann, 2007; Read, 2007). My argument here, however, is *not* against the specific use of medication or other treatments; rather I wish to illuminate the potentially harmful effects and assumptions of the medical model. These include the individualising of distress; ignoring socio-cultural-familial causes of distress such as abuse, racism and poverty; and, perhaps most critically, the colonisation of SDCs' experience through the imposition of alien narrative frameworks, thereby disempowering and silencing individuals' own understandings, while implying that the experience of distress lacks the potential for meaning.

The biomedical story is strongly contested by many PDMIs, activists, researchers and clinicians (O'Hagan, 1994; Parker et al., 1995; Fee, 1999; Newnes et al., 1999, 2001; Tew, 2005a); opposition includes a strong body of opinion within the 'psych' professions (Johnstone, 2000; Boyle, 2004; Read et al., 2004a; Healey, 2008; Bentall, 2009; Moncrieff, 2009). The extensive evidence against the medical model has been well detailed elsewhere, and there are many readily available texts which readers can access in order to inform themselves of this critical work (O'Hagan, 1994; Parker et al., 1995; Newnes et al., 1999, 2001; Tew, 2005a). Critiques interrogate the notion of 'illness', reframing it as common, if extreme, human distress, caused not by biological or genetic dysfunction but by traumatic events or structural oppressions. Madness and distress, therefore, are conceptualised as reactions to concrete external causes, and the distressed individual as existing on a continuum with other 'normal' human beings. Yet, despite the large body of research detailing, for instance, the relationship between trauma and so-called 'schizophrenia', as well as other 'conditions', this evidence has still not provoked a radical step-change in treatment (Hammersley et al., 2003; Read et al., 2003; Read et al., 2004b, 2004c; Garno et al., 2005; Rosenberg et al., 2007; Shevlin et al., 2007).

Narrative identity and standpoint knowledges

My arguments here emerge from an engagement with the theoretical paradigm known as 'narrative identity', which argues for the central importance of stories to human beings' lives and identities (Ricoeur, 1984, 1991, 1992; Polkinghorne, 1988; Bruner, 1990). Nuanced versions of this paradigm include a recognition that the stories within which we live, and by means of which we orient our actions, are dependent upon, and emerge from, stories extant in culture. Often, particularly if we are from a marginalised and oppressed group, we will find ourselves the subject of others' stories – that is to say, we will be someone whose story is told rather than the one who tells the story. Moreover, the story which prevails in culture is often the one told by the most powerful storyteller. The corollary of this is that such a 'master story' is hard to resist when we conceptualise our identities, and we may find ourselves colonised by others' narratives (McLean, 2008). An example of this is the biomedical story of 'mental illness', in which a powerful story about the origins of distress occludes and silences alternative understandings (Beresford, 2005).

My arguments here also proceed from my own 'standpoint knowledges' (Harding, 1993, 1998; Kenney and Kinsella, 1997; Tew, 2005b). I am myself a PDMI, have been a user of mental health services for over 30 years, and have a great deal of personal experience of various therapies and medications. I have often been an SDC; I have known and know many other SDCs/PDMIs. My standpoint knowledges emerge from my own experience and the many relationships and conversations I have had with others who have experienced madness and distress. It is significant that this chapter is being written by a PDMI. PDMIs are well used to being talked about by a wide variety of professionals and having frameworks of understanding imposed on them which 'deny their own knowledge and expertise' (Tew, 2005b: 17). It is still rare for PDMIs to be given an opportunity to speak authoritatively from their own knowledges; this exclusion from public discourse is further evidence of oppression and discrimination (Beresford, 2003; Stone, 2004a).

Narrative understanding, context and choice

The therapist engaging with an SDC must take into account the narrative context of the therapeutic encounter. It is likely that SDCs will not feel themselves to have authority over the ways in which they are able to represent themselves, and their framework of self-understanding may not account adequately for their experience (Stone, 2004a, 2008a, 2008b). Yet, notwithstanding reservations about the medical model, it is also critical that therapists understand that for a client who is using it to understand their experience, it would be inappropriate and possibly dangerous to challenge this model if this is not done with great sensitivity. A narrative understanding of the person notes the human need for frames of understanding, with this need especially urgent at times of acute crisis (Bruner, 1990; Frank, 1995; Holstein and Gubrium, 2000; Stone, 2004a). Many of us who receive serious psychiatric diagnoses find, initially at least, the medical model to be a source of comfort and reassurance; the likelihood is that the only story on offer to us when we arrive at a health facility will be that of the illness model (Beresford, 2005; Stone, 2009). To dislodge the medical story, without offering alternative means of framing understandings, is to strand the client in a void without sense, meaning or waymarkers.

It is also critical that no matter how negative therapists' own views of the medical model are, they allow the client to come to their own position of understanding with which they feel comfortable, and which fits with their own perceptions (Spence, 1982). To replace one imposed narrative frame with its opposite is simply to perpetuate the original problem of colonising the client with a narrative they have not constructed for themselves (Knight, 2005). The key point here is that clients need to be helped towards understanding that they have a *choice* in how they conceive of their distress. If they then choose to frame their experience using the medical model, this position must be respected.

Readers may begin to see why a narrative approach to conceptualising distress and the client–therapist encounter is important. Narrative approaches to understanding experience emphasise the *plurality* of stories – that is to say, a variety of stories can be told about the same situation; and all stories are contingent, contestable and mutable (Rimmon-Kenan, 2006). Therefore this approach, *in itself*, is in opposition to the principles informing the medical model, which claims for itself 'validity' and 'truth', thereby disregarding alternative understandings. A narrative understanding of this, when put alongside the evidence that the medical model is fatally flawed in making such claims, argues that 'validity' in this instance emerges not from 'evidence' but rather from the power of the story-tellers, their access to resources, funding, media outlets and the like, and also the exigencies of a process in which vested and powerful interests, such as the pharmaceutical industry and current political imperatives, authorise some stories and not others (Beresford, 2005).

Schizophrenia – some consequences of the medical model

In order to understand the deleterious implications of the medical model, a good place to start is with the work of the originator of the diagnostic category of *dementia praecox*, Emil Kraepelin (1981 [1907]). The history of this diagnosis, now reframed as 'schizophrenia', is a paradigm case from which we can learn a great deal about attitudes towards people diagnosed with a range of psychiatric 'conditions'. Kraepelin held, and his heirs continue to follow suit, that 'schizophrenia' is a purely organic condition. In this view, psychological manifestations of the 'illness' are random malfunctions of the brain, and therefore unworthy of the kind of hermeneutic study which we would routinely accord to 'normal' human feelings or cognitions. If behaviours and feelings are understood as resulting from malfunctioning neurophysiology, then meaning cannot be gleaned from studying them. The clinical psychologist Louis Sass notes how this mechanistic cast of thought constructs the 'schizophrenic' as akin to a 'malfunctioning ... machine' characterised by a 'deterioration' and 'enfeeblement' of the highest human faculties, with the corollary that individuals are 'not only *difficult* to interpret but in some sense *beneath* interpretation, since their behaviour and expression must lack the intentionality and meaningfulness of normal human activity' (1992: 18).

Many current medical interventions treat the 'symptoms', or as I would prefer, 'content', of mental illness as of little importance, and proceed from a view it is something to be 'recovered' from. It is true that in the UK in recent years there has been a drive to expand the provision of psychological therapies, and one might argue that this represents a move away from a rigorously medicalised model. However, these treatments are largely being delivered in the form of very brief and highly focused cognitive behavioral therapies (CBT), and CBT, *in this manifestation*, poses little if any challenge to the medical model. While CBT per se, and when used alongside other therapies such as mindfulness-based therapy (Segal et al., 2002; Fulton et al., 2005) or acceptance and commitment therapy (Hofmanna and Asmundson, 2008) can help clients to reframe their understandings at a fundamental level, CBT as it is being developed focuses on the learning of instrumental means of changing thought patterns, rather than providing avenues of interpretation and understanding (Wakefield, 2005; Knight, 2005; Smail, 2007; James, 2007; Rowe, 2008; House and Loewenthal, 2008). In avoiding linking the present signifiers of distress with signifieds in the SDC's history (including the political history of her oppression), CBT, in this guise, is an anti-narrative form of therapy in which little, if any, time is allowed for autobiographical reflection and analysis.

Living with distress

'Mental illness' is not like other illnesses (Read et al., 2006). Whereas physical illness typically affects a part of the self, 'mental illness' is often seen and experienced as a condition which potentially affects the whole person. This emphasis is evident in a wide range of narrative reports of the experience of distress, and also in academic and clinical writing on the subject both from the mainstream of psychiatric opinion and more critical commentators (Stone, 2004a, 2004b, 2004c). Importantly, when an individual's 'mental illness' is most acute, her experience will be that there is little other than the 'symptoms' of 'illness' present in her identity: to all intents and purposes she *becomes* her 'illness'.

The medical model is largely structured teleologically: whether using drugs or CBT, or a combination of the two, treatment is directed towards an 'end', with the content of distress construed as a problem to be overcome, or as waste which must be cleared so that living can restart. (Even the currently fashionable 'recovery' model of treatment, which claims that remission of 'symptoms' is less important than 'empowerment' and re-establishing a sense of 'purpose', has powerful echoes of 'cure' in its very designation (Anthony, 1993).) In the throes of an acute distress which is co-extensive with an individual's very existence, effectively the whole of present experience and selfhood is constructed as harmful waste which must be discarded: the individual thus learns that *she* is a problem without value, a symptom to be overcome. This pathologising of selfhood is exacerbated by the language of diagnosis and treatment (Goffman, 1961; Scheff, 1984; Thoits, 1985). If my experience is defined by distress, the label attached to that experience will subsume all that I am. Although my experience is unique, refracted as it is through the complexities of my history, my class, age, gender, race, education and so on, diagnostic labels do a violence to its richness and consign me to a pre-defined category.

Those who become subjects of the medical model story will invariably do so while in a highly vulnerable state, in a setting in which they have little sense of power, with the clinician's authoritative narration apparently backed by scientific expertise. The route to this first clinical encounter will usually have been via mounting anguish, and may have been impelled by the insistence of family or employer. The individual will arrive as a supplicant, petitioning not only for help, but – on her behalf or others' – a means of accounting for troubling experiences. Thus, this formative moment is undergirded by the intensely felt human need for stories to contextualise and link together disparate experiences, and thereby integrate these into the larger narrative of an identity.

Because of the urgent need for a story, and because the medicalised language of illness is a discourse sanctioned by power, it is likely that in the limit-state of radical vulnerability individuals will accept the medical narrative, especially if alternatives are unavailable. The individual may feel an intense relief that a story has been offered which accounts for her suffering. If a treatment is offered, then this may suggest that the medical narrative promises more lasting relief, and be a further reason to grasp the proffered understanding. The individual, having had her need for a story met, may experience her distress as having been to some extent relieved, and, in the weeks which follow, when her suffering returns, she or others may reiterate the story told about her, and cling to this framework as a means of accounting for the trials of madness. Remembering medicine's promises of relief, she will be urged to continue her treatment and not to lose heart.

In this way the medical story is gradually incorporated into the fabric of a life. It becomes a means by which the individual interprets and understands significant aspects of her experience, fitting the various manifestations of distress into its template, and orienting her responses and actions. So too, those close to her may refer to the medical story and act according to its precepts. All of this means that the story becomes integrated into the individual's sense of selfhood, woven into the weft of her narrative identity.

Introjecting the dominant story

While the medical story may provide a welcome framework by which to understand troubling experience, the process of introjection may be far from harmless. The SDC's distress has been homogenised, hollowed out of meaning and nuance; no longer an individual whose experience is refined by her history and imagination, she has become an instance in a category which defines something without value, something to be moved through as quickly as possible. With treatment aimed towards 'recovery' much of present existence appears to be without value or meaning, and deprived of these signifiers of humanity, she has become a thing – hoping for revivication. Eventually the powerful story through which she has been authorised to understand herself becomes who she is. Labelling the richness of her experience as symptomatic, she ceases to perceive its unique textures.

This process might be described as 'self-stigmatisation', but this is not simply a matter of explaining the low self-esteem of PDMIs (Corrigan and Watson, 2002). Rather, we need to understand the harmful implications for the ways in which individuals relate to and understand their experience. The therapist must be aware that this will affect what is said and thought (and not said and not thought) in the therapeutic encounter. PDMIs and SDCs may have ceased to hope that their experience is meaningful, and therefore may no longer be easily able to describe, perhaps even perceive, the texture of selfhood.

The importance of social discourse

I will close with two further points. First, the experience of PDMIs is overwhelmingly one of isolation. This is so for various reasons, including chronic levels of unemployment, poverty, and lack of access to education (Thornicroft, 2006a, 2006b). But in addition, the medical model's individualisation of distress means that the (narrative) connections between self and world may have been severed at a profound, epistemological level. PDMIs relate to themselves as individually dysfunctional, and as painfully different. Therefore, the possibility of engaging in meaningful social relations is curtailed. In order to overcome this, it is critical that PDMIs have access to the experience and knowledge of others like themselves. The social nature of the self, and the experience of other minority liberation movements, teach us that in order to construct alternative understandings of ourselves and our oppression, we need to act together, in solidarity with others who have walked a similar path (O'Hagan, 1994; Wallcraft et al., 2003; Icarus Project, 2006). The prevalence of negative images of and stories about PDMIs means that these cannot be combated effectively alone, nor can alternative understandings of distress be constructed without the help of others (Stone et al., 2008). A therapeutic relationship alone, I would argue, is unlikely to suffice. The therapist, then, needs to understand her own limits, and to advertise these to the SDC, perhaps helping the client to form relationships with others, and alerting her to the groups and literature which counter the medical model with alternative narratives. Alternative understandings of madness and distress are vital counters to the hegemonic medical narrative; but equally vital is that these understandings are formulated by SDCs and PDMIs, rather than imposed on us, or given to us – even when this is done by well-meaning therapists or academics.

Second, the pervasiveness of the medical model's assumptions cannot be underestimated. It is inevitable that the therapist, no matter how well versed in the critiques, will also have been shaped by this dominant discourse. Thus, it is vital that she scrutinises herself and is attentive to her own prejudicial assumptions. This process of 'critical elaboration' (Gramsci, 1971: 323) is crucial. Even for SDCs who have an understanding of the implications of the medical model, it is difficult, perhaps impossible, to resist its influence. For myself, I am aware that its precepts continue to affect the way in which I relate to my experience (Stone et al., 2008; Stone, 2008b). I still inadvertently reiterate harmful assumptions about my own and others' experiences of distress which have insinuated themselves into me. Without the support and critical insight of others 'like me' I would not recognise this and continue to operate under the influence of stories which, consciously, I have rejected.

Exercises to explore anti-discriminatory therapeutic practice with SDCs and PDMIs

1 Evaluate the differences between discrimination against PDMIs and discrimination against other minority groups.
2 'Critically elaborate' the traces which cultural discourses towards PDMIs have deposited in you, and consider how these influence your behaviours, attitudes and choices.
3 Explore examples of support literature produced by self-help groups, such as the Icarus Project, and evaluate how this differs from clinical approaches.
4 Evaluate the views of distress found in autobiographical writings by PDMIs. Gail Hornstein's *Bibliography of First-Person Narratives of Madness in English* is available online at www.mtholyoke.edu/acad/assets/Academics/Hornstein_Bibliography.pdf.

Useful links

Writings by the activist/advocate Mary O'Hagan:
www.maryohagan.com/mental-health-service.html

Publications by the PDMI-led network The Icarus Project:
http://theicarusproject.net

The Mental Health History Timeline
www.studymore.org.uk/mhhtim.htm

Mental Health and Survivors' Movements and Context:
http://studymore.org.uk/mpu.htm

The Critical Psychiatry website has links to many papers which critique the medical
  model:
www.mentalhealth.freeuk.com/

The Social Perspectives Network website includes links to many useful publications:
www.spn.org.uk/

Writings by the radical psychotherapist David Smail:
www.davidsmail.info

References

Anthony, W. (1993) 'Recovery from mental illness: The guiding vision of the mental
    health service system in the 1990s'. *Psychosocial Rehabilitation Journal*, 16.4: 11–23.
Baumann, A. (2007) 'Stigmatization, social distance and exclusion because of mental
    illness: The individual with mental illness as a "stranger"'. *International Review of
    Psychiatry*, 19.2: 131–5.
Bentall, R. (2009) *Doctoring the Mind*. London: Allen Lane.
Beresford, P. (2003) *It's Our Lives: A short theory of knowledge, distance and experience*.
    London: Citizen Press.
Beresford, P. (2005) 'Social Approaches to Madness and Distress: User Perspectives and
    User Knowledges', in Tew (2005a) (op. cit.): 32–52.
Boyle, M. (2004) *Schizophrenia: A Scientific Delusion*? London: Penguin.
Bruner, J. (1990) *Acts of Meaning*. Cambridge, MA: Harvard University Press.
Byrne, P. (2000) 'Stigma of mental illness and ways of diminishing it'. *Advances in
    Psychiatric Treatment*, 6: 65–72.
Corrigan, P. and Watson, A. (2002) 'Understanding the impact of stigma on people with
    mental illness'. *World Psychiatry*, 1: 16–20.
Dietrich, S. (2004) 'The relationship between public causal beliefs and social distance
    toward mentally ill people'. *Australian and New Zealand Journal of Psychiatry*, 38.5:
    348–54.
Fee, D. (ed.) (1999) *Pathology and the Post-Modern: Mental Illness, Discourse, and
    Experience*. London: Sage.
Frank, A.W. (1995) *The Wounded Storyteller: Body, Illness, and Ethics*. Chicago:
    University of Chicago Press.
Fulton, P., Germer, C. and Siegel, R. (2005) *Mindfulness and Psychotherapy*. New York:
    Guilford Press.
Garno, J., Goldberg, J. and Ramirez, P. (2005) 'Impact of childhood abuse on the clinical
    course of bipolar disorder'. *British Journal of Psychiatry*, 186: 121–5.
Goffman, E. (1961) *Asylums*. Harmondsworth: Penguin.
Goffman, E. (1968) *Stigma: Notes on the management of spoiled identity*. Harmondsworth:
    Penguin.

Gramsci, A. (1971) *Selections from the Prison Notebooks.* London: Lawrence and Wishart.

Hammersley, P., Dias, A., Todd, G., Bowen Jones, K., Reilly, B. and Bentall, R. (2003) 'Childhood trauma and hallucinations in bipolar affective disorder: Preliminary investigation'. *The British Journal of Psychiatry,* 182: 543–7.

Harding, S. (1993) 'Rethinking Standpoint Epistemology: What Is Strong Objectivity?', in Alcoff, L. and Potter, E. (eds) *Feminist Epistemologies.* London: Routledge: 49–82.

Harding, S. (1998) *Is Science Multi-Cultural? Postcolonialisms, feminisms and epistemologies.* Bloomington, IN: Indiana University Press.

Healy, D. (2008) *Psychiatric Drugs Explained.* London: Churchill Livingstone.

Hill, D. and Bale, R. (1981) 'Measuring Beliefs About where Psychological Distress Originates and Who is Responsible for its Alleviation', in Lefcourt, H. (ed.) *Research with the Locus of Control Construct,* Vol. 2. New York: Academic Press.

Hofmanna, S. and Asmundson, G. (2008) 'Acceptance and mindfulness-based therapy: New wave or old hat?' *Clinical Psychology Review,* 28.1: 1–16.

Holstein, J. and Gubrium, J. (2000) *The Self We Live By: Narrative identity in a postmodern world.* New York and Oxford: Oxford University Press.

Hornstein, Gail (2008) *Bibliography of First-Person Narratives of Madness in English* (4th edn). Available at www.mtholyoke.edu/acad/assets/Academic/Hornstein_Bibliography.pdf, accessed September 2009.

House, R. and Loewenthal, D. (eds) (2008) *Against and For CBT: Towards a constructive dialogue*? Ross-on-Wye: PCCS.

Icarus Project (2006) *Creating Community Mental Health Support Networks.* New York: Icarus Press. Available at http://theicarusproject.net/icarus-downloads/friends-make-the-best-medicine+, accessed September 2009.

James, O. (2007) *Affluenza: How to be successful and stay sane.* London: Vermilion.

Johnstone, L. (2000) *Users and Abusers of Psychiatry: A critical look at psychiatric practice.* London: Routledge.

Kenney, S. and Kinsella, H. (eds) (1997) *Politics and Feminist Standpoint Theories.* New York: Haworth.

Knight, T. (2005) 'You'd better believe it: Accepting and working within the client's own reality'. *Clinical Psychology Forum,* 155: 38–42.

Kraepelin, E. (1981 [1907]) *Clinical Psychiatry* Vol. 7. Trans. A. R. Diefendorf. New York: Scholars' Facsimiles & Reprints.

Leff, J. and Warner, R. (2006) *Social Inclusion of People with Mental Illness.* Cambridge: Cambridge University Press.

McLean, K. (2008) 'The emergence of narrative identity'. *Social and Personality Psychology Compass,* 2/4: 1685–1702.

Mehta, S. and Farina, A. (1997) 'Is being sick really better? Effect of the disease view of mental disorder on stigma'. *Journal of Social and Clinical Psychology,* 16.4: 405–19.

Moncrieff, J. (2009) *The Myth of the Chemical Cure.* London: Palgrave Macmillan.

Newnes, C., Holmes, G. and Dunn, C. (eds) (1999) *This is Madness: A critical look at psychiatry and the future of mental health services.* Ross-on-Wye: PCCS.

Newnes, C., Holmes, G. and Dunn, C. (eds) (2001) *This is Madness Too: Critical perspectives on mental health services.* Ross-on-Wye: PCCS.

O'Hagan, M. (1992) 'On being "not quite human": A psychiatric survivor's perspective on stigma', in Patten, D., *Public Attitudes to Mental Illness.* Wellington, NZ: Department of Health: xvii–xxii.

O'Hagan, M. (1994) *Stopovers On My Way Home From Mars.* London: Survivors Speak Out.

Parker, I., Georgaca, E., Harper, D., McLaughlin, T. and Stowell-Smith, M. (1995) *Deconstructing Psychopathology.* London: Sage.

Polkinghorne, D. (1988) *Narrative Knowing and the Human Sciences*. Albany, NY: SUNY Press.

Read, J. (2007) 'Why promoting biological ideology increases prejudice against people labelled "schizophrenic"'. *Australian Psychologist*, 42.2: 118–28.

Read, J. and Baker, S. (1996) *Not Just Sticks and Stones*. London: MIND.

Read, J. and Haslam, N. (2004) 'Public Opinion: Bad Things Happen and Can Drive You Crazy', in Read et al. (2004a) (op. cit.): 133–46.

Read, J., Agar, K., Argyle, N. and Aderhold, V. (2003) 'Sexual and physical abuse during childhood and adulthood as predictors of hallucinations, delusions and thought disorder.' *Psychology and Psychotherapy: Theory, Research and Practice*, 76.1: 1–22.

Read, J., Mosher, L. and Bentall, R. (eds) (2004a) *Models of Madness: Psychological, social and biological approaches to schizophrenia*. Hove: Brunner-Routledge.

Read, J., Goodman, L., Morrison, A., Ross, C. and Aderhold, V. (2004b) 'Childhood Trauma and Stress', in Read et al. (2004a) (op. cit.): 223–52.

Read, J., Seymour, F. and Mosher, L. (2004c) 'Unhappy Families', in Read et al. (2004a) (op. cit.): 253–68.

Read, J., Haslam, N., Sayce, L. and Davies, E. (2006) 'Prejudice and schizophrenia: A review of the mental illness is an illness like any other approach.' *Acta Psychiatr Scandinavica*, 114: 303–18.

Ricoeur, P. (1984) *Time and Narrative*, Vol. 3. Trans. Kathleen McLaughlin and David Pellauer. Chicago: University of Chicago Press.

Ricoeur, P. (1991) 'Life in Quest of Narrative', in David Wood (ed.) *On Paul Ricoeur*. London: Routledge.

Ricoeur, P. (1992) *Oneself as Another*. Trans. Katherine Blamey. Chicago: University of Chicago Press.

Rimmon-Kenan, S. (2006) 'Concepts of Narrative.' *Collegium*, 1: 10–19.

Romme, M., Escher, S., Dillon, J., Corstens, D. and Morris, M. (2009) *Living with Voices: 50 Stories of Recovery*. Ross-on-Wye: PCCS.

Rosenberg, S., Lu, W., Mueser, K., Jankowski, M. and Cournos, F. (2007) 'Correlates of adverse childhood events among adults with schizophrenia spectrum disorders.' *Psychiatric Services*, 58: 245–53.

Rowe, D. (2008) 'Cognitive behavioural therapy.' *Psychminded*. Available at www. psychminded.co.uk/news/news2008/October08/dorothy-rowe004.htm, accessed 20 August 2009.

Sass, L. (1992) *Madness and Modernism*. Cambridge, MA: Harvard University Press.

Scheff, T. (1984) *Being Mentally Ill*. Chicago: Aldine.

Segal, Z., Teasdale, J. and Williams, M. (2002) *Mindfulness-Based Cognitive Therapy for Depression*. New York: Guilford Press.

Shevlin, M., Dorahy, M. and Adamson, G. (2007) 'Childhood traumas and hallucinations: An analysis of the national comorbidity survey.' *Journal of Psychiatric Research*, 41.3–4: 222–8.

Smail, D. (2007) 'Clinical Psychology and Truth.' De-Medicalising Misery Conference, University of East London, 14 September.

Spence, D. (1982) *Narrative Truth and Historical Truth: Meaning and interpretation in psychoanalysis*. New York: Norton.

Stone, B. (2004a) *Starting to Speak: Madness and the narration of identity*. Unpublished PhD thesis. Sheffield: University of Sheffield.

Stone, B. (2004b) 'How can I speak of madness? Narrative and Identity in Memoirs of Mental Illness,' in Brian Roberts (ed.) *Narrative, Memory and Identity: Theoretical and methodological issues*. Huddersfield: University of Huddersfield Press: 49–59.

Stone, B. (2004c) 'Towards a writing without power: Notes on the narration of madness.' *Auto/Biography*, 12.1: 16–33.

Stone, B. (2008a) 'Why Fiction Matters to Madness', in David Robinson (ed.) *Narrative and Fiction: An interdisciplinary approach*. Huddersfield: University of Huddersfield Press: 71–8.

Stone, B. (2008b) 'The Content of our Distress: What Happens When You Abandon Illness?' Paper given at Asylum! Conference, Manchester Metropolitan University, 10–12 September.

Stone, B. (2009) 'Running Man'. *Qualitative Research in Sport and Exercise*, 1.1: 67–71.

Stone, B., Wilson, A. and Beresford, P. (2008) 'Madness and Distress: From Individual to Collective Narratives'. Paper given at Disability Studies Conference, Lancaster University, September.

Tew, J. (ed.) (2005a) *Social Perspectives in Mental Health: Developing social models to understand and work with mental distress*. London: Jessica Kingsley.

Tew, J. (2005b) 'Core themes in Social Perspectives', in Tew (2005a) (op. cit.): 13–21.

Thoits, P. (1985) 'Self-labeling processes in mental illness: The role of emotional deviance'. *American Journal of Sociology*, 92.2: 221–49.

Thornicroft, G. (2006a) *Shunned: Discrimination against people with mental illness*. Oxford: Oxford University Press.

Thornicroft, G. (2006b) *Actions Speak Louder … Tackling discrimination against people with mental illness*. London: Mental Health Foundation.

Wakefield, M. (2005) 'Person-centred practice in primary health care'. *Person-Centred Quarterly*, 1–5.

Walker, I. and Read, J. (2002) 'The differential effectiveness of psychosocial and biogenetic causal explanations in reducing negative attitudes toward "mental illness"'. *Psychiatry: Interpersonal and Biological Processes*, 65.4: 313–25.

Wallcraft, J., Read, J. and Sweeney, A. (2003) *On Our Own Terms: Users and survivors of mental health services working together for support and change*. London: The Sainsbury Centre for Mental Health.

Warner, R. (1985) *Recovery from Schizophrenia: Psychiatry and political economy*. London: Routledge.

9 Counselling, Psychotherapy and Religion

William West

Nietzsche famously said 'God is Dead' which may have been true in the mid-19th Century but in the early 21st Century God is certainly báck with a vengeance. Religious identity and the rights of religious minorities within a Secular culture are becoming increasingly important political and legal issues in many Western countries and internationally. (Religion Law UK, 2009)

Whether we like it or not, most of the world's population hold a religious view of life. Even in Britain today, which most regard as a secular society, the vast majority of the population believe in God and value their spirituality whatever they mean by this word (Hay and Hunt, 2000). Consequently, the secular stance which is still the dominant narrative within counselling and psychotherapy is in contrast to most people's values and beliefs. This is of overwhelming importance to a profession that claims to value the client's perspective and which places a high premium on accurate empathy.

In this chapter, I will explore what religion and spirituality are; their relevance to practice; counsellors in training; mental health and spirituality; present some examples from practice; discuss how we might change practice for the better; and I include some exercises and useful resources for students and practitioners.

It is apparent that the world of counselling and psychotherapy in Britain (and indeed elsewhere in what is referred as the 'West') has a problematic relationship with regard to religion, indeed to the broader area of spirituality (Richards and Bergin, 2005; Swinton, 2001; Thorne, 2002; West, 2004). This represents I believe, at least in part, a problem that resides within the broader majority white culture. It would be valuable to trace the cultural roots of this problem, some of which goes back, I suspect, to the religious wars in Britain that began under the Tudors in the mid-16th century, if not earlier. However, such an exploration is beyond the scope of this chapter.

Of course not everyone within the world of therapy would accept that there is a problem. I have sometimes been told, 'None of my clients presents issues relating to religion or spirituality', to which my response is to ask 'How have you silenced them?' Perhaps worse than this are therapists who follow Freud in regarding religion in neurotic terms: 'The derivation of religious needs from the infant's helplessness and the longing for the father aroused by it seems to me incontrovertible' (Freud, 1963: 9).

There are other more recent voices that urge us not to explore spirituality. Smail, a notable critic of modern therapy, suggests that with regard to spirituality we follow Wittgenstein's advice 'Wherefore one cannot speak, therefore one must be silent' and states 'That is to say, the place of spirituality in psychotherapy must remain, I think, largely unspoken' (Smail, 2001: 47). This begs a number of questions, including the challenge of being present to that which is unspoken within the therapeutic encounter.

In the last decade or so there has been an increasing literature and debate around the role of spirituality in counselling and psychotherapy (e.g. Gubi, 2002; Lines, 2006; Richards and Bergin, 2005; Rowan, 2008; Thorne, 2002; West, 2004; Whitmore, 2000), but still the issue of religion tends to get a bad press. Therapists seem more willing to acknowledge the value of spirituality and spiritual experiences to their clients and sometimes themselves, but the idea of organised religion is still often unacceptable.

What is religion and spirituality?

At this point it would be helpful to begin to define spirituality and religion. Most people seem to use the word 'religion' to cover the organised group of people, religious leaders and buildings that are used by a faith group. In contrast 'spiritual' is often seen as being about the individual's personal beliefs and experiences, which may well be in some kind of tension with the faith group they belong to, if any. Indeed, Jungian analyst James Hollis (1996) says 'Religion is for those who fear going to Hell, spirituality is for those who have been there'.

Not everyone accepts these distinctions but they do reflect common usage and dictionary definitions. For example, in Wikipedia (accessed 10.3.2009) religion is defined: 'A religion is an organized approach to human spirituality which usually encompasses a set of narratives, symbols, beliefs and practices, often with a supernatural or transcendent quality, that give meaning to the practitioner's experiences of life through reference to a higher power or truth.'

And spirituality: 'The spiritual is traditionally contrasted with the material, the temporal and the earthly. A perceived sense of connection forms a central defining characteristic of spirituality – connection to a metaphysical reality greater than oneself, which may include an emotional experience of religious awe and reverence, or such states as satori or nirvana. Equally importantly, spirituality relates to matters of sanity and of psychological health. Spirituality is the personal, subjective dimension of religion, particularly that which pertains to liberation or salvation.' For a more detailed consideration of definitions of spirituality in relation to therapy, see West (2004).

So spirituality as defined above may be part of religion or even in tension with religion and 'secular spirituality', a somewhat confounding term, becomes a possibility. It should be noted that this separation of spirituality from religion is not readily accepted by all people. I have met several rabbis who insist that their spirituality and religion are not separate and also some African Caribbean Christians who use the word 'religious' and 'spiritual' interchangeably.

This suggests it is very important to understand how clients are using these terms. Indeed, I would extend this care to what a client might mean by the word Christian, Muslim, Hindu, Sikh, Jew, Pagan, and so on. These are alive words whose meanings alter. For example Sufis, who represent the mystical tradition within Islam and whose religious practice often includes devotional music and dancing, convey a very different view and image of Islam to the more stereotypical media representation of Islam. Or contrast the views of Christ found among Quakers with those of Anglicans or Roman Catholics.

It is my contention that membership of a religious group and/or personal spiritual beliefs and practices are very relevant to the practice of counselling. Ideally, this matter would be uncontroversial, but many counsellor training courses give little time towards careful consideration of religion and spirituality in modern society. This goes back to my opening comments on the problem that religion and spirituality presents to modern Britain. So why should counsellors be any different?

The relevance of religion and spirituality to practice

Despite the training of counsellors and the theories that underpin counselling often ignoring, underplaying or undermining religion and spirituality, it is striking how spiritual many counsellors are. Peter Gubi (2002), in his research into prayer and counselling, did a survey of British Association for Counselling and Psychotherapy (BACP) registered counsellors. Of the 247 respondents (43 per cent return rate), 12 per cent had used prayer overtly with Christian clients and 59 per cent had used prayer covertly. Of those using prayer covertly, 37 per cent had prayed for guidance during a session, 25 per cent prayed for their client during a session, 49 per cent outside of a session and 51 per cent had used prayer to prepare themselves. However, only 24 per cent of those using prayer had ever discussed it in supervision.

These findings suggest that perhaps counsellors are more religious than their trainings and theories are, and worryingly are using spiritual interventions like prayer without adequate supervision. Indeed, Gubi (2002) speaks of their fear of not being understood, of being judged, losing the respect of others and fear of how their supervisor will react.

Of course it could be argued that Gubi's respondents were those with a keen interest in prayer, although his 43 per cent return rate suggests this represents a significant minority, at least of BACP counsellors. Indeed, the Association for Pastoral and Spiritual Care and Counselling (APSCC), which is the Division of BACP for those interested in spirituality and religion, currently (March 2010) has an individual membership of 800 and 41 organisational members. BACP itself has a membership of over 20,000.

Prayer and other spiritual techniques have been used for healing within many faiths (see, for example, Moodley and West, 2005). Within Islam, traditional healers have used spiritual techniques and prayer for generations, and these practices are fundamental to notions of healing in Islam.

Barbara Smith draws our attention to Razali et al. (2002), who undertook a randomised control trial incorporating socio-cultural and religious aspects in the management of anxiety among Muslim patients. The therapists used a cognitive behavioural therapy approach and aspects of the Holy Qur'an and Hadith with which to guide clients. Their guidelines included encouraging patients to be close to Allah through prayer and reading the Qur'an; advising patients to change their lifestyle to emulate that of the Prophet Muhammad and to accept the patients' interpretation of symptoms. They found that religious-cultural psychotherapy rapidly improved anxiety symptoms in Muslim patients with a strong religious background, when used in conjunction with standard treatment for general anxiety disorder.

Barbara suggests that these results concur with the findings of King and Dein (1998), who suggested that people who are religious experience better psychological health in the face of difficult life events than non-religious people. Razali et al. (2002) call attention to the meditative qualities of praying five times a day, promoting relaxation and a feeling of well-being (Woon, 1984).

Other authors who have led the way in incorporating spirituality into therapy include: Fukuyama and Sevig (1999), who promoted spirituality into multicultural counselling; Leseho (2007), who sees therapy as a spiritual activity in itself; and my own research (West, 1997, 1998) into healing and spirituality in therapy. Yaqoob (2000) laments the absence of spiritual and religious endorsement in the Western psychological literature: 'there is a taboo in mixing faith with treatment – it is not acceptable or considered professional.'

Counsellors in training

This question of the attitude of counsellors in training to religion is further explored by Banks (2003), who describes trainees' reactions to a case study of a woman with strong religious feelings who tolerated emotional neglect from her husband and teenage children because 'through suffering one will find the true meaning of God'. Banks describes the 'many angry feelings' expressed by trainees, some from a feminist viewpoint and from those who felt stunted by their own religious upbringings. Some stated that they had 'no time for religious [nutters]'. Banks comments, 'A heated debate arose in which others attempted to get the dismissive individuals to reflect on whether their experience was unfortunate and distorted or whether this could be generalized to the experience of all ... in some cases this self reflection was not possible' (Banks, 2003: 106).

This unfortunately is not an isolated incidence, as Jenkins discovered in conversation with a counsellor: 'The message there [on the PD group] was that a lot of counsellors had anti-religious feelings ... So I suppose there too there is a message being given that it is not okay to talk about your spirituality ... certainly never in my [counsellor] training have we talked about religion' (2006: 80) In my own experience as a trainer, I was recently shocked to have witnessed some strident anti-Christian remarks made in the presence of trainees who had previously declared their Christian beliefs and church belonging. I could not imagine similar anti-semitic, Islamophobic remarks being acceptable to a counselling trainee, so why anti-Christian?

The danger of such negative attitudes is that they spill over into practice, as one former psychiatric patient reports: 'When I was ill, I certainly learned VERY quickly to keep the spiritual side of myself separate from the rest of myself whenever I met with any of the "professionals"' (Jenkins, 2006: 80). In other words, to be actively engaged with one's spirituality or religion can be seen as a *symptom* of one's illness rather than something healthy. Indeed, the non-acceptance of the value of religion and spirituality to mental health service users within the NHS is a major cause for concern (Swinton, 2001).

Mental health and spirituality

The issue of mental health and spirituality is difficult. I will offer a light-hearted example of the challenge of diagnosis, albeit with serious implications. My wife, who has studied transactional analysis (TA) for some years, recently decided that my personality adaption in TA terms (Stewart and Joines, 1987) was schizoid. 'No,' I replied 'I am a mystic.' Unfortunately mystic is not one of the TA personality adaptions. Mystic is quite a useful way of understanding myself, as it happens. We could both be right of course – I might be a mystic with schizoid features or a schizoid with mystic features!

There is a very real issue here, that people undergoing change involving spirituality – something Grof referred to as 'spiritual emergency' (Grof and Grof, 1989) – can be misdiagnosed, mistreated and misunderstood by practitioners who pathologies religiosity and spirituality. Allman et al. (1992) did a survey of 650 members of the American Psychological Association who were in full-time practice. From the 285 respondents it was apparent that 4.5 per cent of their clients had reported a mystical experience in the previous year. In this survey the authors presented a case vignette of a client reporting mystical experience with some troubling psychotic features. Respondents were asked how they would treat this client. Humanistically inclined respondents tended to overlook the psychotic features, while others chose to ignore the mystical aspects. It was apparent that many respondents were judging the case on the basis of their own attitude to mysticism.

A reflective exercise

1 Soraya, a young Muslim woman, comes to the counselling service wearing a veil. As the sessions progress, she says that she is experiencing increasing levels of verbal abuse which often coincide with Islamophobic media items. She is generally supported by her faith and her belief in the afterlife. However, she is now suffering high levels of anxiety and considering removing her veil.

   Q: *What do you think the implications are for Soraya in making her decision?*

2 Janet, a strong evangelical Christian, was severely troubled that her husband was losing interest in their church and she seriously faced the dilemma from her faith that he will not therefore be with her in heaven when he dies. It would be so easy to challenge the theology involved rather than face the discomfort of listening empathically to Janet's very real problem. It can be hard as a counsellor to accept that this kind of dilemma is very real and very painful for the client involved, especially when we might well view her belief system as absurd. It is important to note that the client has not chosen to speak to her minister but has come to a counsellor who does not share her evangelical faith.

   Q: *What do you imagine would be your own response to Janet's situation?*

3 Mariyam, a young Muslim woman at university, is exploring with her counsellor whether to suspend her studies and prioritise a marriage arranged by her parents.

The therapist questions Mariyam about whether she 'wants' this marriage, making the common and offensive error of confusing 'arranged' with 'forced'.

Q: *Are you aware of some of the values embraced in the Holy Qur'an that might help you to understand Mariyam's dilemma, i.e. family, education, parental influence?*

4 John, a deeply religious client, became anxious when his counsellor suddenly started wearing a crucifix – fearful of what judgments he faced as the harsh God of the Old Testament from his Christian upbringing was activated inside him. Despite the therapist wearing the cross as a fashion accessory, some useful therapeutic work resulted about his inner God figures.

Q: *Are you aware of the religious or spiritual beliefs of your own clients, including their relationship with religions from childhood?*

An agenda for change

1 Counsellors need to cultivate a willingness to learn about their clients' culture beyond merely being open to being taught by their clients.
2 The anti-Christian and pro-secular bias in many counsellor training courses and amongst many counsellors in Britain need to be effectively challenged.
3 We need to cultivate a positive and respectful attitude towards clients' spiritual and religious beliefs, certainly not viewing them as immature.
4 It is important to understand the relationship between the clients' culture and their faith. For example, Christianity among Black African Caribbean people was, and is, an important part of their resistance to white oppression. It is a shaming part of British history that African Caribbean immigrants to Britain in the 1950s onwards, who were often Christians, were made so unwelcome by the Church of England. Tales of their ostracisation, in those early days, are still prevalent today among the African Caribbean community.
5 Most people in Britain and elsewhere in the world have some religious or spiritual faith and this truth needs honouring, understanding and exploring within counsellor training, practice and supervision.

Exercises for students

1 Define what spirituality means to you. What implications does this definition have for the practice of therapy?
2 Consider the role of religion, if any, in your upbringing. What did, and does it mean to you today?
3 What do you know about the main faiths practised in Britain? Are you familiar with the four noble truths of Buddhism? With the concept of Karma in Hinduism? The call to prayer within Islam? How religious Jews observe the Sabbath and Passover? What Christ means to Christians?

Conclusion

Religious faith seems like the last taboo in a counselling world willing to discuss sex, gender, race, death, suicide and drug addiction. The vast majority of the people in the world have a religious faith, and even more of them have spiritual experiences. Although, as with any human endeavour, spirituality can be pursued in a neurotic unhealthy way, to many people it is an important part of their lives and certainly worthy of respect and understanding with the counselling encounter.

Acknowledgements

Although I am responsible for the ideas expressed here, it is important that I acknowledge how much I have learnt from the many people who have contributed so much to my understandings. These include, first, my editors, Colin Lago and Barbara Smith – Barbara in particular drew my attention to the role of Islamic traditional healers and some of the work presented in this chapter draws on her forthcoming doctoral thesis. Also, my teachers include: Lynda Ankrah, Allen Bergin, Terry Biddington, Fevronia Chistodoulidi, Kam Dhillon, Dawn Edge, the late Grace Jantzen, Chris Jenkins, the late Pittu Laungani, Roy Moodley, Abdullah Popoola, Richard Summers and Dori Yusef.

Useful resources

For helpful information on new religious groups, contact INFORM: www.inform.ac.uk
The website of the Special Interest Group on Spirituality of the Royal College of Psychiatry is well worth a visit: www.rcpsych.ac.uk/college/specialinterestgroups/spirituality/publications.aspx.
There are some interesting novels emerging reflecting the experiences of second-generation British people that reflect many of the challenges faced in terms of culture and religion, for example:
Syal, M. (1997) *Anita and Me.* London: Flamingo.
Sanghera, S. (2008) *If You Don't Know Me by Now.* London: Penguin.

References

Allman, L.S., De Las Rocha, O., Elkins, D.N. and Weathers, R.S. (1992) Psychotherapists' attitudes towards clients report mystical experiences, *Psychotherapy,* 29(4): 654–9.
Banks, N. (2003) Counselling and religion, in C. Lago and B. Smith (eds) *Anti-Discriminatory Counselling Practice,* London: Sage.
Freud, S. (1963) *Civilisation and its Discontents,* New York: Basic Books.
Fukuyama, and Sevig, (1999) *Integrating Spirituality into Multicultural Counseling* (Multicultural Aspects of Counseling And Psychotherapy), London: Sage.
Grof, C. and Grof, S. (1989) *Spiritual Emergency – When Personal Transformation Becomes a Crisis,* Los Angeles, CA: Tarcher.

Gubi, P. (2002) Practice behind closed doors – challenging the taboo of prayer in mainstream counselling culture, *Journal of Critical Psychology, Counselling and Psychotherapy*, 2(2): 97–104.

Hay, D. and Hunt, K. (2000) Understanding the Spirituality of People Who Don't go to Church, Centre for the Study of Human relations, Nottingham University.

Hollis, J. (1996) *Swamplands of the Soul: New Life in Dismal Places*. Toronto: Inner City Books.

Jenkins, C. (2006) A Voice Denied, Clients' Experience of the Exclusion of Spirituality in Counselling and Psychotherapy, PhD Thesis, University of Manchester.

King, M.B. and Dein, S. (1998) The spiritual variable in psychiatric research, *Psychological Medicine*, 28: 1259–62.

Leseho, (2007) A critical discussion of recent texts in child counselling, *International Journal of Children's Spirituality*, 10(1): 101–8.

Lines, D. (2006) *Spirituality in Counselling and Psychotherapy*, London: Sage.

Moodley, R. and West, W. (2005) *Integrating Traditional Healing Practices in Counselling and Psychotherapy*, Thousand Oaks, CA: Sage.

Razali, S.M., Aminah, K. and Kahn, U.A. (2002) Religious cultural psychotherapy in the management of anxiety patients, *Transcultural Psychiatry*, 39(1): 130–6.

Religion Law UK (2009) Home page, available at www.religionlaw.co.uk, accessed 1 November 2009.

Richards, P.S. and Bergin, A.E. (2005) *A Spiritual Strategy for Counselling and Psychotherapy*, 2nd edition, Washington, DC: APA.

Rowan, J. (2008) *The Transpersonal; Spirituality in Psychotherapy and Counselling*, 2nd edition, London: Routledge.

Smail, D. (2001) On not being able to eff the ineffable, in S. King-Spooner and C. Newnes (eds) *Spirituality and Psychotherapy*, Ross-on-Wye: PCCS Books, 47–51.

Stewart, I. and Joines, V. (1987) *TA Today: A New Introduction to Transactional Analysis*, Nottingham: Lifespan.

Swinton, J. (2001) *Spirituality and Mental Health Care*, London: Jessica Kingsley.

Thorne, B. (2002) *The Mystical Path of Person-Centred Therapy: Hope Beyond Despair*, London: Whurr.

West, W. (1997) Integrating psychotherapy and healing, *British Journal of Guidance and Counselling*, 25(3): 291–312.

West, W. (1998) Developing practice in a context of religious faith: a study of psychotherapists who are Quakers, *British Journal of Guidance and Counselling*, 26(3): 365–75.

West, W. (2004) *Spiritual Issues in Therapy – Relating Experience to Practice*, Basingstoke: Palgrave.

Whitmore, D. (2000) *Psychosynthesis Counselling in Action*, London: Sage.

Woon, T.H. (1984) Therapeutic exercise, *Journal of Malaysian Society of Health*, 4: 60–2.

Yagoob, S. (2000) Muslim Women in Science: A Better Future. Presented at International Conference on 'Muslim Women in Science: A Better Future' Fez, Morocco, 22–4 March 2000; organised by the Royal Academy of Science International Trust (RASIT) and The Islamic Educational Scientific and Cultural Organisation (ISESCO).

Counselling Older People

Stephane Duckett

Ageism, as opposed very often to other forms of discrimination, rarely presents itself in the speaker's mouth as overt hostility let alone conscious awareness, but its capacity to wound and belittle is nevertheless just as strong. It is perhaps for this reason that it has proved itself to be the most resistant to societal change and in this respect it is the most insidious.

What is age discrimination?

> Ageism is the defining of another by virtue of your limiting beliefs on what it means to be a particular age, whether young or old. It is the failure to acknowledge or allow for the possibilities of what that individual might or might not be.

The focus of this chapter is on reducing the ways in which our therapeutic practices may prove unhelpful in facilitating older clients from achieving their therapeutic objectives. However, not all forms of discrimination should be considered necessarily ageist. Indeed, I will argue that in some critical respects, ignoring or not acknowledging a client's age may be inimical to promoting psychological wellbeing. Put simply, therefore, it is not enough to ignore the client's status as an older adult but rather as a counsellor one needs to reflect upon the impact that the fact of the client's age may or may not have for them (Rayle, 2004; Woods, 2003).

Thinking in categories and short-cuts to thinking

Prejudicial thinking is, one could argue, inevitable given that we do not approach each new situation as a clean slate. We make sense of the here and now via the experience of the past. Occasionally that past may be such that it distorts our ability to view the present clearly. Those distortions apply to varying degrees and generalize to a greater or lesser extent. In the absence of overt experience we often draw upon our wider culture to make sense of new experiences. For instance, what you tell yourself about older people will be greatly influenced by the amount of contact you have with older people (Duckett, 2005a). Without that experience, you may draw upon popular portrayals through television, newspapers and novels. How accurate is this going to be? The Screen Actors Guild and the Federation of TV and Radio Artists sponsored a study (Gerbner et al., 1994) in which they noted that despite the fact that adults over 60 comprise nearly 17 per cent of the population, they made up only 5.4 per cent of prime-time characters (4 per cent for daytime serials). Therefore, in the absence of direct and indirect experience of what it means to be older, we may fall back upon prejudice and stereotyping.

Exercise 10.1

Itemise what the word 'old' means to you. Think about somebody close to you that you think of as old and list the defining qualities of that person. In what ways does your experience of that individual either confirm or disconfirm what it means to be 'old'?

Prejudice, discrimination and stereotyping

Cuddy and Fiske (2004) suggest a tripartite categorization:

- Prejudice (affective)
- Discrimination (behavioural)
- Stereotyping (cognitive).

These three categories within this model are interlinked. Therefore, to understand one requires an understanding of all. The cognitive component (stereotyping) is said to emerge from our need to organize our experience and engagement with the world. Citing Allport, 'The human mind must think with the aid of categories. Once formed, categories are the basis for normal pre-judgement. We cannot possibly avoid this process. Orderly living depends upon it' (1954: 20). Categories themselves may emerge from multiple sources, however, Cuddy and Fiske highlight two primary sources: *prototypes* and *exemplars*. *Prototype* refers to wider cultural ideas which need not be based on particular individuals, whereas *exemplars* are drawn from direct experience.

Prototypes may be 'implicitly' embedded within our minds. As evidence of this, Bargh et al. (1996) noted that subjects who were primed on a computer task with the faces of elderly subjects altered their behaviour (moving more slowly) when they left the lab. Fiske and Taylor (1991) suggest that whilst we may be subliminally influenced by cues, whether we pay attention to those cues or not depends upon our conscious motivation. If we have reason to pay attention we will not fall back on cognitive shortcuts such as stereotyping in taking an action. As the authors express it, 'people are not fools ... [they] are motivated tacticians, strategically choosing situations that warrant additional mental resources when they are motivated and able to do so' (1991: 14).

The question inevitably poses itself, why would we therefore be motivated to do otherwise, or is it just down to cognitive laziness as these authors suggest? Cognition does not operate alone but is fuelled by emotion (prejudice) and finds expression in behaviour (discrimination). There has been much debate in recent years around the impact of ageism on health care provision generally ('Age discrimination in heart care', BBC News, 15 November 2000, GMTV) and within the medical literature (Rivlin, 1995).

But what of mental health services? Regrettably, there is ample evidence to suggest that our attitudes do influence our actions as mental health workers. This will be examined in some detail further on when we look both at the reasons why an older adult may be denied access to counselling, the form that counselling can take, and how the client's presenting problems are conceptualized.

What are the sources of old age discrimination?

To better understand the nature of discrimination as already noted we need to consider what fuels our cognitive biases, namely what we tell ourselves of what it means to be old. Becker (1973) argued that our knowledge of our own mortality presents a threat to us that we are reluctant or unwilling to face head-on. Our knowledge of this finality has the potential to lead to a 'paralyzing terror' for which the only mechanism of defence is denial. Older adults, or at least our conception of ageing, present us with a constant reminder of our own finality and hence our wish to distance ourselves. This we achieve through acts of discrimination. The first step towards discrimination is dehumanizing your subject, in other words allowing them to be defined as something less than human. J.P. Sartre in *Being and Nothingness* ([1943] 2003) spoke of 'bad faith' that is the individual's capacity to allow themselves to be defined (define another) by a trait, something less than the totality of their being. Erving Goffman (1970) referred to this as stigma, which when it forms part of a class of individuals becomes tribal stigma (Duckett, 2007). For Sartre what drove this bad faith was our anxiety when faced with the need to exercise our freedom; for Becker it is the threat of our annihilation. I would wish to argue that this is largely a by-product of our sanitization or dehumanization of death (Duckett, 2008a). Consider, for instance, that despite the ubiquity of death how many of us get to see somebody die, not on television but in person? I suspect relatively few of us, yet the portrayals of death in our entertainment are everywhere. But if you look carefully the dead are less than human, particularly with police dramas. They are simply vehicles for us to ogle obscenely at or marvel at the cleverness of the criminal or the detective. Most deaths in the West occur within hospitals, but even here we go to great lengths to distance and protect ourselves from the contamination of dead and dying people.

Exercise 10.2

What has been your experience of death? To what degree were you 'protected' from it? What was your involvement? Do the comments above reflect your experience? Do you believe that the person's age was relevant in your experience of their death?

Protecting ourselves against ageing

Cuddy and Fiske (2004) cited the following, what they term 'proximal defences to the "elderly"'.

1 *Physical distance*: for us as clinicians this may come in the form of ensuring that older clients do not show up in our office by denying access to services or, arguably, by creating specialized services to which individuals may be relegated or corralled.

2 *Psychological distancing*: this may come in both the way we conceive of our older clients (cognitive shortcuts) but also in the language we utilize.

3 *Psychological distancing in seeing attitudes, interests and personality traits as different*: Pyszczynski et al. (1995) noted that subjects that were asked to rate another were influenced in their perception of personality differences if they believed the subject to have cancer. Similarly, Simone de Beauvoir (1977) noted that defining somebody as elderly results in their not being seen as 'a real person' but as another being.

Mental health workers are not immune to the above (Shapiro, 1993; Sonderegger and Siegel, 1995; Steuer, 1982; Zivian et al., 1994). The link between psychotherapy as we practice it and unexplored themes around issues of death and loss has been raised eloquently by Becker (1973), but neither knowledge of your subject alone, nor your own age or maturity obviate the need for you to examine your own thoughts, feelings and attitudes around death – the danger of failing to examine these issues is that you may implicitly respond in a discriminatory fashion to these fears and prejudices (Duckett, 2005c).

Exercise 10.3

Think about your engagement with older clients. Have you distanced yourself (or not) in any way, physically or psychologically? How? What caused this? What was the effect?

Denying access to counselling

In March 2001, the Government set out its strategy for improving services to older people through the *National Service Framework for Older People* (DoH, 2002). Within this framework mental health services are specifically targeted (*Standard* 7): 'Older people who have mental health problems [should] have access to integrated mental health services, provided by the NHS and councils to ensure effective diagnosis, treatment and support, for them and their carers'. Access to specialists is noted as a key intervention and yet there are significant hurdles to such access. The following focuses on problems in access as they relate to the client, the therapist and more widely systemically.

The client

'Why are you bothering with an old codger like me?'

Internalized ageism is often overlooked since most first-hand accounts written about the effects of ageism stem from individuals who have a voice within our society and therefore are usually far from disenfranchised. However, unfortunately some of the most egregious expressions of ageism I hear come directly from the clients themselves. Erving Goffman in his seminal book *Stigma* (1970) notes that where individuals who previously formed part of the wider normative population become, for instance, disfigured, and as a result part of the discriminated group, they import the discriminatory values that they held prior to being stigmatized.

There is, indeed, much written on what has come to be known as *identification with the aggressor*, but less as it applies to older adults. Older adults are no exception to this. It often comes in the form of apologies for 'taking the time' of a therapist, to poor self-esteem (Roth 1978) and depression, or more problematically to not accessing services all together. Carers, likewise, may contribute to this. I was recently told by the daughter of a client who was severely depressed 'He is 90, of course he is going to be depressed'. Such attitudes need to be challenged vigorously when they arise, certainly with other professionals but also sensitively with both carers and clients alike. Internalized ageism and scepticism as to the effectiveness of treatment are not the only reasons for clients not seeking services. Sibicky and Dovidio (1986) have noted how fear of rejection itself, even when the perceived need for those services is there, may prevent an individual from seeking psychological services.

The therapist

Freud infamously stated that psychological therapy for anybody aged 50 and above was a waste of time. Unfortunately this has cast a long shadow on the way we go about our business (Brodie, 2004; Rainsford, 2002). Although some recent studies have suggested changing attitudes of trainee therapists towards working with older people (Lee et al., 2003), others have highlighted the discrepancy that can exist between stated perceptions and the actions or beliefs that may follow. These observations do not simply apply to trainees but to qualified clinicians as well (Larsen, 1986; Zank, 1998). This may manifest itself as under-detection of mental illness, particularly in depression (Freeling et al., 1985; Iliffe et al., 1991), or in the sort of diagnosis an older adult may receive. Other considerations may also apply as it relates to age, gender and race (Social Services Inspectorate, 1998).

> **Robert**, an older Caribbean man, had developed an infection that rendered him temporarily delirious. The delirium cleared with antibiotics but because he had spoken about being guided by his wife's dead spirit, he was transferred to inpatient psychiatry. No 'allowance' had been made for the differing cultural beliefs around spiritualism which forms an integral part of his cultural background.

Therapists denying access to services as explained in the previous section may be motivated by their own fears, however, Lewis and Johansen (1982) suggest that resistance to treatment may also emerge paradoxically from both pathologizing normal ageing experience, but also more fundamentally as an empathic failure. This will be explored further on.

Systemic ageism

Despite significant recent changes in employment law, systemic discrimination remains a reality whether in the finance industry or in the way community services are delivered. There is insufficient room within this chapter to cover these points. However, where it applies specifically to mental health provision, this may be both at the planning stage in a failure to recognize need but also at implementation (Bytheway, 1995). However, even in instances where provision is given there may be a lack of infrastructure which prevents older people from accessing those services, for example through lack of transport (Sharman, 1998). On occasion, unnecessarily rigid theoretical beliefs, for instance around boundary issues as they relate to home visits, may also contribute to a failure to accommodate access needs for certain clients (Duckett, 2005b). Access problems to services for older clients may also occur within specialist services for particular patient groups. For instance, Pearce (2008) noted under-utilization of cancer peer-support groups amongst older women. A variety of reasons may be contributing to this, which may include the attitudes of other younger patients.

How ageism may influence the way counselling is conducted

Tom Kitwood is one of those seminal figures within our profession who, despite his death more than 10 years ago, continues to exert an influence in ways that may not have occurred to his readership when first published (1997). Although Kitwood's work was specifically with the experience of dementia, I believe that some of these ideas should be more widely applied. For instance, central to his model is the notion of a person-centred approach. It emerges from a profoundly empathic notion that the experience of dementia is guided not just by the disease process alone but by the personal history of the individual. As such, intervention becomes less about the disease process occupying centre stage and more about the sense that the individuals themselves make of their experience. The difficulty here for clinicians is two-fold. First, there is safety in allowing a client to be defined by their disease. It effectively robs them of their humanity, allowing us to distance ourselves from the client's suffering. Second, somewhat controversially, therapeutic models can on occasion take centre stage in promoting familiar or cherished concepts to the detriment of the patient. For instance, Blanchard et al. (2009) challenged the notion of a recovery model when working with older clients. These authors argued that the application of ideas imported directly from adult models of psychotherapy is inappropriate, given that many of the clients we serve may be confronting significant loss both in their interpersonal lives as well as in their own abilities which carry irreversible consequences. Previous life-span developmental models (Erickson, 1980) have often failed to acknowledge this in placing too much emphasis on resolution and equanimity as the benchmark to psychological wellbeing in later life. As Gloria Steinhem expresses it:

> Age is supposed to create more serenity, calm, and detachment from the world, right? We'll, I'm finding just the reverse. The older I get, the more intensely I feel about the world around me, including things I once thought too small for concern. (1994: 249)

Blanchard et al. (2009) argue that acknowledging the full range of emotions that realistically accompany our lives, particularly in the face of significant losses, may be desirable for many of our clients. To do otherwise may be setting your client up to interpret their distress as failure rather than an affirmation of their humanity.

Gill felt really embarrassed at being referred to a psychotherapist by her GP. Whilst we take psychotherapy for granted as a point of 'modern living', for Gill and the world she emerged from, the notion of mental illness necessitating a professional referral is profoundly stigmatizing. On first encounter she apologized profusely and attempted to minimize the obvious depression she had experienced recently following the death of her husband. She was therefore keen not to prolong this encounter. She was also, given her poor self-esteem, anxious to do well, that is to be a good patient. She therefore listened intently to what her counsellor had to say and followed diligently with his requests and assignments. Upon 'successful' completion of the six-week intervention she went home to grieve quietly and out of public view.

Blanchard et al. are not alone in calling for a more flexible approach in not merely goal-setting but also in the manner in which a client may chose to conceptualize their presenting complaint (Rainsford, 2002). Occasionally this may present the therapist with beliefs that may challenge their world view. This may require that the therapist remains open to include within their work topics or areas of experience that they may not find comfortable, such as spiritualism (Duckett, 2008b) or sexuality in later life (Bouman and Arcelus, 2001). Even when such topics do get covered, there is evidence to suggest that clinicians simply do not take them as seriously when contrasted with younger clients (Ivey et al., 2000).

Likewise, when working within particular models it is important not to be overly prescriptive with their application (Evans, 2007). Psychotherapy is very much part of our mainstream culture now. However, for many of our older clients it remains intensely stigmatizing. Indeed, their contact with you may be the first contact they have had with a mental health professional and may inadvertently contribute to their sense of shame or failure. Coping strategies that have served them well for an entire lifetime no longer work quite so well, often because they don't have other resources to fall back on such as work, family life, or indeed friends. Thus, the sense of shame that may arise for these clients in simply presenting themselves at your office may be acute. This is coupled with a feeling of lack of entitlement and disenfranchisement generally. It is crucial that you do not inadvertently contribute to their experience of failure by not accommodating the client's abilities and needs flexibly.

Experiencing the client's despair set against often irreversible and overwhelming losses can be enormously uncomfortable for the therapist, as already noted. You may respond by wanting to do something concretely when the client is often fully aware that you are not a magician and nothing overtly can be done. Loss brings with it an extraordinary sense of loneliness. Our meaning stems from the relationships we have both in our personal lives and also in our professional lives. When these relationships begin to dissipate for various reasons we are afloat and without anchor, adrift in an impersonal ageist world. To have these strong emotions that emerge from this experience acknowledged through an empathic engagement affirms our humanity and our sense of belonging. It allows us to reinterpret those strong emotions not as failure but as part of what it means to be human in the fullest sense. Do not therefore undervalue that skill above the need to look busy as a way to mitigate your own anxiety faced with the void of the patient's losses (Sobel, 1980; Terry, 2008).

Exercise 10.4

Do you have preferred counselling approaches? What are they? Can you imagine a situation in which they may not be the best approach in working with an older client? What might be the reasons? How can you determine if your approach is a 'good fit' for your client? Are there any subject areas that you would feel uncomfortable raising with an older client? Imagine how you would handle the situation.

Communicating with clients

Language, or communication more broadly, comes in several forms. Verbal communication is its most overt expression, hence it is perhaps not surprising that there is much more written about the age discriminatory use of such language; but it may also arise in the manner in which a client is addressed. We take for granted the current practice of addressing a stranger on a first-name basis, but this may be seen as demeaning or disrespectful by some. It is good practice to ask a client how they wish to be addressed. Therapists who look very youthful in appearance must take note of this and be prepared to address this issue directly or indirectly non-defensively if broached. Here again the cultural diversity literature has addressed this issue (Wong, 2007). Awareness of difference is key.

Another important consideration with respect to communication is sensory and cognitive losses. Again, the client may experience profound feelings of shame about this. Men in particular, for instance, may not want to wear hearing aids and therefore will opt to try to hide (mask) their hearing loss by guessing at what is being said.

Likewise, cognitive impairment can make maintaining a conversation difficult due to gaps in memory, slowed processing skills or more unusual manifestations of neuropsychological deficits. Not all clients will necessarily be aware of their deficits. There are various ways a therapist may accommodate these challenges. Brief written summaries at the end of each session, for instance, may help facilitate clients retaining and carrying over work from one session to another.

Exercise 10.5

How might you recognize in an older client's communication with you that their senses are impaired? How would you address this issue if required?

Discrimination in formulation

Ageism as a concept has been slow to take hold since Butler first coined the term (1975). The world we occupy is ageist, but we as a society are largely unseeing of this. Today we look back at the comedies of the 1970s and cringe at their racist and sexist content. Will society look back in 30 years at the comedies of today and cringe at their ageist content? David Smail, in his keynote address to the 2004 PSIGE Conference, spoke eloquently of the subtle and not so subtle ways in which one discovers one is 'old': in the small ways in which the behaviour of others alters – sometimes good, sometimes bad – to its wider expression with the occasionally brutal comments within the media about burden of care, for instance Baroness Warner's repeated comments in the House of Lords in support of euthanasia. As we are defined interactively through others we take on this 'flawed identity' (Duckett, 2007) and become apologetic for ourselves. When you are employed and youthful it is enormously difficult to know what it means to be without meaning within a world that sees you as expendable. Kitwood was acutely aware of this when he noted 'personhood is bestowed by others' (1997).

Most of us are aware in one form or another of the finality of our lives. We wish to accept this not necessarily with equanimity, but we are aware in our own fashion. How we see this may be a personal matter. However, what we may not be aware of is that within our world there are two deaths: the first is social and the second physical. Most commentators on the experience of ageing are anything but disenfranchised members of society. As such they will be much less aware of the social death (which precedes the physical) where we find ourselves gradually dissolving into irrelevance within an ageist world. Most of my clients, I would argue, are accepting of the biological terms of their existence, particularly in later older adulthood. However, it is the preceding social death which is the cruellest of them all. What our older clients gain through empathic engagement of psychotherapy is a reaffirmation of their humanity, of the validity of their emotions which, contrary to being evidence of failing, is an assertion of that humanity. The ultimate betrayal or expression of discriminatory practice would be in an attempt to protect yourself from the enormity of those emotions by failing to acknowledge the reality of the world your client occupies and their place in it, *whatever that may be.*

References

Allport, G. (1954) *The Nature of Prejudice*, Reading, MA: Addison-Wesley.

Bargh, J., Chen, M. and Burrows, L. (1996) 'Automaticity of Social Behaviour: Direct Effects of Trait Construct & Stereotype Activation on Action', *Journal of Personality and Social Psychology*, v.71, pp: 230–44.

Beauvoir, Simone de (1977) *Old Age*, Harmondsworth: Penguin.

Becker, E. (1973) *The Denial of Death*. New York: Free Press.

Blanchard, M., Serfaty, M., Duckett, S. and Flatley, M. (2009) 'A Reintergrative Model for Old Age Psychiatry', *International Journal of Geriatric Psychiatry*, v.24 pp: 202–6.

Bouman, P. and Arcelus, J. (2001) 'Are Psychiatrists Guilty of Ageism when it comes to Taking a Sexual History?', *International Journal of Geriatric Psychiatry*, v.16 pp: 27–31.

Brodie, C. (2004) 'Trainee Clinical Psychologist Attitude Towards Adults over the Age of 65', *PSIGE Newsletter*, No. 87, pp: 20–25.

Butler, R. (1975) *Why Survive? Being Old in America*. New York: Harper and Row.

Bytheway, B. (1995) *Ageism*, Buckingham: Open University Press.

Cuddy, A. and Fiske, S. (2004) 'Doddering but Deasc: Process, Content, and Function in Stereotyping of Older Persons', in *Ageism* (ed. Nelsom, T.), Cambridge, MA: MIT Press.

Department of Health (2002) *National Service Framework for Older People*, London: DoH.

Duckett, S. (2005a) 'Does Age Influence the Perception of Age?', *PSIGE Newsletter*, No. 91 October.

Duckett, S. (2005b) 'Boundary Crossings vs Boundary Violations', *Self and Society*, v.33, No. 1 August.

Duckett, S. (2005c) 'Death of the Client', *Clinical Psychologist*, March.

Duckett, S. (2007) 'Tribal Stigma', *PSIGE Newsletter*, No. 99 Spring.

Duckett, S. (2008a) 'Divorced from Dying', *Psychologist*, v.21/No. 8 (Letter).

Duckett, S. (2008b) 'Ghosts: From a Socio-Ecological Perspective', *Clinical Psychology Forum*, No. 197 November.

Erikson, E. (1980) *Identity and the Life Cycle*, New York: W W Norton.

Evans, C. (2007) 'Cognitive-Behavioural Therapy with Older People', *Advances in Psychiatric Treatment*, v.13 pp: 111–18.

Fiske, S. and Taylor, S. (1991) *Social Cognition* (2nd Edition), New York: McGraw-Hill.

Freeling, P., Rao, B.M., Paykol, E.S., Sireling, L.I. and Burton, R.H. (1985) 'Unrecognised Depression in General Practices', *BMJ* v.290 pp: 1880–183.

Gerbner, G., Gross, L., Morgan, M. and Signorielli, N. (1994) 'Growing up with Television', in J. Bryant and D. Zillman (eds), *Media Effects*. Hillsdale, NJ: Lawrence Erlbaum.

Goffman, E. (1970) *Stigma*, Harmondsworth: Penguin.

Iliffe, S. Haines, A., Gallivan, S., Booroff, A., Goldenberg, E. and Morgan, P. (1991) 'Assessment of Elderly People in General Practice', *British Journal of General Practice*, v.41 pp: 9–12.

Ivey, D., Wieling, E. and Harris, M. (2000) 'Save the Young – the Elderly Have Lived Their Lives: Ageism in Marriage and Family Therapy', *Family Process*, v.39 pp: 163–75.

Kitwood, T. (1997) *Dementia Reconsidered: The Person Comes First*, Buckingham: Open University Press.

Larsen, W. (1986) 'Providing Psychotherapy to Older Adults: Therapist Reluctance and Societal Opinion', *Dissertation Abstracts International*, v.47 Issue 1-B(379).

Lee, K., Volans, P. and Gregory, N. (2003) 'Attitudes Towards Psychotherapy with Older People Among Trainee Clinical Psychologists', *Ageing and Mental Health*, v.7 pp: 133–41.

Lewis, J. and Johansen, K. (1982) 'Resistances to Psychotherapy with the Elderly', *American Journal of Psychotherapy*, v.36 pp: 497–504.

Pearce, N.J. (2008) 'Older Adults Living with Cancer: Supportive Care Needs and Utilisation of Peer Support Services', *Dissertation Abstracts International*, Section A: Social Sciences and Social Services, 68/12-A (5174).

Pyszczynski, T., Greenberg, J., Solomon, S. Cather, C., Gat, I. and Sideris, J. (1995) 'Defensive Distancing from Victims of Serious Illness: The Role of Delay', *Personality and Social Psychology Bulletin*, v.21 pp: 13–20.

Rainsford, C. (2002) 'Counselling Older Adults', *Reviews in Clinical Gerontology*, v.12 pp: 159–64.

Rayle, A. (2004) 'Counselling Older Adults', in *Cross-Cultural Psychotherapy: Towards a Critical Understanding of Diverse Clients*, Reno, NV: Bent Tree Press.

Rivlin, M. (1995) 'Protecting Elderly People: Flaws in Ageist Arguments', *BMJ*, v.310 pp: 1179–82.

Roth, N. (1978) 'Fear of Death in Ageing', *American Journal of Psychotherapy*, v.32 pp: 552–60.

Sartre, J.P. ([1943] 2003) *Being and Nottingness: An Essay on Phenomenological Ontology*, London: Routledge.

Shapiro, S. (1993) 'Gender-role Stereotypes and Clinical Process: Commentary on Papers by Greenthal and Hirsch', *Psychoanalytic Dialogues*, v.3 pp: 371–87.

Sharman, J.M. (1998) *A Brief Narrative Approach to the Treatment of Depression for the Elderly*, Dissertation Abstracts International Section B: The Sciences and Engineering 58/8-B (4472).

Sibicky, M. and Dovidio, J. (1986) 'Stigma of Psychological Therapy: Stereotypes, Interpersonal Reactions, and the Self-fulfilling Prophecy', *Journal of Counselling Psychology*, v.33 pp: 148–54.

Smail, D. (2004) *PSIGE Conference*, Nottingham, 7–9 July, Keynote speaker.

Sobel, E. (1980) 'Counter-Transference Issues with the Later Life Patient', *Contemporary Psychoanalysis*, v.16 pp: 211–22.

Social Services Inspectorate (1998) *They Look After Their Own, Don't They?*, London: SSI.

Sonderegger, T. and Siegel, R. (1995) 'Conflicts in Care: Later Years of the Lifespan', in *Ethical Decision Making in Therapy: Feminist Perspectives*, New York: Guilford Press.

Steinhem, G. (1994) 'Doing Sixty', in *Moving Beyond Words*, London: Bloomsbury.

Steuer, J. (1982) 'Psychotherapy with Older Women: Ageism and Sexism in Traditional Practice', *Psychotherapy: Theory, Research and Practice*, v.19 pp: 429–36.

Terry, P. (2008) *Counselling the Elderly and their Carers* (2nd Edition), Basingstoke: Palgrave Macmillan.

Wong, P. (2007) 'The Inscrutable Doctor Wu', in *Dialogues on Difference: Studies of Diversity in the Therapeutic Relationship*, Washington, DC: APA Books.

Woods, R.T. (2003) 'What's so Different about Older People?', *Clinical Psychology and Psychotherapy*, v.10 pp: 129–32.

Zank, S. (1998) 'Psychotherapy and Ageing: Results of Two Empirical Studies Between Psychotherapists and Elderly People', *Psychotherapy: Theory, Research and Practice*, v.35 pp: 531–6.

Zivian, M. Larsen, W., Gekoski, W., Knox, V.J. and Mackette, V. (1994) 'Psychotherapy for the Elderly: Public Opinion', *Psychotherapy: Theory, Research and Practice*, v.31 pp: 492–502.

11 Working with Refugees

Human Rights Therapy

Jude Boyles

> In my culture we don't know our friends and family by talking, talking, talking; we know by watching and being with them – you will learn to know me in this way so why would I need to talk to you, can't you see? (Iyabo, African torture survivor)

These words were said to me many years ago when I began working with refugees. It was our second session together and I was attempting to explain to Iyabo what counselling was and why it may help him. He had been raped and tortured and was alone in the UK, separated from his family and community and terrified for his wife and children back home. His bewilderment at my description of counselling was the beginning of a steep learning curve in my work with refugees over the last decade, which remains almost as steep to this day.

In this chapter, I aim to share some of my experiences in working with refugees, exploring how we might work anti-oppressively and how we can prepare ourselves for the challenges the work presents without becoming overwhelmed. Throughout I will use the term 'refugee' to mean both those seeking protection in the UK and those granted some form of asylum. The term 'asylum seeker' has been widely used in recent years to undermine the credibility of those seeking protection in the UK and has contributed to the culture of hostility towards this group.

Why people flee

In 2003, it was estimated that there were 35 recognised conflicts and 132 countries still practising torture (Amnesty International, 2003). At the beginning of 2007, the number of people of concern to the United Nations High Commissioner for Refugees (UNHCR) was a record 32.9 million, with a total of 740,000 people seeking asylum at the beginning of 2007 (UNHCR, 2007–2008). Refugees flee to the UK for a variety of reasons other than war and conflict. They flee torture and inhumane treatment, persecution and harassment, death sentences and oppressive regimes. Women flee gender-based abuses including female genital mutilation (FGM), honour killings and sexual slavery.

Internationally, women and children experience violence, sexual abuse and trafficking on a massive scale. The military advisor to the United Nations (UN), Major General Patrick Cammaert, commented 'It is now more dangerous to be a woman than to be a soldier in modern conflict' (UNHCR, 2007–2008).

The relatively small numbers of refugees who manage to make it into the UK apply for asylum under the 1951 UN Refugee Convention, and in 2007 Europe hosted just 10 per cent of the world's refugees, with Asia hosting 45 per cent and Africa 30 per cent (UNHCR, 2007–2008).

A safe haven?

Applicants for asylum are interviewed by the Home Office on arrival in the hope of receiving a decision on their claim for protection. The length of time this can take varies hugely. Those arriving since 2007 can receive a decision within a few months, but many of the clients I see at the Medical Foundation for the Care of Victims of Torture have been here for many years and are still awaiting a decision on their claim for protection.

Once a refugees' claim for protection has been exhausted, that is, refused by the Home Office and all appeal rights exhausted, their accommodation and income is terminated and effectively the refugee becomes destitute. It was estimated in 2007 that there were 20,000 destitute refugees in the UK (Refugee Action, 2007). Those seeking protection are unable to work or claim benefits, and are not entitled to public housing. They face weekly or monthly 'signing' at police or Immigration Centres so the Home Office can monitor their whereabouts.

Home Office decision-making continues to be widely criticised at national and international level by human rights and refugee organisations, and many refugees are refused asylum and face return to the countries where they have fled from.

A new challenge for counsellors

Following the Immigration and Asylum Act (Home Office, 1999), those seeking asylum began to be accommodated outside of the South East of England and were 'dispersed' to live in communities across the country. This dispersal has resulted in many counselling and therapy services being faced with an unfamiliar group of clients whose experiences may be new to them, such as those who have fled torture and war, are under threat of return, living in poverty and without support networks. In addition, most of the time refugees do not speak English and therapeutic work is being offered through an interpreter. Even for refugee and/or bilingual therapists, the range of languages spoken in the refugee population is so huge that all counsellors will be expected to work with an interpreter at some point in their therapeutic work with refugees. In addition to living with the impact of past experiences of torture, persecution and conflict, clients also face huge losses. These include losses of community, culture, family and friends, and loss of work, status and political affiliation.

It is within this context of pre-flight human rights abuses and inhumane treatment by the UK authorities that refugees are referred or refer themselves for help. Increasingly, mental health and counselling services are faced with traumatised and isolated people with multiple social problems, and we are often expected to offer some form of help within brief or short-term models.

How can we prepare?

Any therapist who is thoughtful about working anti-oppressively and aware of their own structural or societal position and its impact will already think about gender, race, sexuality, disability and class when considering offering an assessment to any new client. With a refugee client, it is important to find out about the country the client has left behind. We have a responsibility as therapists living in the host country to learn about the political and social contexts our clients have fled from, otherwise we risk separating the individual from their history and culture. Equally important is learning about our clients' cultural beliefs if we are to ensure that we can offer safety and containment and understand the context of disclosures.

For any woman to disclose rape is painful, and most describe profound feelings of shame. It can take women many years to disclose sexual violence. For women in some cultures, disclosing rape may risk her losing her entitlement to marry and have children and could resign her and/or her family to exclusion and harassment.

> **Fawzia** is from Afghanistan. In Fawzia's culture, being raped is seen to have dishonoured the family and women are obliged to marry the rapist in order to maintain the family's honour. It took some time for Fawzia to disclose her rapes to me. I was a stranger from a different society. A stranger who might tell her family, GP or the Home Office. The potential negative consequences of her disclosure were profound.

It is important to prepare ourselves for what atrocities we might hear. We risk shutting down our clients if we are wholly congruent and express horror at what may be for our clients a daily experience.

> Until we have sat with someone who knows the capacity of human beings to inflict pain, who knows the depth of physical, emotional and mental pain that can arise in situations of war, we cannot be totally sure just how we will react. (Bryant-Jefferies, 2005: 15)

Alongside the research and reading we may do about the cultural and political histories of the countries our clients flee from, gaining an understanding of the asylum process is also important. This is especially the case if you are working with a newly arrived refugee. Refugees are thrown into a legal system where they have no understanding of the process with rare access to an interpreter. Often we can provide some very basic information about UK systems that can immediately reduce anxiety. The Refugee Council have a multilingual information site that offers up-to-date information for you and your client on the asylum process.

Those who are socially isolated may only have access to a trained and confidential interpreter once a week when they have an appointment with the counsellor. It is therefore important to have knowledge of key refugee advice and advocacy projects in your area, to ensure that your client can access help in their first language.

Taking a position

When counselling refugees, there are additional layers of power issues to be explored as they are amongst the most disempowered and marginalised groups in the UK. The dynamics of the relationship between your own country and theirs will enter the therapy room and refugee clients will often want to know your position. As a human rights therapist, I believe in having those dialogues with refugee clients. Prepare not to be neutral, to be able to support your clients to explore the meaning of their experiences both in their country and in the UK. The meaning is political, just as torture and conflict are political, processes.

An African client and I have recently spent many hours exploring his justifiable rage about the UK's role in the oppression of his people. He was not an activist prior to fleeing, but tortured in his country purely because of his ethnicity. The harsh racism of the process from his arrest to his current status has politicised him: he is discovering his political self, which includes his rage at his treatment in the UK.

Assessment

> The core experiences of psychological trauma are disempowerment and disconnection from others. Recovery therefore is based upon the empowerment of the survivor and the creation of new connections. Recovery can only take place within the context of relationships; it cannot occur in isolation. (Herman, 1992: 133)

Refugees often have no understanding of counselling as a form of support or treatment, or even an awareness of the concept of confidentiality in their culture, sometimes confusing it with secrecy.

The very act of a seemingly one-way conversation with a stranger about personal matters can be a stigma in many cultures. Considerable time is needed therefore to establish who you are and what counselling is, and allowing time in your assessment for the client to gain trust in the interpreter. This three-way dynamic can lead to the client feeling more distrustful and worried about the confidentiality and attitudes of the interpreter than of the counsellor. They may not even look at you for several sessions, always watching the interpreter to ensure that they are not being judged, particularly if the interpreter is from their community.

Offering a client an opportunity to 'explore their difficulties' may leave them confused and wondering what they are expected to do. Taking time to provide a framework for the work you are going to do together is important, as is being mindful of imposing your own cultural perceptions of what is causing illness or difficulty. Every culture and society has its own beliefs and traditions which determine how people cope with suffering and how to seek help. Be mindful of not judging what is traumatic by your own cultural bias, as within Western individualistic cultures, persecution and torture is experienced as an individual experience, but in collectivist-based cultures persecution damages a community.

Ahmed, a Kurdish refugee, explained that talking about private matters was a taboo in his village and that he shouldn't be talking to a woman in this way. He felt he was being unfaithful to his wife back home, breaking the rules whereby men and women who are not married should not meet alone. He felt he was shaming his family by his disclosures, being embarrassed and ashamed that he had cried and couldn't understand how on earth getting upset once a week could help! He was tired, hungry, terrified of being returned and in pain from a back injury following torture. He was also shocked at the strength of his feelings towards me, they were confusing and unexpected – he described his tongue running away with him whenever we talked.

Ahmed's situation highlights that what we offer can be mysterious. Demystifying our work allows our clients some choice about how much they may say. Without care we risk over-exposure before a client has fully come to terms with what you are offering and your potential position in their life. Ahmed and I assessed over six sessions, and by the end of this process he had some sense of what counselling was and was able to make a choice to continue.

Undertaking casework in counselling

> For the client who is traumatised, suffering from a lack of sleep, frequent forgetting, lacking concentration, and disorientated with a lost sense of who they are, navigating the asylum, housing, benefit and legal systems often brings further despair and desperation. (West, 2006: 11)

At times clients may bring forms and letters to appointments so that the counsellor can help make sense of them. Newly arrived refugees often don't know the rules of Western society and keep discovering they have broken them. If they experience breaking the 'rules of counselling' by asking for practical help, you risk exacerbating their sense of failure and rejection if you say 'no' before you know what is being asked of you and why.

If you simply send a client away with their letter or ask them to make a call themselves via a GP or advocate, you risk alienating a client desperately trying to find answers and source information and help. A letter might be from the Home Office or an appeal determination; it could be a refusal or a lost appeal. They may have little time to act, and to suggest they take the letter elsewhere may put them at risk. Sometimes undertaking advocacy and practical tasks for your client may be appropriate, and in early sessions can help with engagement.

> Their perception that the therapist's intervention will enable greater access for them is (also) reasonable, especially given the current political climate, with its consequent growth of prejudice. By using what they know and asking for help they are not relinquishing autonomy but acting with autonomy. (West, 2006: 12)

Alain was a torture survivor from the Democratic Republic of Congo (DRC). In our assessment he arrived with a Red Cross letter to show me. He had kept the letter in the envelope for six weeks. He believed the letter informed him whether his wife and children were dead, as he was attempting to trace his family through the Red Cross Tracing Service. When he had received our letter offering him the assessment he realised that he had a chance to ask someone to read it to him with an interpreter. The first thing he did was to ask me to read the letter to find out if his family were alive or dead.

Therapeutic work – a holistic approach

When we hear stories of atrocity and human rights violations we can make assumptions about where the therapeutic work might lie. What are the refugees' perceptions of their difficulties and what is causing their distress? The difficulties that are brought by refugees will vary hugely, and it is important to be prepared for the chaotic and crisis-ridden nature of your refugee client's life. One week you both may be exploring loss, and the next week poor housing conditions and what can be done. *Both are important.*

Flexibility is crucial, as is pacing the work. The lives of refugees are often controlled by others and they can be moved without notice – bad news and change is frequent.

Therapists need to be realistic about what it may be possible to achieve in counselling given the refugee context. Loss and grief is life-long, especially when the experience for many refugees is that they may never know what has happened to their family and community members. Therapeutic help can be very important, but we must not ignore our client's own traditional concepts of healing and survival, and for most refugees, social, faith-based and community support is vital.

A flexible approach to working with trauma

Many trauma models require traumatised individuals to be living in relative safety. Such models are not always relevant to the lives of refugees. For them the trauma is not over and they remain under threat with their families still being at risk or living in conflict. The threat is heightened when they go to the police station or Immigration Centre to sign, or when others in the refugee community disappear.

> Working with trauma requires the therapist to be aware of the particular models that exist for such work and often involves some additional training or education. That said, a contextually sensitive application of such models is essential if this work is to be helpful to (refugee) clients. (Burchell, 2005: 6)

My own experience is that refugees who are traumatised can and do process past experiences effectively whilst still in the asylum process faced with an uncertain future. What is needed is a collaborative approach and considerable flexibility. It is important to explore what tools and resources clients have and to use and work on increasing them, *whilst at the same time* giving opportunities to explore what is painful and distressing. The promotion of control and choice is fundamental to the work.

Jean was a Congolese woman (DRC) who came for assessment three weeks before her appeal against her refusal of protection by the Home Office. She was terrified at the knowledge that the rapes would be mentioned in court and how she would be 'publicly shamed'. She had stopped sleeping and was acutely anxious. Our short-term work together focused on the appeal and its possible result. It involved exploring her fears and shame, normalising her feelings as well as supporting her to manage her anxiety by teaching breathing and relaxation techniques. My aim was to give her as much information and support as I could to prepare her for the appeal and offer containment and safety during this frightening time.

Missed sessions

It is often said that drop-out or non-attendance rates for this client group are high. This has not been my experience. If a refugee client misses a session it is often with good reason rather than a decision not to attend. We should be mindful of how we might respond to a missed session and what assumptions we may be making. A client may have no bus fare, be unwell and have no credit on their phone to ring you or may have been detained, moved or have to 'sign', or simply be frightened. In addition, practical and social problems may be so huge that these quite rightly take precedence. If we accept this as a simple choice not to attend, we risk losing a vulnerable client who may need help to get to our service, and clients may think that they have dishonoured or disrespected you in some way and feel too ashamed to return. It is crucial to remember our position of power as a professional in the host country, where for some refugee clients our position and perceived status may induce subservience, leading clients to fear disapproval or withdrawal of care.

Working with interpreters in therapeutic encounters

> For some refugees and asylum seekers language carries a particular resonance, as it may be through what has been said about them in the past, or through things they said themselves, that they were forced to flee their country of origin. (Tribe, 2007: 159)

For most therapists, working with interpreters is a necessary and important part of refugee work. Training is crucial, as is consideration of the gender, ethnicity and class of your interpreter, in addition to continuity with a qualified interpreter working to a code of ethics. Explanation by the interpreter of their agency policy relating to confidentiality might reassure the client of their professionalism. Many counsellors are 'making do' with community interpreters who are not trained and may not fully interpret all that is said – in the way it is said – reflecting both of your tones and interpreting in the 'first person'.

It is my contention that clients have a right to an interpreter who reflects all that is said. Tolerating an unskilled interpreter who is summarising or adding to your client's words, risks the client losing this important opportunity and exacerbating their disempowerment. 'The experience of being unable to express oneself verbally can be a frightening and disempowering experience for anyone' (Tribe, 2007: 160). Many refugee clients have described poor and inaccurate interpreting at their Home Office interview or with the GP, and may have little faith in interpreters.

It is crucial to prepare your interpreter for the work and that you both brief and de-brief them. Interpreters need containment too. It can be frightening for an interpreter to interpret for a client in the midst of a flashback, and important for their sense of safety that they understand what you are doing and why. Refugee interpreters are often themselves survivors of torture and conflict and may find interpreting histories of torture and conflict extremely painful. Interpreters are not 'cultural experts' and whilst we have much to learn from our interpreting colleagues, only your client can teach you about their world.

There are times when clients engage more quickly with the interpreter who shares the same culture and language, and this can result in counsellors initially feeling excluded and impotent.

Endings

Loss and separation are central to the lives of refugees, and so ending counselling is likely to bring up painful reminders of past and present losses. Ending such a close and significant relationship may also be culturally unfamiliar and experienced as painful and unwanted. Encouraging and supporting connections both in the host and refugee's own culture (if appropriate and safe) can be a crucial part of the work. For refugees who have built up strong networks and a place in the community, ending is a positive process and a sign of independence and hope. Of course, our own experience of ending with clients who are terrified or at risk of return and facing an uncertain future can be challenging, leading to a reluctance to let go.

Exploring power – self-awareness

Work with survivors of torture requires a commitment to ongoing critical self-reflection and exploration of our biases, histories, motives and our experiences and re-enactments of power. (Patel and Mahtani, 2007: 164)

There are many dangers in this work for counsellors, particularly the potential to unintentionally oppress and further victimise refugee clients seeking our help. As a therapist, it can be easy to forget when confronted with such high levels of need that therapy can be a tool of oppression. For many clients, a counselling assessment can feel like a Home Office interview, where information and histories are given without consent or commitment. Histories are told because it seems expected, and clients fear that support will be withdrawn if their story is not told.

There is the danger that counselling itself can reduce refugee experiences of war, torture and oppression to the individual and therefore reduce or separate the individual from a sense of collectivity or community and the reassurance that can bring. Conversely, therapists can over-empathise before having come to understand their experience and its meaning for them. In cultures where emotions are expected to be displayed in private, we risk our clients thinking that they have shocked and upset us, and they may fear that we will not be able to bear hearing what they have survived.

For refugee and black and ethnic minority therapists, clients' experience of racism and oppression can be linked so closely to the therapist's own experience that staying separate can be challenging. For refugee therapists, a client's experiences can be too close to their own for the sessions not to feel overwhelming and painful. Loss of homeland and cultural bereavement is a lifelong process, and hearing others grieve for home can be painful for refugee and migrant therapists. For white therapists and practitioners, disempowered refugees can believe the counsellor knows more and is worth more. Exploring internalised oppression and our client's own prejudices towards others can be a familiar feature of work with refugees.

I find myself continually examining my responses to clients to ensure that I do not re-victimise my clients or act too quickly because I am so horrified by their experiences and so angry at what has been done in the UK. Acting on behalf of a client is not empowering if it is done to relieve our feelings of inadequacy or guilt. Retaining an awareness of abuses that may have been perpetrated by the client as well as what has been survived can be challenging. Aiming to practice from an empowerment-based model is fundamental to refugee work. However, it is really important to remember that your client may actually have no power in some situations. You may be one of the few people who has the power and position or knowledge of the client to act. Sometimes we have the information or can access it easily. At these times, our priority should be to share our knowledge or to act and then explore why we have power and our clients don't. However, the sense of indebtedness that some clients feel at these times can create a complex dynamic that will need to be explored.

Writing a letter of support, a counselling or psychological report to support a claim for protection, or making a call to housing can give your client the message that this is not just a private pain but a social injustice that can be resolved or challenged.

> Empowerment is claimed to be at the heart of therapy. But the ability of an individual to change his/her personal circumstances through therapy is dictated, limited, or moulded by social power. (McLeod, 2004: 375)

Refugees are often dehumanised and rendered powerless in the asylum process, and counsellors with a strong human rights commitment can express outrage too soon and be over-helpful. This can further humiliate and create a dynamic in the relationship that is distressing but uncomfortably familiar to many clients. Many refugee torture survivors have begged for the torture to stop and begged for help from a torturer. Having to ask for repeated help from you or for a bus fare can re-ignite feelings of shame, powerlessness and anger.

Bracken and Petty (1998) emphasise that what is important in client's recovery is finding meaning – social and political meaning. But finding meaning is not only important for the refugee, it is important for the practitioner too. A human rights perspective enables us to engage in a political discussion about why we can act and why the system deliberately renders our clients powerless, living in poverty and under threat. We can name the social and political processes that ensure refugees are deliberately kept in poverty to 'discourage' others from coming and to encourage voluntary returns.

Self-care

> Trauma is contagious. In the role of witness to disaster or atrocity, the therapist at times is emotionally overwhelmed. She experiences, to a lesser degree, the same terror, rage and despair as the patient. (Herman, 1992: 140)

Listening to multiple atrocities can be shocking and has the potential to vicariously traumatise the counsellor. There are now many counsellors throughout the UK who have considerable experience of working with refugee communities, and a growing number of specialist refugee counselling services. Many black and ethnic minority and women's services are immersed in this work, and having contact with other counsellors and practitioners undertaking work with refugees can be validating and reassuring. Most cities now have refugee forums and networks which can be a good source of information and support. 'The need for supervision is especially clear for individual therapists as well as teams of professionals in institutions who assist traumatised refugees' (Lansen and Haans, 2004: 137). Many therapists have found they have either needed specialist individual or group supervision or additional supervision in order to manage the impact of the work.

It is important *not* to embark on this work lightly and for those still in training to ensure that you are closely managed and supported. Over the last 10 years, undertaking this work has changed me, and it has changed the therapists and interpreters I have worked with or supervised. Working alongside a survivor in recovery is such rewarding and important work, but we must keep in mind those that do not survive or who cannot escape. As witnesses, this is our responsibility.

> However this war may end, we have won the war against you; none of you will be left to bear witness, but even if someone were to survive, the world would not believe him. (Wiesenthal, 1968: 293)

References

Amnesty International (2003) *Combating Torture – A manual for action.* London: Amnesty International.

Bracken, P. and Petty, C. (1998) *Re-thinking the Trauma of War.* London: Free Association.

Bryant-Jeffries, R. (2005) Counselling Victims of Warfare, *Person-Centred Dialogues.* Oxford: Radcliffe.

Burchell, S. (2005) BACP Information sheet, *Counselling Asylum Seekers and Refugees.* London: BACP.

Herman, J.L. (1992) *Trauma and Recovery: From domestic abuse to political terror.* London: Pandora.

Home Office (1999) *Immigration and Asylum Act.* London: HMSO.

Lansen, J. and Haans, T. (2004) Clinical Supervision for Trauma Therapists. in B. Drozdek and J.P Witson (eds), *Broken Spirits The Treatment of Traumatised Asylum Seekers, Refugees, War and Torture Survivors.* UK: Brunner-Routledge.

McLeod, J. (2004) *An Introduction to Counselling,* 3rd edition. Maidenhead: Open University Press.

Patel, N. and Mahtani, A. (2007) The Politics of Working with Refugee Survivors of Torture. *The Psychologist,* Vol. 20, No. 3 pp. 164–7.

Refugee Action (2007) *The Destitution Trap – Research into destitution among refused asylum seekers in the UK.* London: Refugee Action.

Tribe, R. (2007) Working with interpreters. *The Psychologist,* Vol. 20, No. 3 pp. 159–61.

UNHCR (2007–2008) *Protecting Refugees and the Role of UNHCR.* Geneva: UNHCR.

West, A. (2006) To do or not to do – Is that the question? *Therapy Today,* Vol. 17, No. 06 pp. 10–13.

Wiesenthal, S. (1968) *The Murderers are Among Us.* London: Bantam.

12 Class and Counselling

Anne Kearney

Recent writing for counselling/therapy has addressed itself to developing a greater understanding of different types of oppression, which are part of our social world. This chapter looks at an aspect of potential oppression which is largely ignored in such discussions – that of social class. Giddens invites us to consider 'two phenomena, which should be conceptually separate – *class and class consciousness*. Class differences exist regardless of whether people are conscious of them' (1993: 227). Dominelli, writing about racism in social work, describes a 'colour-blind approach' where white workers ignore the colour of black people's skin: 'It is not that they are unaware of the colour of a person's skin, but that they discount its significance' (1988: 36). I am suggesting here that this equally applies to class, and that the counselling profession and its members are largely 'class-blind'. This chapter is an invitation to confront our class-blindness and consider the implications of class difference in our counselling, supervision and training activities.

Class differences

Controversy surrounds most discussions of class within the social sciences where there is frequent disagreement between protagonists as to what social class actually is. The theoretical disagreements between researchers, whilst relevant, are not the focus of this chapter, though I have discussed them in greater detail elsewhere (Kearney, 1996).

There are three main approaches to discussions about social class. The first, that of Karl Marx, is based on the ownership of wealth (capital, as he calls it). There are two major groupings of people in society, he argues: those who own capital and those who do not – the bourgeoisie and the proletariat. Those who own capital in the form of land, plant and equipment employ those who do not. They exploit workers through making profit from their labour and pay them as little as they can get away with. Apart from the two major groupings, Marx identified two other groupings, much smaller in number than the bourgeoisie or the proletariat. These are what he called the 'intermediate classes' and the 'lumpen proletariat', what present-day writers sometimes refer to as the 'underclass', who are neither owners of capital nor employed by owners. The second major description of social class is given by Max Weber who, though he did not disagree with Marx, did feel that Marx's description 'missed out' some important features of class, such as status and power. Weber saw the class system as being similar to a ladder, with a different group on each step.

The steps differ from each other not only in terms of wealth, but also in terms of lifestyle, status and the amount of power they have. This seems superficially to be very different from Marx's view, but like Marx, Weber claimed that it is wealth and our position on the ladder that determines our 'life chances' (our experiences, opportunities) and general 'way of being'.

The third approach to describing the class system is not a historical one, rather it is a 'snapshot' description of what the class system looks like in terms of the ladder or hierarchy as described by Weber. This view – the Registrar General's classification of social class – looks at the occupational system and categorizes people on the basis of the job they do. It consists of five main groupings of jobs arranged on a hierarchy from the 'top' jobs such as lawyers and doctors, to the 'bottom' jobs, such as unskilled labourers. It is basically a bureaucratic view of social class, designed to provide administrative and policy guidelines (such as the number of council houses we may need to build), rather than an attempt to understand the class system, as Marx and Weber were trying to do. As such, the Registrar General's categorization of jobs has limited use as an aid to understanding; it is based on the 'head of household' for instance, and makes no reference to people who are not in the occupational system, such as unemployed people or those with full-time care obligations.

For the purpose of this discussion I am using a very broad definition of class which is fairly arbitrary. I am using the concepts of 'middle class' and 'working class' to describe the differences between those people who, while they are not owners of wealth, in Marx's terms, do occupy different positions in the class structure. By 'middle class' I mean those people who do 'white-collar' jobs as distinct from those who do 'blue-collar' (or manual) jobs. I am aware of the crudeness of this distinction, in that there are many variations of income, status and power *within* each of these groups. Nevertheless, research suggests that the great divide is between those who do non-manual and those who do manual work. I am also aware that the most deprived and disadvantaged people are those who, for whatever reason, have no job and that in recent years this group has grown massively. That unemployment itself creates deprivation and consequently psychological problems for people is not in question. There is no doubt whatever in my mind that the constraints imposed by unemployment and poverty directly and indirectly create and sustain emotional difficulties for people. I suggest that they are difficulties which are different in degree rather than in kind from those of employed people who are exploited and impoverished – and often disenfranchised, too. These difficulties include problems of ego development, poor self-esteem, feelings of unworthiness, self-loathing and shame.

Social class is a major determinant of our life experiences. Our socio-economic position, and consequent lifestyle, our values, attitudes and traditions, and our life chances all impact on who we become and what we might bring to therapy. It is well documented that income, standard of education, language use, health and leisure opportunities are all influenced by the class position that we occupy. There is general agreement that there are huge disparities of power, status and money between the two major classes and that each of us is positioned in either one or the other grouping (Hutton, 1995). I am suggesting here that it is these very things that often *create* the conditions that bring clients to counselling.

The impact of class difference on the counselling profession and on clients

Class and counsellor training

On beginning counsellor training we are embarking on a process of acquiring skills, knowledge and values, which form the basis of our 'expertise'. Training has already been contaminated, however, by class issues in a number of ways:

- Most trainers occupy middle-class positions which give them social power by virtue of their role.
- Trainees are disproportionately middle class, since training is expensive and many cannot access it.
- The training itself is influenced by predominantly middle-class assumptions and values which are rarely explored during the course.
- The emphasis on individualism, personal choice and personal responsibility are informed by (and in their turn form) an ethos of training which is class-based.

These factors have very direct consequences for *all* trainees, whether middle class or working class. For middle-class trainees it may result in their not being challenged and invited to explore the class-based assumptions they may (unwittingly) hold about people and which may impact on their future work with clients. The impact on working-class trainees is different but equally important. I offer an example from my own practice when a trainee in supervision said 'I feel I don't know anything about people any more, and I always thought I was perceptive'. What emerged on further exploration was her sense that her 'knowledge' of people was valued less highly than 'knowledge' being exhibited by other trainees from more prestigious social class backgrounds.

We can gain 'knowledge' in a number of ways: by experience, by observation, by intuition, by being 'given' it, or by reading. We tend to assume that there is an absolute difference between what is 'known' publicly (in other words, what people generally agree is the case) and what we know privately, from 'gut feeling', personal experience or personal observation. It is very likely that those people who share a similar class position will observe and experience in broadly similar ways, and this becomes the 'knowledge' that this group share in a taken-for-granted way. It is at this point that social power differences become very important because the shared 'knowledge' of middle-class people is imbued with the greater authority allocated to them in class terms. It is middle-class perceptions, middle-class experiences and middle-class interpretations which are seen to *be* knowledge, and working-class knowledge is thereby demoted to 'folklore' or 'being canny'. A similar process takes place between women and men, where 'men's knowledge' is seen as superior to 'women's knowledge' which is demoted and devalued as inferior. I suggest that what passes for 'knowledge' is socially constructed and is widely influenced by social class considerations. I prefer to think that there are 'knowledges', rather than only one legitimate 'knowledge'. In the process of knowledge construction, the greater power and status attributed to being middle class promotes certain kinds of knowledge and legitimizes it over others. What this trainee was expressing was her internalized devaluing of her own knowledge – her perception and intuition – ironically a fundamental quality for counsellors.

Ideally, there should be no need on any training course to address issues of oppression on the basis of gender, class and race, and so forth as 'add on' modules. These would all be dealt with in the main body of the training and would be central to it. While there is now a growing volume of work and literature on, for example, transcultural counselling (Pedersen and Ivey, 1994; Lago and Thompson, 1996) there is no specific attention paid to class as an external form of oppression. Our awareness of class as a major source of oppression in therapeutic work seems less advanced than our awareness of other types of oppression and seems to be less well understood in its detail than other forms. What I am claiming here is that the training world of counselling/psychotherapy operates from essentially middle-class assumptions and values, assumptions that are rarely (if ever) challenged, and perceived to be apolitical and universal. It may be difficult for individual trainees to challenge the ideological basis of their training where the very people doing the training are those who will assess and judge their work and who probably belong to professional organizations which fail to challenge the underlying premises of the work they legitimize. In other words, the counselling community, as trainers, counsellors and supervisors, seems reluctant to recognize that we as a profession are positioned in a wider world where inequalities are normalized and taken for granted. We take a stance (by default, if not actively) in relation to these inequalities – a stance that either challenges them (both as professionals and as citizens) or endorses them by our *failure* to challenge them.

One of the outcomes of this for working-class counsellors is a feeling expressed by one training supervisee that he felt 'silenced' by a sense of alienation from the very 'middle-class niceness' that he experienced in his training. His concerns were as much with what was missing from his training – its absences – as with what was present. He had come from a world where poverty was a daily struggle for most people he knew, to one where poverty was rarely, if ever, mentioned. His community of origin was one in which poor housing and irresponsible landlords were part of the everyday experiences of people, yet awareness of these experiences was 'absent from his training'. He withdrew from his training on the grounds that 'counselling is not about people like me, we don't figure'.

Clients, shame and class

The counselling community's failure to confront class inequalities and the different experiences of class-disadvantaged people (trainees as well as clients) results in counselling becoming an elite activity, aimed at other privileged people whilst paying lip service to the equal value of every unique individual, at odds with the actual day-to-day practice of counselling/psychotherapy. This is not to doubt the integrity of individual trainers and therapists, but to argue that our reluctance as a professional group to take on the difficulties and challenges of these aspects of our work and to see them as having relevance to oppressed people may well result in our being part of the process of oppression (Hutton, 1995).

In the remainder of this chapter, I want to explore the actual ways in which the 'class-blind' approach to our work may impact on clients, in particular where the client is working class and the counsellor/psychotherapist is middle class. I will examine some of the areas where I believe the impact may be greatest, though the areas I have selected are illustrative and not exhaustive. From the moment the client makes contact with us, our class differences or similarities are apparent – and significant. Our initial contact may be either by telephone or (in the case of GP or other organizational settings) they may involve face-to-face contact which gives more visual 'clues'. Telephone contact draws attention to accent, language use, the degree of warmth and/or formality and will mobilize a whole set of stereotypic assumptions on both sides which may facilitate or hinder further contact. A middle-class accent and use of language may reinforce a working-class client's internalized classism, and the same process may be activated for the counsellor. Middle-class accents and language use are differently powered; they are perceived as 'superior', as having status and as conveying 'expertness' which in turn may add to the power imbalances between the counsellor (who is likely to be skilled and experienced at making verbal contact with clients) and a client who may be feeling anxious and vulnerable anyway. A very perceptive and able working-class client recently said to me 'As soon as I heard you, I knew you'd know how to help me, I knew you'd know what to do.' Processing this when the client came for her session enabled us both to separate out the impact of my middle-class accent and her class-based assumption that middle-class people automatically 'know best', and in so doing we could talk very early on about the power issues which were an important theme in her therapeutic work. It can operate in the other direction too. As a client said in her first review, 'I wasn't sure I'd be able to tell you the things I needed to, you might be shocked, you might think I was awful.' Again, processing this enabled both of us to be aware of the class differences between us and how they might impede (or enhance) our work together.

The settings in which we work also make statements about class differences. I am aware for instance, in my GP-based work, that the medical setting contributes to a sense of class difference, particularly for working-class clients. There seems to be a 'spin-off effect' of status from the doctors in the surgery to me, so clients have a tendency at first to be more distant and formal when saying why they have come. The medical setting seems to have the effect of clients describing their lives in terms of 'symptoms' and to feel, at least initially, that they cannot be 'real' with me.

When I work from home the setting is still not free from class clues and clients will often make comments which outline this, such as 'Have you read all those books?' These observations present us with ideal opportunities to explore the client's underlying assumptions and their own and my own class positions, which I believe have a definite impact on the therapeutic work. I have become convinced that these differences have an impact on how we, as counsellors, actually hear clients and how they hear us. Given that middle-class language (i.e. Bernstien's 'elaborated code', 1971) is more highly valued generally, the client may feel doubly disempowered by the differences between us. In the first place I, as a middle-class woman, will selectively choose what parts of the client's content to reflect back. In doing that I may unwittingly be attributing a middle-class meaning structure to what has been said and, when that is combined with the already existing power differences between the client and myself, the chances that the client will feel empowered enough to challenge my understanding are greatly diminished.

When we fail to take into account that this might happen, we take the risk of 'missing' the client (Hargaden and Summers, 2000). These authors cite the work of Sterne, who gives the example of client X who was brought up in a working-class family. X tells the therapist of an incident that she knows happened when she was an infant but does not have a memory of.

> X: My parents came to collect me from the hospital but I did not recognize them. I just sat between them sighing [*sounds sad and a little lost*] ... I had lost them forever ...
>
> *Therapist*: That little baby, sitting there, feeling lost and hurt, sitting in the car between her mummy and daddy but not knowing that they were her mummy and daddy.

> Upon hearing the word 'car', X froze and felt embarrassed. Her family had never owned a car and her parents could not drive. She felt paralyzed by a sense of shame and confusion. (1985: 153)

The client's story and its attendant feelings are at risk, then, of becoming a multi-layered process of self-rebuke by the climate in which s/he sees him/herself as somehow 'lacking' something. Of course, the 'lack' in the case of working-class clients is that of a middle-class framework within which to interpret experiences. For the (middle-class) counsellor, too, there is a lack – of a working-class framework. But the therapeutic setting is not an objective area where different frameworks compete on equal terms when class differences exist between therapist/client. It is an area in which the therapist's framework is given much greater legitimacy by virtue of his/her 'expertise' and, just as importantly (and maybe even more so) by virtue of his/her 'middle-classness'. In other words, what happens in the therapy room parallels what happens in the outside world – middle-class people are given (and internalize) greater status, power and authority than working-class people.

One consequence of this is that it can (and I suspect, often does) result in the counsellor/therapist holding (probably unconsciously) a 'deficit model' of the client. The client may be seen as being deficient in experiences or deficient in insight or even deficient in feeling when compared with the therapist's own measures. Of course, from the perspective of the client, the same would be the case from his/her perspective; the counsellor/therapist could be seen as deficient in the area of experience, knowledge and even feelings that the client has. Again, this might not seem to matter too much; after all, this happens very commonly when people from different backgrounds interact socially. But it does matter, greatly, in the therapeutic context where the therapist/counsellor is already more powerful than the client and where it is the job of the therapist to enter into the meaning structure of the client – on the client's terms. It is almost impossible for this to be achieved if the therapist fails to take account of and raise awareness of the class differences between them. The failure to do that creates the risk that the client believes him/herself to be 'wrong' in some way; to somehow not be feeling what s/he 'should' be feeling. It is too big a responsibility to impose on the client the expectation that s/he will 'hold on to' his/her sense of self, experiences and interpretations when they are not being validated by the therapist. This is the therapist's responsibility, and it is one that most of our training and our professional organization fails to prepare us for. Unless we become and remain aware that social class structures our experience and expectation and greatly informs our learning framework, we run the risk of inaccurately imputing meaning to the client's story. If we are unaware of the impact of social class we may not be alert to the potential 'mis-hearing' and/or misunderstanding, and the distance between us and the client becomes greater.

This could be avoided if training involved a component which required trainees to become familiar with the relevant information about how society is organized, how social class operates and how power inequalities are created and sustained by such divisions. Let us take, for example, the experience of counsellors in prisons or in drug counselling agencies, which are largely populated by working-class clients. It is important to question what part social class played in each of the lives of these clients. What cultural and socio-economic influences – for example locality, poor housing, peer group, poor education, unemployment and poverty – were the backdrop to *this* client's story and their current situation? So far we have looked at theories of class, the impact of class differences on counsellors and on clients, and we have looked at how we might unwittingly shame clients about class issues.

What I want to look at in the remainder of this piece is how we need to look even further than recognizing and acknowledging class and its consequences for our work. I want to explore how the focus on the internal world of the client precludes not only a focus on class, but ignores too how class stratification is embedded in structures which are often taken for granted and yet we construct and are constructed by in ways we internalize and normalize. The capitalist structure of our society generates a system of beliefs and values which justifies its existence. In spite of this we often persist in privileging the personal, subjective world of the client over the social world that constitutes the inner world. As a client recently said,

> I suppose you'll tell me that I have choices and I can have responsibility for my own life. I even believe that sometimes. But the big world out there seems to put me back in my place whenever I try to take control …

I could sense the anger that underlies that view, and it seems to me to be justifiable anger since it comes close to 'blaming the victim' for any distress or sense of powerlessness the client felt to be part of her frustration.

If we fail to process the appropriateness of the clients' feelings in the light of social constraints deriving from structures outside him/herself we risk pathologizing the client's attempts to gain on central greater parts of their lives. This risk is sometimes manifest in our tendency to label the client's behaviour in ways that minimize his/her distress. We may also use 'professional' language in ways that disrespect the often creative ways in which we all try to cope with the circumstances of our lives. We can see this sometimes in the ways in which a counsellor coveys information about the client.

> *Supervisee*: The client is over-anxious and gets depressed easily and seems a bit …
> *AK*: A bit?
> *Supervisee*: A bit over-fragile.

> *AK*:   'Over' in what sense?
>
> *Supervisee*: [*Paused, looked embarrassed*] Yes, I suppose I'm implying that there's a level of anxiety and fragility I'm seeing as acceptable and any more than this is 'over', I think, for me.

In fact, the supervisee had previously described the client as coming from a background of poverty through the illness of the family breadwinner. She had also said that the client had had two jobs in the past eight months and had been made redundant from both.

The supervisee's honesty and willingness to be open and reflective enabled her to see that the client's 'fragility' and 'anxiety' may not have been intrinsic to him but may be a response to the precariousness of his employment and the fact that he was responsible for supporting his three children – in other words, his emotional state was a rational response to his situation.

Recent developments in the economic sphere have highlighted the precariousness of the existing economic system and as such are likely to generate great levels of just the sort of feelings we might mistakenly frame as pathological. We cannot fail to recognize (in the light of the current depression) just how fragile our economic and social well-being is, and how our welfare may depend on the vagaries of the system of global capitalism.

Recent developments have made it clear that while we will all be affected by the economic depression, some will be more severely and more directly affected than others. This is, our class position either exposes us to the full impact of the depression or it may protect us from the worst short- and long-term consequences. Generally, more working-class people (and people disadvantaged in other ways) will be affected by unemployment than will middle- and upper middle-class people, who may well have more reserves to cushion themselves from the worst impacts.

It has become clear, too, that banks and other institutions will be massively subsidized at vast expense to the taxpayers. Even as this is happening, senior members of those organizations expect (and will receive) sizable bonuses despite their failure, while managerial workers in the finance industries continue to receive huge salaries on the grounds that if they do not receive huge sums of money in return for their skills(!) they may go elsewhere. What this shows is that the class system continues to protect some groups over others, even when it is obvious that the differential in pay cannot be justified by their superior skills or their demonstrable successes. We can make sense of these things only if we challenge the ideology that some workers are intrinsically more deserving of reward than others.

As therapists we can see how we ourselves are affected by social changes. We can see, for instance, how the emphasis on cognitive-behavioural therapy (CBT) is not based on evidence of its superior efficacy, but on the advantages that accrue to the state because of its relative brevity and because it can be audited more effectively by a cost–benefit analysis than can other methods of therapy. In the process, of course, choices are further removed from poor clients by how it implies a 'one size fits all' policy. Whilst CBT is undoubtedly effective for certain purposes, it definitely is not the panacea the government would like it to be. As a client said, having completed a CBT programme 'well, I can function enough to go back to work, but now I'd like to do the therapy I needed in the first place, and I can only have that by paying for it.'

Whether we like it or not, as therapists we are ourselves affected by how we are positioned in the class system. We see this being played out in miniature, so to speak, in the creation of a hierarchy of therapies (legitimated, sadly, by BACP), which is very similar in structure to how social class generally is mediated to us.

The position we occupy as therapists within the broader social context (what some would call the 'dominant discourse') puts us at risk of becoming a form of social control by locating emotional difficulties in the subjectivity of the client. Because a major feature of the dominant discourse is the construction and sustaining of the oppression in various forms, there is a real danger that we could become part of what oppresses clients and part of normalizing gross inequalities between individuals and between groups.

Summary

I have claimed in this chapter that the literature of therapy has (up to very recent times) concentrated on the inner world of the client, on his/her subjectivity. Yet we know at a common-sense level that the client lives (as we do!) in a wider social world of economics, politics, sometimes religion, gender, 'race', and so on. Each one of these positions the client in its hierarchy and in doing that, each one affects and even constructs the clients' experiences, his/her sense of self and life opportunities.

I have suggested that the class system is one of the major external systems in this process, ordering and giving meaning to the client's experienced inner-world as well as his/her life chances. A client recently described her therapy as 'being introduced to herself in a new way' as she became more aware of her class position and how it influenced her expectations of, for instance, her relationship with her partner, whose class position was a different one.

It is the opacity of the class system that makes it difficult for us to identify it as a major source of the distribution of power, and of course it is in the interests of those who benefit from the inequality of its distribution not to make it transparent.

As therapists we can align ourselves with the view that suggests our life experiences are largely self-generated – particularly the positive ones. Alternatively, we can align ourselves with the view that it is part of our obligation to clients to enable them, not only to make effective choices but also to recognize the limits within which those choices are made. The choice we, as therapists, do not have (although many would probably dispute this, perhaps) is to avoid either choice: there is no neutral place we can occupy while we work. It seems to me that we need to decide 'which side we're on' so that we can be transparent to clients, supervisees and trainees. It is the least we can do, and probably the most we can do.

References

Bernstein, B. (1971) *Class, Codes and Control.* Vol. 1. London: Routledge and Kegan Paul.

Dominelli, L. (1988) *Anti-Racist Social Work.* London: Macmillan.

Giddens, A. (1993) *Sociology* (2nd edition). Cambridge: Polity Press.

Hargaden, H. and Summers, G. (2000) 'Class, Shame and Self-righteousness'. Conference Papers *Embracing Life's Differences*. ITA Conference.

Hutton, W. (1995) *The State We're In*. London: Johnathan Cape.

Kearney, A. (1996) *Counselling, Class and Politics – Undeclared Influences in Therapy*. Manchester: PCCS Books.

Lago, C. and Thompson, J. (1996) *Race, Culture and Counselling*. Buckingham: Open University.

Pedersen, P. and Ivey, A.E. (1994) *Culture-Centered Counseling and Interviewing Skills*. Westpoint, CT: Greenwood/Preager.

Sterne, D.N. (1985) *The Interpersonal World of the Infant*. New York: Basic Books.

13 Therapy, Disability and Ethnicity

Power and Powerlessness

Zenobia Nadirshaw

Having a disability is rarely a welcome event and in the first half of the twentieth century it was viewed as a 'tragedy' with professionals portraying nothing but a negative impact on the family and community. Thankfully those days are over and support offered to the disabled population has increased two-fold. Legislation in the form of the Disability Discrimination Act (1995), the Race Relations Amendment Act (1968) and the Human Rights Act (1998) have each ensured that people with disabilities have the same rights to ordinary living as the rest of the population in employment, education, dignity and respect. However, access to fair and equitable services for these vulnerable groups still remains a challenge – despite the fact that they have particular psychological needs and experience feelings of being over-whelmed, depressed, anxious, socially isolated with low self-esteem as a result.

Given the multitude of challenges this group of people face it is important that appropriate psychotherapy and counselling is offered to them. This chapter will make such a case by highlighting (a) the double discrimination suffered by those who are disabled and who, simultaneously, belong to black and minority ethnic (BME) groups, and (b) suggesting the actions that anti-disabling counselling services and therapists can take at individual and professional levels.

The Office for Disability Issues (2009) identified over 10 million disabled people in Britain, of whom 5 million were over state pension age and 800,000 were chil-dren. This estimate covers the number of people with a long-standing illness, dis-ability or infirmity and who have significant difficulty with day-to-day activities.

Disabled people, as defined by government, account for about one-fifth (20 per cent) of people in the UK, with many people having more than one impairment (hearing loss, vision loss, difficulty with walking and climbing stairs, learning dis-ability, mental health problems, literacy difficulties, and so on).

Additionally, for some, there is stigma attached to the concept of mental ill health, and BME people frequently view access to mental health care within the statutory services with suspicion.

We do know that there is inequality in service provision to health and social care between women and men, disabled and non-disabled, people from different ethnic backgrounds, people with different sexual orientations, people of different ages and people with different religions or beliefs (East Midlands Regional Assembly, 2009).

The ideas of Wolfensberger (1972) and colleagues (Wolfensberger and Glen, 1983) on normalisation and social role valorisation in the learning disability field is a force for good and can be applied to all vulnerable groups. However, it holds atti-tudes, values and expectations reflecting the dominant population and disregards the unique culture and cultural thinking of the disempowered group. The idea inherent within the philosophy of social role valorisation, that people must aspire to the 'normal', presupposes many judgements. There is no acknowledgment in the above model of the unique features of a person who is marginalised, both on the grounds of being labelled as long-term disabled and coming from a minority ethnic background. In reducing one's stigmata/differentness, one is expected to attain more valued membership and goals of the dominant society.

Unfortunately, blanket assumptions can so easily be made about what is considered 'normal' or 'valued' in society. According to Ferns (personal communication, 2000), 'human services operate in an inherently racist society and as a set of principles, normalisation and social role valorisation do not take into account the fact that the dominant sections of society are racist in covert ways and not least in their value systems and norms.' Although the theory purports to revalue people, it is rooted in hostility to and a denial of difference and it exerts a threshold of intolerance, which, in essence, asserts that there is a limit beyond which it is not reasonable to expect majority populations to continue with their 'normal' level of tolerance.

In the author's view, disabled people continue to be discriminated against by:

- psychological and psychotherapy services not proving easy to access;
- the systemic maintenance of a 'colour-blind approach' in services where 'one size fits all' still results in a lack of formal recognition of the diverse and varied needs of this 'broad group' of people;
- being discriminated against on the grounds of 'special' needs by statutory services; and
- their needs being seen as 'different', diverse and invalid and therefore negative value being attributed to those needs.

The argument presented here is that people with (learning and other) disabilities (like other vulnerable groups) should have the same rights as others to choice and freedom, be socially accepted and valued, be treated with dignity and respect, and have community participation and integration.

Despite Britain being a multi-racial, multi-lingual and multi-cultural society, authority and decision-making powers still rest in the hands of the dominant majority. People with learning disabilities, like other disempowered groups, remain oppressed and vulnerable in society – suffering discrimination and disadvantage in the course of their everyday lives through socially constructed concepts of 'difference' and 'differentness'.

Discrimination leads to the formation of negative self-concepts, feelings of rejection and stigmatisation, confusion about one's sense of inclusion, and has long-term implications for emotional and psychological well-being.

An action plan for social cohesion and social inclusion

A case for change needs to be made for BME disabled people who remain socially excluded, with their emotional and psychological needs not being met by statutory psychotherapy and mental health services. Very often they struggle to access appropriate psychological and psychotherapeutic care and all too often have to reach a crisis point to do so. Contact with helping professionals needs to be made at an appropriate time to achieve better outcomes for this group. Some of the issues that have been addressed (but continue to require more systemic attention) are:

- How are services to be made accessible?
- Who should provide the help and assistance?
- What kind of methods and psychotherapeutic interventions are chosen to alleviate difficulties and solve the problems?
- Who should provide these interventions and what are the anticipated outcomes?

Similarly, how these ideas could be implemented at a policy level within the helping organisations also needs to be addressed. In keeping with a person-focussed planning philosophy and principles, the user's voice should dictate what happens at practitioner, administrative and policymaking levels.

I now lay out an action plan for social cohesion and social inclusion in mental health settings.

Listening to the user's voice

Clients, as users of professional services, have important contributions to make to service delivery. Where possible, it is important for clients to become involved with groups who can become advocates for improved services. All clients suffering disability and from BME backgrounds should be encouraged to become involved. These groups have been characterised as having more problems with systems of service delivery (including poor access to and under-utilisation of therapeutic services), and have reduced participation in the planning and co-ordination of services.

Research into current methods of working strongly suggests that the existing 'workforce' must develop 'cultural competence' in order to arrest and reverse the prevailing pattern of discriminatory practices. A truly cross-cultural approach means an acceptance, understanding and respect for different patterns of human behaviour and for institutions of racial, ethnic, religious or social groups. The word 'competence' implies having the knowledge, skills, attitudes and capacity to function effectively.

Practitioner level: understanding, knowledge, awareness and skills

In the world of disability it is suggested that psychologists and therapists (particularly those working within the Health Service) must have:

- a thorough understanding of the lived experience of (ill) health and disability of the clients they serve;
- knowledge and awareness about the social and political context in the development, expression and care of illness/injury. They need to understand how 'race',

culture, spirituality, sexual orientation and the impact of poverty and displacement can have on the client and his/her well-being;

- working knowledge of the pathophysiology and progression of injuries and diseases, the medical treatments and procedures usually carried out and the psychological significance these may have for the client with reference to the process of adjustment, vulnerability resilience and self-help;
- the confidence, as part of their therapeutic practice, to undertake long-term risk assessment with members of the other multi-disciplinary team involved with their client;
- skills that can adapt their input flexibly across different healthcare environments in which they see their clients (for example, in intensive care units, GP clinics, in the client's own home and other special circumstances);
- interpersonal and supervisory skills that support others involved in looking after their client;
- skills in engaging with the client in the planning and delivery of care and promoting the client's priorities (for example, choice of intervention, timeliness and accessibility of care);
- research and audit skills in establishing and supporting clinical governance procedures as applied in acute, intermediate and primary healthcare settings;
- a thorough understanding of their work in accordance with the code of ethics and conduct as defined by their professional bodies and to work within the limits of their own competencies, within an appropriate structure of professional support and supervision;
- developed skills and confidence in maintaining resilience in the face of strains of dealing with their clinical caseloads that includes trauma, disfigurement, severe distress and death in some circumstances; and
- continuing professional development which include not only keeping up to date with the evidence-base, clinical interventions and other therapeutic practices, but also undertaking equality impact assessments of policies and programmes in relation to disability, ethnicity and gender.

Equality impact assessment

It is essential that the helping professional develops knowledge and skills in equality impact assessment as part of their training and continuing professional development plan.

Equality impact assessments, when done properly, will identify unlawful/unjustifiable discrimination and harassment, promote equality and foster positive relationships between different groups of people.

The helping professional's practice must be guided by the principles of empowerment practice, which are grounded in a well-informed appreciation of the effects of oppression on the lives of their clients and their carers. They need to have a familiarity with key concepts such as power, powerlessness, privilege and disadvantage. The challenge for the helping professionals is that their clients may be oppressed on several grounds at the same time. (See Chapter 14 by Moodley and Murphy.)

The helping professionals could ask themselves the following questions whilst undertaking a 'needs assessment' of a disabled black client, for example:

- Has my 'assessment of need procedure' acknowledged recognition of disablism and racism and its effects, whether overt or covert?
- What steps have I taken to critically examine my own values and perception of a disabled black female client in the assessment and therapeutic context?
- How do I respond to the black woman client when she challenges me or criticises my assessment – constructively or defensively?
- How do I define the needs of this black woman with disability and ensure that my assessment is based on her experience and reality and not on my values and perceptions?
- Do I assess the strengths of this black person and her family or community as well as her weaknesses, problems and needs?
- Does my assessment make explicit distinctions between my client's possible control of personal problems versus the external constraints beyond her control? What are those distinctions?
- How can my assessment and resulting therapeutic intervention empower my client?
- How do I evaluate my assessment and the outcome of it?

Ethics and values

The helping professional must be guided by the ethical principles of autonomy, beneficence, fidelity, justice, non-maleficence and accountability. These are principles that have been developed by professional bodies and have thus been written in an apparently neutral form. However, professional ethics, by their very nature, are socially constructed and inevitably have inherent values by which 'right' and 'wrong' are judged. The author's concern is that the values embedded in these professional codes are likely to be those reflecting the dominant majority in which these professions developed. There can exist a myth of neutrality that can be used to legitimise the disablist and racist traditions of the helping professions whist cloaking their activities in the language of professionalism and science (Patel, 1999).

The helping professional needs to consider their client's differences and be aware of how their own cultural values might impact on the way therapy is offered and undertaken.

Professional power and empowerment

Individual practitioners, by the end of their training, must have a good understanding of the professional power that resides with them. They need to show, as part of their knowledge, skills and attitudes, the change in emphasis of professional power from their hands into the hands of the disadvantaged groups they serve. Professional power resides in:

- access to relevant knowledge, experience and expertise, which it is claimed is only available to members of the professional group;
- the authority to make decisions over the lives of others;
- being able, on terms available to the professions, to dispense with or withhold information from service users; and
- being able to structure face-to-face interactions (interviews, meetings, reviews) in ways which are advantageous to the professional person.

In developing abilities in the form of skills, knowledge and attitudes alongside personal characteristics and qualities, the helping professional could ensure competencies and maintenance of high standards of care in their work with their clients (Nadirshaw, 1999). For example, in therapeutic work with BME clients, the author suggests following a culturally competent framework of moving and working towards cultural competence as depicted in Figures 13.1 and 13.2. This model is based on the human services literature that was developed by Cross et al. (1989).

By developing the competencies in Figures 13.1 and 13.2, individual therapists will be able to develop confidence in offering psychotherapy services which match their client's needs and be cognisant of the cultural and other socio-political factors that may influence the presentation of psychological problems.

Cultural destructiveness

Acknowledging only one way of being and purposefully denying other cultural approaches.

Cultural incapability

Supports the concept of separate, but equal, marked by an inability to deal personally with multiple approaches but a willingness to accept their existence elsewhere.

Cultural blindness

Fosters an assumption that people are all basically alike, so what works with members of one culture should work within all other cultures. Liberal philosophy of 'one size fits all'.

Cultural pre-competence

Realises its weaknesses and encourages learning and understanding of how to develop new ideas and solutions to improve performance or service to specific populations.

Cultural competence

Involves actively seeking advice and consultation and a commitment to incorporating new knowledge and experiences into a wider range of practice. Acceptance and respect for difference and continuous expansion of knowledge and resources.

Cultural proficiency

Involves holding cultural differences and diversity in the highest esteem, pro-active regarding cultural differences and promotion of improved cultural relations amongst diverse groups and knowledge base of culturally competent practice by conducting appropriate research, developing new therapeutic practices.

Figure 13.1 Moving towards cultural competence

1 Exploring one's background and becoming aware of one's own cultural biases towards 'race', culture and disability.
2 Seeking and obtaining knowledge of various cultural beliefs on and about the various disability issues.
3 Gaining the skill to conduct a cultural assessment.
4 Engaging in an abundance of cultural encounters.
5 Having the desire of 'wanting' to, not 'having' to deliver culturally competent care.

Questions that one can ask about one's level of cultural competence:

- Am I aware of my biases and prejudices towards other diverse and cultural groups as well as racism and sexism in health care and general society?
- Do I have the skill of conducting a cultural assessment in my native language or achieve a better outcome using a second language? (This question explicitly includes the consideration of appropriate use of sign languages.)
- Am I knowledgeable about the worldviews of different cultural and ethnic groups regarding mental health and mental well-being?
- Do I really 'want to' become culturally competent?

Figure 13.2 Working towards cultural competence

Therapists need to examine and focus on their client's presenting problems as a result of the nature of their 'situatedness' in society, for example housing, education, poverty and unemployment, and conduct their interventions accordingly.

Therapeutic work with disabled and BME clients will be greatly enhanced:

- through therapists renouncing their professional power and seeking to share it with clients;
- by making the professional's therapeutic practice more accessible and appropriate to the diverse needs of this population (Johnson and Nadirshaw, 1993);
- through generating a culturally competent workforce who have the confidence to use their critical analysis of prevailing theoretical models and therapeutic approaches in judging their applicability to their client's needs;
- in working from the perspective of cultural competence to ensure the rights of service users in terms of privacy, confidentiality, self-determination and autonomy which will be aligned with the helping professional's updated code of professional ethics that respects the rights and dignity of the person, their competence, responsibility and integrity; and
- if by the end of their training and commencing clinical practice the helping professional has become more confident of adopting and working within an inclusive practice in which they would expect and feel comfortable with the diversity that is in the local population.

Organisational level

Professional bodies and academic departments for clinical psychology, psychotherapy and counselling will need to show the paradigm shift detailed in Table 13.1.

Table 13.1   Paradigm shift for academic departments in the helping professions

From	To
Subject of social exclusion, racism, disability being treated separately.	Being mainstreamed within the overall agenda of social inclusion with a clear vision, aims and objectives, principles and action plans, clearly laid out with an identified lead champion on equality and diversity on the board of directors.
Treating disability and disabled communities as a homogenous group.	Acknowledging the extensive diversity that exists within these various groups.
Moving from consultation with community groups.	Moving into the world of action in working with community groups and the other voluntary sector agencies. Working with and learning from these groups models of good practice, including being equal partners in decision making and power sharing which is vital.
Providing eurocentric models of therapeutic practice.	Providing a culturally competent therapeutic service which enhances recovery, self-esteem, self-worth and self-confidence as key resultant outcomes.
Treating disabled group (including BME as a problem and weakness).	Recognising and working with the issues of fairness and equity as part of the overall solution to the organisation's strategic plan and objectives. Service users to be seen as a fundamental resource and strength in their own care and in determining the outcomes of the therapeutic practice and to feel empowered by getting involved in committee work relating to research and evaluation of services as well as service plans.

Source: Nadirshaw, 2000: 225

Psychotherapy policy, practice and research have to be informed by views of users and recipients of services. A coherent strategy that is governed by the principles of equality, anti-discrimination and anti-racist practice should be developed through the incorporation of views of *all* sections of society. A key senior manager should be given the responsibility to undertake the detailed work necessary to developing a coherent and effective strategy, including an implementation plan. Clear leadership within the helping professional body will need to ensure the important shift from the firmly entrenched status quo to reveal the language of exclusion and segregation behind the language of inclusion and elitism.

The training, accreditation and validation committees of the different professional bodies must invite evidence from supervisees on how they are prepared to meet the psychological and mental health needs of the varying communities, and also provide guidance on preparing supervisees to work in a multi-ethnic and multi-racial context. It would be helpful to look at Lago and Smith's (2003) guidelines on supervision and how to avoid the vicious cycle (Nadirshaw and Torry, 2004).

The committee needs to identify and incorporate statutory/mandatory requirements to ensure the inclusion of a module on 'values' within the curriculum, which could detail principles, criteria, competencies and a clear interpretation of responsible practice in relation to working with disability.

The accreditation teams and the equality and diversity committees could offer guidance on criteria by which training courses would be accredited/recognised as competent in their teaching and practice area of difference and equality. These topics need to be monitored rather than being seen as a 'specialist' one-off topic. This would include evidence of individual and group work with clients and increasing the number of supervisees from BME backgrounds and disabled communities.

Individual heads of department within the NHS could regularly monitor their own services by:

- reviewing the ethnic composition of local communities and existing personnel and identifying the steps that need to be taken to get to know the vulnerable communities within their area;
- identifying the training and supervision needs of the department in relation to the ethnic make-up of the population it serves;
- comparing a cohort of their referred clients with the expected referral profile based on epidemiological data and the social demography of their catchment area;
- acknowledging a better understanding of how disabled people are under-served by the use of inappropriate psychological therapy and interventions despite progress made within various fields (e.g. in behavioural/cognitive therapies with different client populations); and
- making their services more accessible by establishing and maintaining links and credibility with the community groups and the black voluntary sector with relation to the shared expectations of training requirements and services offered as a result.

Qualified and trainee therapists, as part of their contribution to addressing the needs of a diverse, multi-ethnic society, need to develop: accurate assessment; meaningful and appropriate interventions which are culturally contextualised; deal with differences in language and meaning; and explore the role of the 'change agent' in their work with the voluntary sector.

Implications for training and continuing professional development (CPD)

The following learning outcomes could be sought:

- To be aware of the bias in service provision and service delivery in clinical psychology and its origin in the Eurocentric value base of the helping professional.
- To understand the history of psychotherapy and to revisit the value base against which the work of therapists can be understood (patient's rights, consent to treatment/effects of psychotropic medication, balancing the personal and political, addressing inequalities based on power and domination).
- To have a better understanding of the barriers to access to mental health and psychotherapy services as experienced by disabled, BME people.
- To understand the role and responsibility of psychotherapy services in developing appropriate and culturally competent models of service to disabled, BME clients by relocating the problem from the purely individual to the socio-economic and socio-political nature of psychological problems.

- To understand the psychotherapy role as 'change agent' in the provision and delivery of services (e.g. networking with the black voluntary sector, primary care teams, patient's councils, use of legislation and government acts like the Patient's Charter, Disability Discrimination Act and the Race Relations Act).
- To be aware of ways in which a culturally sensitive, anti-discriminatory perspective can be incorporated in all aspects of service delivery (assessment, formulation and intervention and monitoring).
- To develop a more pluralistic approach that reflects psychological reality more adequately for all sections of British society and to refocus from the scientific framework of psychology and psychotherapy to the personal.
- To understand the limitations of the current theoretical frameworks for practice and academic research which continue to be developed from within the narrow confines of a universalist approach.

Teaching/academic departments

It is incumbent on academic departments of clinical psychology, psychotherapy and counselling to set up diversity sub-groups and ensure that their students are competent by the end of their training to be a confident workforce in the field of difference and diversity.

Items for consideration include:

- increasing the selection of supervisees from the disabled communities and making the profession of psychotherapy a 'marketable commodity' from school and undergraduate level;
- engaging with local disability voluntary groups within the community and get supervisees to undertake placements with them;
- developing knowledge and skills in working with interpreters and community leaders.
- ensuring that supervisees see at least one person from a specific group/background in each of the placements.
- video-recording accounts of service users using psychotherapists and their services; and
- auditing CPD records and staff/exit interviews.

Academic teaching staff, supervisors and supervisees need to show that they have acquired the ability and confidence of the diverse clients they serve as being met in different contexts and different specialities. They need to demonstrate knowledge of service delivery issues, current legislation, policies and guidelines that cover clinical therapeutic practice and gain the confidence of the service users accordingly. Service users need to be assured that practitioners and academic staff have developed skills in recognising institutional barriers to equitable and fair access to services.

Teachers and trainers of psychotherapy need to evidence that their curriculum has included subjects relating to difference in relation to racism, sexism, class, physical and intellectual disability and that these issues are discussed as mainstream teaching topics, not one-off specialist topics.

Examination questions need to be set which:

- assess critically the analysis of prevailing theoretical models and therapeutic approaches in judging their applicability and finding a fit between the therapeutic model and client's needs;
- assess the trainees'/students' understanding of the historical and social processes relating to disability and the multiple discrimination resulting from the previously stated double discrimination that is prevalent and experienced by the disabled and BME communities;
- questions the assumptions about similarities and difference and their therapeutic alliance; and
- work through the power differentials between the helper and the helped person on grounds of social class, gender, 'race', disability, ethnicity, religion, age and sexual preference.

Teachers and trainers need to be confident that their students develop the ability to ask appropriate questions and to record answers sensitively and flexibly. For example, in the area of assessment, formulation and intervention for disabled BME clients, the following checklist of assessment of needs could be undertaken:

- Does the trainee recognise 'disabilism' and its effects in assessment process?
- Have steps been taken to critically examine one's own values and perception of this group?
- How does the person ensure that assessment is not based on negative stereotype views and attitudes shaped by society?
- How does the person respond to black clients challenging or criticising their assessments constructively or defensively?
- How does the trainee respond to anxieties without blaming the client?
- How does the trainee define the needs of disabled BME users and other groups to ensure that their assessment is based on the person's experience and reality?
- Do assessment processes assess strengths of the disabled BME person and his family and community as well as weaknesses, problems and needs?
- What has the person done to ensure that the assessment responds to different and specific needs of user – not just 'special' needs?
- Does the person actively seek and or use guidance from BME expertise?
- How do you evaluate your assessment of the BME client and outcome of your assessment on the person?

Undertaking the above would reveal students' ability to reflect on their own beliefs and attitudes, demonstrate their awareness of difference and 'differentness' by incorporating these into their formulations and intervention planning.

Conclusion

The helping therapeutic world and the individual practitioners within it need to have a collective and individual responsibility to reduce and eliminate the impact of social inequalities and develop anti-oppressive practice. They need to move away from the world of words into real action that leads to positive outcomes for individuals whose lives and experiences have been shaped by social inequalities. The therapeutic world needs to move on from the traditional ways of thinking and working and imposing an overwhelming ethno-centric perspective. Solutions must replace myth and old adages. Therapists, service providers and planning commissioners must present themselves as part of the solution. Therapeutic organisations with clearly identified monitoring mechanisms need to take responsibility. If it is not done, we are doomed to continue the boring trudge towards professional credibility and political neutrality at the expense of our humanity.

References

Cross, T.L., Bazron, B.J., Dennis, K.W. and Isaacs, M.R. (1989). *Towards a Culturally Competent System of Care* (Volume 1). Washington, DC: National Center for Technical Assistance: Center for Children's Mental Health, Georgetown University Child Development Center.

East Midlands Regional Assembly (2009). *Cross-Cutting Challenges: Addressing Inequalities*. Available at www.emra.gov.uk/what-we-do/housing-planning-transport/irs-framework/challenges-and-integrated-policy/cross-cutting-challenges/addressing-inequalities, accessed November 2009.

Ferns, P. (2000) Personal communication with the author, October 2000.

Johnson, A.W. and Nadirshaw, Z. (1993). 'Good practice in transcultural counselling: an Asian perspective'. *British Journal of Guidance and Counselling*, 21 (1): 20–29.

Lago, C. and Smith, B. (2003). *Anti-Discriminatory Counselling Practice*. London: Sage.

Nadirshaw, Z. (1999). 'Clinical psychology', in K. Bhui and D. Olajide (eds), *Mental Health Service Provision for a Multi-cultural Society*. London: Saunders.

Nadirshaw, Z. (2000). 'Professional & organisational issues', in N. Patel, E. Bennet, M. Dennis, N. Dosanjh, A. Mahtani, A. Miller and Z. Nadirshaw (eds), *Clinical Psychology, 'Race' and Culture: A Training Manual*. Leicester: Blackwell/BPS.

Nadirshaw, Z. and Torry, B. (2004). 'Transcultural health care practice: Transcultural clinical supervision in health care practice'. Available at www.rcn.org.uk/development/learning/transcultural_health/clinicalsupervision, accessed December 2009.

Office for Disability Issues (2009). Family Resources Survey (FRS) Disability prevalance estimates 2007/8. Available at www.officefordisability.gov.uk/docs/res/factsheets/disability-prevalance. pdf, accessed 12 May 2010.

Patel, N. (1999). *Getting the Evidence. Guidelines for Ethical Mental Health Research Involving Issues of 'Race', Ethnicity and Culture*. London: Transcultural Psychiatry Society: UK and MIND Publications.

Wolfensberger, W. (1972). *The Principles of Normalisation in Human Services*. Toronto: National Institute of Mental Retardation.

Wolfensberger, W. and Glen, G. (1983). 'Social role valorisation: a proposed new term for the principle of normalisation'. *Mental Retardation*, 21, 6.

14 Multiple Identities and Anti-Discriminatory Counselling Practice

Roy Moodley and Lee Murphy

The psychology of identity and how we attempt to make sense of it in clinical practice has been the preoccupation of the counselling and psychotherapy profession in the last few decades. Particularly, the multicultural and diversity scholars have been attempting to draw our attention to the multiple ways in which clients construct their subjective positions, mainly in relation to their experiences of oppression within these identities. An essential aspect of understanding the subjective nature of identity is the recognition that each individual is impinged upon by social structures which operate differentially depending on one's personal and unique set of circumstances. Part of human existence is a tendency to categorize ourselves and each other (i.e. place ourselves into 'boxes') according to an infinite set of socially constructed paradigms that contribute to our identity: 'These social constructions are essential elements within which the identity of the client is negotiated and the inter-subjective relationship is constructed' (Moodley and Palmer, 2006: 4).

Much is researched and written about the 'big 7' socio-cultural identities or categories (gender, race, class, sexual orientations, disability, religion, age) (see Moodley and Lubin, 2008), and their intersections and convergences in therapy (see Robinson-Wood, 2008). These sites have also become the place where scholars, researchers and practitioners can examine, understand and analyse the oppressive experiences of people who identify with the 'big 7' categories. However, the categories themselves are highly complex and problematic, not least because they are embedded in ideological and the dominant culture hegemony. Further confounding matters, counsellors are likely to subscribe to dominant cultural ideals and even well-intentioned therapists 'introduce cultural bias into the counseling process in ways that are inadvertently harmful' (Arthur and Collins, 2005: 68).

While acknowledging the danger of presenting a culturally biased influence, Johannes and Erwin (2004) have cautioned against the fragmentation that a difference-based approach may produce in the counselling field if Euro-American therapeutic practices are viewed as being in opposition to other cultures. To develop multicultural competence, the authors emphasize counsellor self-awareness in terms of ethnocultural heritage and working to identify accompanying assumptions as pertinent to diversity of culture, ethnicity, race, gender, class, religion and sexual orientation (Corey, 2001, cited in Johannes and Erwin, 2004: 335). The literary discourse has positioned these identities as the site or place within which discriminatory practices are deployed, experienced negatively or internalized (see Moodley, 2003). Indeed, it is these places that counsellors turn to when attempting to make sense of the client's experiences of racism, anti-Semitism, sexism, misogyny, homophobia, disabilism, ageism and many others. Consequently, counsellors and psychotherapists have been examining the individual effects of these oppressions in their effort to make their practice anti-oppressive. The movement towards a more broad-based anti-discriminatory practice encompassing the 'big 7' identities seems to be gaining momentum as it appears to be an advance on cultural competency and cultural sensitivity models and the previous anti-racist approaches.

However, the effects of a combination of oppressive experiences (incorporating the multidimensionality of the 'big 7' identities) have not been researched adequately, nor given much attention in the counselling and psychotherapy literature. We still know very little about the complexity of affective experiencing that takes place when these forces act together. In social science, however, where these issues are beginning to be interrogated, black feminists like Collins (1990) and Lorde (1984) have emphasized the various ways in which racism, anti-Semitism, sexism, disabilism, homophobia and ageism interconnect and overlap as agents of oppression.

Clearly, the notion of a plural or multiple identities is now more acceptable and takes precedence over the conventional idea that a person's identity is singular, fixed or static. How these multiple socio-cultural and political identities are understood, experienced and 'worked with' in counselling is a critical question for therapists. For example, what happens in the therapeutic relationship with a client who discloses one of the multi(ple) cultural identities (class, gender, race, sexual orientation) but not the other(s)? Can an authentic therapeutic relationship be experienced without one or the other of their identities being marginalized and rendered invisible, and the client feeling oppressed through this experience? Can the present practice of counselling cope with the multiple cultural identities that may be disclosed and shared in therapy? (Moodley, 2003).

This chapter sets out to explore these issues in the following ways. First, by considering the constructions of the 'big 7' socio-cultural identities. Second, it examines the problematic of the 'Other' to suggest that there is no hierarchy in terms of religion, sexual orientations, race, gender, class, disability and age. Through a brief examination of the current practice of counselling, the chapter considers therapists' attitude towards the 'Other' and asks whether the present multi(ple) cultural therapies can comprehend the complexity of experiencing that goes on in clients who feel multiple oppression. The chapter concludes with a look at the strategies clients adopt in therapy and that therapists can employ with clients to understand their multiple oppressions (Moodley, 2003).

Multiplicity of the 'big 7' identities

Post-modernism appears to indicate that the 'big 7' identities are not fixed, transhistorical or essentialistic, but are flexible, dynamic and multiple. An individual's identity is a mixture of his or her gender and race, as well as ethnic, class and sexual orientation identity, and no one identity takes precedence over the other in an individual's inner world (Moodley, 2003). Thus, 'an individual *simultaneously* inhabits not just one but a great range and variety of contesting and overlapping cultural frames' (Moodley, 2007: 13). This individualized internalized culture is what becomes significant psychologically (Ho, 1995, cited in Arthur and Collins, 2005: 63) and ultimately contributes to the formation of one's identity. If all these discursive practices are influential in the personality make-up of the individual, then it seems reasonable to assume that in counselling a client who chooses to disclose one or more of their multi(ple) cultural identities, in different moments and movements in therapy, is undertaking this process to answer ontological and existential questions (Moodley, 2003).

The representation, presentation and interpretation of one's identity in therapy is complex, and a number of variables may act and interact together to produce a particular transference relationship. But how do culture and the interplay of multiple identities influence the therapeutic alliance and the therapist's ability to engage with the consciousness of the 'Other'? Will being black, or deaf, or gay or lesbian with a therapist depend on the client's or therapist's ethnocultural history, the presenting problem, the therapist's personality or the therapeutic approach? It seems likely that in addition to a balance of these factors, the client's own multivariate and individual culture acts in an elaborate manner to create the unique identity that is conveyed and perceived.

In *Counselling – The Deaf Challenge*, Marian Corker (1994) discusses an American study on identity which found that 87 per cent of black deaf people who were questioned about their 'double immersion' identified as black first and deaf second. Those who identified as deaf first were largely from deaf families and residential school background. She suggests that as a result of the focus on black cultural history as opposed to deaf cultural history, many black deaf people have a reduced emphasis on deafness. It may also be indicative of the complexity by which race is understood within the deaf community in terms of internalized disabilism, sub-cultural racism and projections of 'Otherness'. This seems to be evident in all the sub-cultures of the 'Other'. For example, Coyle et al. say, 'Research on lesbian and gay men from ethnic minority communities has highlighted the ways in which the particular voices of these groups have been ignored or downplayed within much existing work on lesbian and gay sexualities' (1999: 140–41). There appears to be evidence (at least anecdotally) to suggest that accusations of 'otherness' are levelled against and within these subgroups. For example, the blacks accuse the Jews of being racist, the gay and lesbian community accuses black men of being homophobic, and many others. Such gross generalizations are not only erroneous and dangerous but also tend to reinforce the myths of stereotyping of each other, which are often perpetuated by the dominant hegemonic social classes (Moodley, 2003).

In terms of the hierarchy of social and cultural identities, Kearney (1996) argues that class remains the dominant position in relation to gender or race. However, in 'Pushing against the wind: the recognition of lesbians in counsellor training', Crouan has this to say:

> Highlighting homophobia and heterosexism in counselling training is not meant to imply support for the notion that a hierarchy of oppressive experiences exists, with one group being any more or less deserving of attention and support than another. (1996: 36)

Clearly, there seems to be no hierarchy of identities when we compare and contrast the ways in which the different disadvantaged groups see themselves. As social and cultural categories, race, gender, class, disability, sexual orientation, age and religion have evolved as important signifiers to differentiate and mark out particular spaces for individuals and groups to assert their social, cultural and political 'rights'. As epistemological tools, these categories have been useful in extending the discussion and debate mainly on the critique of hegemonic masculinities, cultural imperialism, racism, sexism and homophobia. In this respect, Marxist–socialist ideas, feminist studies, black consciousness, disability movements and gay and lesbian movements have shifted the debate away from the corridors of intellectual theorization and political platforms to the realities of social policies and their consequences on the personal and psychological lives of people. They have also provided us with the necessary vocabularies to articulate difference critically and not be content with difference as separate and unequal (Moodley, 2003). As Kuper argues,

> Difference multiculturalism is in-ward looking, self-regarding, pumped up with pride about the importance of a particular culture and its claims to superiority. Critical multiculturalism, in contrast, is outward looking, organised to challenge the cultural prejudices of the dominant social class, intent on uncovering the vulnerable underbelly of the hegemonic discourse. (1999: 232)

In counselling, although these categories are not constructed consciously to divide and subdivide human beings in any hierarchical way, they can become problematic when perceptions and conceptualizations create ambiguous and confusing responses, thus leading counsellors and psychotherapists to be unknowingly essentialistic, sometimes falling into the ideological traps of stereotyping negatively. Sashidharan (1986) reminds us that when concepts such as race, culture and ethnicity take on politically loaded meanings, they become powerful tools in the hands of psychiatrists, counsellors and psychotherapists. People's life experiences become reduced to racial, ethnic and gendered categories which appear to fall neatly within the clinical competence of the culturally informed practitioner (Moodley, 2003). When this happens, culture becomes the site within which the counsellor looks for the clinical problem, which can lead to overlooking the structural dimensions of contemporary discriminatory practices. The treatment is then isolated from the day-to-day struggles – racism, sexism, homophobia, disabilism, ageism – of the client.

Therapy and therapists' attitudes towards the 'Other'

Empathy is widely accepted as a critical element in building a close therapeutic alliance. Cultural empathy is a skill that allows therapists to 'understand accurately the self-experiences of clients from other cultures' (Ridley and Udipi, 2002: 318), which must include those borne of oppression. If the therapist is able to transcend the boxes within which s/he finds her/himself and enter the space between persons ('the third space') (see Moodley, 2007, for discussion), by listening attentively and gathering information about the client's self-experience, then s/he may be able to 'put the pieces of the story together as a means of seeing the client from his or her own frame of reference' (Ridley and Udipi, 2002: 320). Biases on the part of the therapist can pose a barrier to achieving cultural empathy for members of marginalized or minority groups and ultimately understanding the experience of the 'Other' (Murphy, 2009).

The very little research that has investigated the attitude of counsellors and psychotherapists towards the black, the disabled, the gay, the lesbian and the working class seems to indicate that negative reactions are shown to certain of these subgroups. For example, on lesbian, gay, bisexual, transgender and queer/questioning issues, Hayes and Erkis suggest, 'The combination of client sexual orientation and therapist homophobia has been found to predict negative reactions to homosexual clients' (2000: 71). Although a substantial amount of non-pathologizing literature has been produced on gay and lesbian issues, since the removing of homosexuality as pathological by the American Psychiatric Association from its *Diagnostic and Statistical Manual* in 1973 (Coyle et al., 1999), the practice of counselling with gay and lesbian clients still appears to be failing in terms of an authentic anti-discriminatory process. The problem, according to Irigaray, lies with some of the earliest writers in this field. For example, in *Speculum of the Other Woman*, Irigaray (1985) critically examines Freud's, Lacan's and other psychoanalytic work for being phallocentric. In a later work, she argues that Freud

> interprets women's suffering, their symptoms, their dissatisfactions, in terms of their individual histories, without questioning the relationship of their 'pathology' to a certain state of society, of culture. As a result, he generally ends up resubmitting women to the dominant discourse of the father, to the law of the father, while silencing their demands. (Irigaray, 1991: 119–20)

Robinson and Howard-Hamilton (2000) also argue that the devaluation of women is ingrained in culture, which according to Harkins et al. (2008) can result in psychological distress for women through their acceptance of a lower status role. Apart from those of Freud, some of the theories of the other 'founding fathers' (*sic*) have also been critically examined for their basis in male-dominated ideology. For example, Dalal (1988) is critical of some of Jung's writing (see also Thomas and Sillen, 1972: 239).

In addition to having negative attitudes about sexual orientation and gender, there is also evidence that counsellors do not always deal competently with the subject of religion (Banks, 2003). Religion in a therapeutic context is an important factor to consider, as 'research shows that the chance of encountering an individual in counselling who has religious beliefs is high' (2003: 101). This perspective is supported by Helms and Cook (1999), who assert that most individuals who partake in counselling are spiritual and possess some moral code that governs their behaviour. Cook and Wiley (2000) recommend bringing a client's religion or spiritual belief systems into therapy and working openly with a client's beliefs rather than allowing them to become an implicit barrier to the therapeutic process.

Religious and spiritual beliefs are ingrained in culture and contribute to the multiple identities of people (Fukuyama et al., 2008). Inasmuch as religion widely holds extreme importance in the lives of clients and that religious beliefs are inextricably entwined with their personal belief systems, according to Banks (2003), clients rarely raise religion in therapy. This is not surprising when one considers that, in general, counsellors tend to be less religious than clients, and as with other aspects of cultural difference, 'religious differences may be dismissed, ignored or minimized by counsellors' (2003: 100). The need for reflexive practice is emphasized for therapists who must beware of their own values influencing the process to the extent of therapy becoming a 'proselytizing activity' (2003: 107).

In general, counselling has been critiqued for being Eurocentric, ethnocentric, individualistic (see Moodley, 1999), middle-class (see Kearney, 1996), generally focusing on heterosexual issues, and in practice for promoting the YAVIS effect (clients who are perceived to be young, attractive, verbal, intelligent and single) (see Holmes, 1993). Furthermore, as a 'talking cure' with an emphasis on the analysis of the 'utterances of distress' through the speech act(ion), counselling relegates other cultural forms of communication to the margins, for example, British sign language of the deaf (see Corker, 1994). Therefore, it seems that counselling practice has been contained by a particular cultural history, a medical objectivity and a clinical subjectivity, which on the surface appears to be liberal, flexible and creative but can also be experienced as oppressive for black, working-class, disabled, gay and lesbian clients. These clients may sense that they have become the crucible, the containing object, where the heterosexual, middle-class, white unconscious is equated with the consciousness of the 'Other'. In terms of race and ethnicity, post-colonial writers such as Said (1978) and Fanon (1952 [1967]) have also critiqued the negative function of the Western European ego which projects on to the 'Other', 'the dark continent', its anxieties and tensions. This expression of the Western European collective projection is textualized in the pseudo-scientific racism which informed the theories of mental (ill) health during in the 19th century (see Thomas and Sillen, 1972).

As a way out of this dilemma, counselling has begun to include issues of race, gender, religion, class, disability, age and sexual orientation in its theory and practice. But each of these inclusions seems to follow a fairly 'straight' and monocultural process, namely, for blacks and ethnic groups there is cross-cultural or inter-cultural counselling, for gay men there is gay counselling, for lesbian women there is lesbian therapy, for some women there is feminist therapy, for the deaf person there is deaf counselling, and many others. In this particular way individuals are grouped, stereotyped and marginalized. Each occupies a social, cultural and political space within which the psychological needs of its members are deemed to be met. Or are they met? Undertaking a critical and developmental analysis of the present practice of counselling for each disadvantaged group is essential to the future of counselling (Moodley, 2003).

Comprehending the complexity of multiple identities

In the social and health sciences, with the exception of psychiatry, psychotherapy and psychoanalysis, the categories race, gender, religion, class, disability, age and sexual orientation appear to be highlighted in research, theory and practice. Counselling appears to fall between these two worlds. On the one hand, with its history of psychotherapy and psychoanalysis, it has tended to avoid or rather emphasize metapsychology and the internal world, while on the other hand, with its roots in education and social sciences, it has always refused to beckon to the call of the unconscious to stay silent about the social and the cultural condition of the client. Yet the only way for counsellors to engage with the categories of race, gender, religion, class, disability, age and sexual orientation has been to separate, isolate and deconstruct them individually so as to contain them therapeutically (Moodley, 2003).

This construction of separate categories has been effective up to a point. The specific labelling of race, gender, religion, class, disability, age and sexual orientation has allowed each of the oppressed groups to find their own socio-political and psycho-cultural voice within the dominant discourse of therapy. But counselling and therapy is more than a social, cultural or political strategy. For therapy to be organized and delivered primarily around the classification of the 'Other' can, in the long term, lead to further oppression. For many disadvantaged clients, it seems that when it comes to their pain, discomfort, distress and illness, these tend to disappear in the interpretation and analysis in therapy and are replaced by the sociology of race, gender, religion, class, disability, age and sexual orientation. These psycho-cultural identities can initially act as variables within mental (ill) health but eventually construct themselves as the source of the problem. This point is also argued by Fernando, when he says 'Cultures that are different become cultures that are problematic, pathological, inferior' (1988: 155). So, for example, the Asian woman in an arranged marriage, the culture shock of an asylum seeker, the 'coming-out' of the final year student, or the dreadlocks of the rapping Rastafarian can be seen as pathological, and counsellors and therapists tend to 'home in' on these issues when the client is understood solely and exclusively within the 'big 7' categories (Moodley, 2003).

Can therapy in its present state comprehend the complexity of being, for example, black, gay, Buddhist, working class and deaf? The answer must be a 'Yes', because as the individual chapters in this volume testify, there is a concern by the professionals that these issues be addressed in counselling. But what of the above hypothetical client? Can the practice of counselling offer a space for these voices? Is the theory sophisticated enough to accommodate the subtle nuances, multiple metaphors and the complex experiencing of a client who chooses to represent all these identities in therapy? If not, then counsellors may find themselves 'hearing (multiple) voices' and not knowing what to make of it. Their only recourse is to find theoretical security in the psychiatrist's fourth 'bag of (diagnostic hat)tricks' (DSM IV) to pronounce the client as having multiple personality disorder, schizophrenia or some other medicalized identification and label (Moodley, 2003).

For counselling to incorporate both the visible and invisible disadvantages, the external and internal voice, the social and the psychological presentations of 'self', the theory, training and the research in this field must accept the idea of multiple identities and pluralities of the self. At this juncture, where the discourse of counselling advances its practice – innovative research methodology, theoretical epistemologies, practice insights – we may find that counsellors can move beyond the singular categories of race, gender, religion, class, disability, age and sexual orientation to one which incorporates the complexity of all these experiences. For example, a black client would not be offered 'multicultural counselling' but rather a 'new multi(ple) cultural therapy', a critical multicultural and diversity psychotherapy (see Moodley, 2007).

If therapists are to 'work' with, through and beyond their cultural, racial, ethnic, sexual, class differences and offer an authentic anti-oppressive practice, then this must be supported by research, theory and training that is inclusive of all aspects of race, gender, religion, class, disability, age and sexual orientation. Practitioners must also be aware that they themselves could easily reproduce the oppressive structures that clients are experiencing (Moodley, 2003). Wilson and Beresford, who examined anti-oppressive social work practice, had this to say:

> We have seen little to indicate that proponents acknowledge their *own* political role within the structures and apparatus of the 'anti-oppressive' machine. By this we mean little acknowledgement that anti-oppressive theorists and practitioners may *themselves* be contributing to oppressive constructions and definitions of service users and their problems *however 'anti-oppressively' they claim they are operating.* (2000: 558; italics in original)

Therefore, reconstituting and redefining the multi(ple) cultural descriptors of counselling may be necessary, although we are aware that emptying out the (multicultural) crucibles may not be entirely possible or desirable for some clients at a particular stage in their therapy. It must be acknowledged that an exclusive focus on any singular issue of race, gender, religion, class, disability, age and sexual orientation is sometimes inevitable, to allow for 'containing objects' of 'cultural inheritance' (Winnicott, 1971) to surface and find meaning in the client. For example, on issues of race, Janet Helms maintains that 'It is by no means clear that the same competencies required to deliver effective services to clients for whom racial group membership is central are equally appropriate for clients for whom Other social identities (for example, gender, age, or religion) are more central' (1994: 163).

Complexity of experiencing and expressing multi(ple) cultural oppressions

Consider the client who may want to discuss issues of race but finds it problematic therapeutically. The client may find it more comfortable or psychologically strategic to use the language, vocabulary, linguistic codes, the epistemologies of gender as a way to engage with the issues of race and ethnicity. This was seen with Mary (not her real name), who was in therapy with a black woman counsellor and who found it difficult to initially accept the counsellor (Moodley, 2003; see Moodley and Dhingra, 1998 for a complete case study and discussion):

> *Mary*: When I first realised that you are different race to me. I did think she can't be able to help me you know she, eh, especially, I used to live in, a big Asian community around a big Asian community in (...) and they were so very different to me.

The strategy that Mary adopted in accepting her black counsellor and being able to talk about issues of race, culture and ethnicity was to employ the notion and the vocabulary of gender. For example:

> *Mary*:   ... but I do feel you understand me
> *Counsellor*: Um
> *Mary*:   I feel understood as a woman

Counsellor: Um

Mary: When especially a lot of my issues in patriarchal society in and stuff like that and I feel you understand me. I can trust you.

To examine race as a variable in therapy can sometimes create a disturbance or turbulence of the unconscious for the client, or the therapist, or both. In a newly emerging relationship, with its sensitive and delicate boundaries, the process of counselling may not be able to contain the contradictions and paradoxes which a discussion on race may bring. So the 'safe' way to engage in therapy for this client is to speak from 'outside' the preconceived ideas and notions of race in counselling, but inside the culture of gender (Moodley, 2003; see also Moodley, 2005). Race then becomes more acceptable because gender provides it with a particular set of vocabularies and epistemologies and linguistic resonance which can be 'held' in the Winnocottian sense. This 'holding environment' gives both client and therapist time to converge to a point of knowing that it will be 'safe' to discuss the questions, issues and traumas, in this case of race, but the same could be applied to gender, religion, class, disability, age and sexual orientation (Moodley, 2003).

We present a second scenario in which discourse within a single dimension of identity (gender) may help the therapist connect with the client, this time as a conduit to a core issue related to religion. Identities based in gender and religion intersect in that gender role messages 'often have inflexible religious overtones [and] affect people's notions of appropriate conduct in relationships' (Robinson and Howard-Hamilton, 2000: 256). Pressures on individuals to conform to gender stereotyping and emerging role conflicts or 'discrepant perceptions between what one is and what one should be' can all result in psychological difficulties (Harkins et al., 2008: 192). Tina (not her real name), a client from a traditional Filipino Catholic family, seemed to exemplify this. She adhered to the research showing that clients tend not to bring up religion in therapy (Banks, 2003), although religious overtones did surface in the material during session (e.g. awaiting punishment). Through examination of issues related to gender role socialization, ideas about male and female attributes became woven into the fabric of Tina's narrative (Murphy, 2009).

For this client, using gender as an entry point to religion led to a rich description that indicated an identity that was firmly rooted in her role as a loving and supportive wife to her (neglectful) husband. Catholicism conveys strong messages about the sanctity of marriage and for many Filipinos and those of other ethnic origin shapes a culture that rejects divorce, often in the face of stark inequities between the sexes (see Yodanis, 2005). This philosophical framework likely presented the prime basis for conflict in this client, faced with imminent divorce despite futile efforts to save the marriage (Murphy, 2009). Again, in focusing the discussion on the 'safe' subject of gender, the dialogue proceeded unimpeded while exercising caution in addressing the religious implications of divorce, a subject that the client was as yet unready to explore.

In theory, working empathically in such a way allows for the multiple layers of a client's 'self' to be privileged and navigated by the client in concert with the therapist. To address the earlier question of whether an authentic therapeutic relationship can be experienced without one or the other of the client's identities being marginalized, potentially resulting in further oppression of the client, the level of collaboration between the client and therapist must be considered a factor. In addition, determining the best course of therapeutic action (homing in on the identity factor with which to engage) indeed requires a formidable level of sensitivity and skill on the part of the counsellor. This approach is contrasted with the stereotyped, trans-historical and bio-medical model which appears to be the norm in counselling.

Conclusion

To explore the interconnections between and amongst various forms of discrimination and oppression in counselling with the 'Other' client, counsellors must not only be multicompetent in the areas of race, gender, religion, class, disability, age and sexual orientation, but also, and more importantly, examine some of their deep-seated prejudices and biases, which is not easy or comfortable to do (Moodley, 2003). According to Robinson and Howard-Hamilton, 'if the counselor is uncomfortable, a typical response is to ignore, discard, or discourage communication' (2000: 112). In the interest of anti-discriminatory/anti-oppressive practice, it is precisely this tendency that must be resisted by the therapist in order to foster growth in multicultural competence.

In examining the multiplicity of identities and their role in experiencing oppression, we argued against the existence of a hierarchy among categories for individuals, which would garner the support of those opposing multiculturalism of difference (e.g. Kuper, 1999; Johannes and Erwin, 2004) and moralistic culturalism (Dalal, 2006). Corker (1994), who reports race as taking precedence over disability in the black community, and Kearney (1996), who emphasizes the importance of class, have submitted evidence to the contrary. In our exploration of the complexity of multiple identities, two vignettes were portrayed to illustrate the uniqueness of an individual's identity make-up and the delicate way the therapist can navigate the layers of identity in respect of the sensibilities that may accompany them. However, the utility of using one identity (e.g. gender) to access another (e.g. race, religion) raises the question 'If, therapeutically, an entry point is required, does this not suggest that there is an inherent personal hierarchy of identities unique to each client?'

To answer this question, we return to a more macroscopic perspective, recalling the manner of presenting issues that clients bring to the discussion: therapy is seldom about discussing the minutiae of race relations, social class structure and theology. It is rather a focus on problems of individuals who exist in a world which, through the influence of the dominant culture, are manifested in a socially constructed way. Corker's (1994) perspective of differing cultural history for black and deaf groups supports the notion of social influence on identity. It follows that if the forces of politics, economics, science, history and media have engendered a collective consciousness that is uncomfortable with the subject of race (or religion, or sexual orientation), this effect pervades in every arena, most assuredly so in the therapist's office. A client who experiences the distress and acute awareness around one or another of the 'big 7' identities as a result of systemic oppression, discrimination, structural violence or abuse reflects this in his or her suffering.

In therapy, the meaning-making or the (re)construction of therapeutic narratives are dependent on both parties not only accepting and acknowledging each others' differences and similarities in terms of race, gender, class, religion, disability, age or sexual orientation, but also to conducting therapy in a human rights framework within which the client's individual and very personal multi(ple) cultural rights and rites are understood and respected (Moodley, 2003). The level of proficiency required on the part of the practitioner calls for all counsellor education programmes to incorporate a strategic and rigorous component that ensures trainees develop the necessary awareness and skills for navigating client multiple-cultural identities. Only in so doing will counselling and psychotherapy have claim to the hallowed ground of anti-oppressive practice.

References

Arthur, N. and Collins, S. (2005). *Culture-Infused Counselling: Celebrating the Canadian Mosaic.* Calgary: Counselling Concepts.

Banks, N. (2003). Counselling and religion. In C. Lago and B. Smith (eds), *Anti-Discriminatory Counselling Practice.* London: Sage.

Collins, P.H. (1990). *Black Feminist Thought: Knowledge, Consciousness, and the Politics of Empowerment.* Boston, MA: Unwin Hyman.

Cook, D.A. and Wiley, C.Y. (2000). African-American churches and Afrocentric spiritual traditions. In P.S. Richards and A.E. Bergin (eds), *Psychotherapy and Religious Diversity: A Guide to Mental Health Professionals.* Washington, DC: American Psychological Association.

Corey, G. (2001). *Theory and Practice of Counselling and Psychotherapy* (6th edn). Pacific Grove, CA: Brookes-Cole/Wadsworth.

Corker, M. (1994). *Counselling – The Deaf Challenge.* London: Jessica Kingsley.

Coyle, A., Milton, M. and Annesley, P. (1999). The silencing of lesbian and gay voices in psychotherapeutic texts and training. *Changes, International Journal of Psychology and Psychotherapy,* 17(2), 132–43.

Crouan, M. (1996) Pushing against the wind: the recognition of lesbians in counselling training. *Counselling, Journal of the British Association for Counselling,* 7(1), 36–9.

Dalal, F. (1988). Jung, a Racist. *British Journal of Psychotherapy,* 4: 263–79.

Dalal, F. (2006). Culturalism in multicultural psychotherapy. In R. Moodley and S. Palmer (eds), *Race, Culture and Psychotherapy:Critical Perspectives in Multicultural Practice.* London: Routledge.

Fanon, F. (1952 [1967]). *Black Skin, White Masks.* New York: Grove Press.

Fernando, S. (1988). *Race and Culture in Psychiatry.* Kent: Croom Helm.

Fukuyama, M., Sevig, T. and Soet, J. (2008). Spirituality in counseling across cultures: many rivers to the sea. In P. Pedersen, J. Draguns, W.J. Lonner and J. Trimble (eds), *Counselling Across Cultures.* Thousand Oaks, CA: Sage.

Harkins, A.K., Hansen, S.S., and Gama, E.M.P. (2008). Updating gender issues in multicultural counseling. In P. Pedersen, J. Draguns, W.J. Lonner and J. Trimble (eds), *Counselling Across Cultures.* Thousand Oaks, CA: Sage.

Hayes, J.A. and Erkis, A.J. (2000). Therapist homophobia, client sexual orientation, and source of client HIV infection as predicators of therapist reactions to clients with HIV. *Journal of Counseling Psychology,* 47(1), 71–8.

Helms, J.E. (1994). How multiculturalism obscures racial factors in the therapy process: comment on Ridley et al. (1994), Sodowsky et al. (1994), Ottavi et al. (1994), and Thompson et al. (1994). *Journal of Counseling Psychology,* 41: 162–5.

Helms, J.E. and Cook, D.A. (1999). *Using Race and Culture in Counselling and Psychotherapy.* Boston, MA: Allyn & Bacon.

Ho, D.Y.F. (1995). Internalised culture, culturocentricism and transcendence. *The Counseling Psychologist*, 23, 4–24.

Holmes, J. (1993). *Between Art and Science: Essays in Psychotherapy and Psychiatry*. London: Routledge.

Irigaray, L. (1985). *Speculum of the Other Woman*, trans. G.C. Gill. Ithaca, NY: Cornell University.

Irigaray, L. (1991). *The Irigaray Reader*. Oxford: Blackwell.

Johannes, C.K. and Erwin, P.G. (2004). Developing multicultural competence: perspectives on theory and practice. *Counselling Psychology Quarterly*, 17(3), 329–38.

Kearney, A. (1996). *Counselling, Class and Politics: Undeclared Influences in Therapy*. Ross-on-Wye: PCCS Books.

Kuper, A. (1999). *Culture*. Cambridge, MA: Harvard University Press.

Lorde, A. (1984). *Sister Outside: Essays and Speeches*. Tramansburg, NY: Crossing Press.

Moodley, R. (1999). Challenges and transformations: counselling in a multicultural context. *International Journal for the Advancement of Counselling*, 21(2), 139–52.

Moodley, R. (2003). Double, triple, multiple jeopardy. In C. Lago and B. Smith (eds), *Anti-Discriminatory Counselling Practice*. London: Sage.

Moodley, R. (2005). Outside race, inside gender: a good enough 'holding environment' in counselling and psychotherapy. *Counselling Psychology Quarterly*, 18(4), 319–28.

Moodley, R. (2007). (Re)Placing multiculturalism in counselling and psychotherapy. *British Journal of Guidance and Counselling*, 35(1), 1–22.

Moodley, R. and Dhingra, S. (1998). Cross-cultural/racial matching in counselling and therapy: white clients and black counsellors, *Counselling. Journal of the British Association for Counselling*, 9: 295–9.

Moodley, R. and Lubin, D. (2008). Developing your career to working with diversity. In S. Palmer and R. Bor (eds), *The Practitioner's Handbook*. London: Sage.

Moodley, R. and Palmer, S. (2006). Race, culture and other multiple constructions: an absent presence in psychotherapy. In R. Moodley and S. Palmer (eds), *Race, Culture and Psychotherapy: Critical Perspectives in Multicultural Practice*. London: Routledge.

Murphy, L. (2009). Multiple identities in counselling practice: case study analysis. Unpublished paper. University of Toronto.

Ridley, C.R. and Udipi, S. (2002). Putting cultural empathy into practice. In P. Pedersen, J. Draguns, W.J. Lonner and J. Trimble (eds), *Counselling Across Cultures*. Thousand Oaks, CA: Sage.

Robinson, T. and Howard-Hamilton, M.F. (2000). *The Convergence of Race, Ethnicity and Gender: Multiple Identities in Counseling*. Englewood Cliffs, NJ: Prentice-Hall.

Robinson-Wood, T. (2008). *The Convergence of Race, Ethnicity and Gender: Multiple Identities in Counseling* (3rd edn). Englewood Cliffs, NJ: Pearson, Merrill Prentice-Hall.

Said, E.W. (1978). *Orientalism*. London: Routledge and Kegan Paul.

Sashidharan, S. (1986). Ideology and politics in transcultural psychiatry, in J.L. Cox (ed.), *Transcultural Psychiatry*. London: Croom Helm.

Thomas, A. and Sillen, S. (1972). *Racism and Psychiatry*. Secaucus, MJ: Citadel.

Wilson, A. and Beresford, P. (2000). Anti-oppressive practice: emancipation or appropriation? *British Journal of Social Work*, 39(5), 555–73.

Winnicott, D.W. (1971). *Playing and Reality*. London: Tavistock.

Yodanis, C. (2005). Divorce culture and marital gender equality: a cross-national study. *Gender & Society*, 19(5), 644–59.

15 Critical Thinking

A first step towards good practice in training

Gail Simon

> I act not simply 'out of' my own plans and desires but in some sense also 'into' the opportunities offered to me to act, or else my attempts to communicate will fail or be sanctioned in some way. (Shotter and Gergen, 1989: 144)

To work sensitively and effectively with and across difference requires a shift from thinking about people as individuals with an internal world in focus to a view of a person in a social world, as members of families, of social, religious, professional and cultural groups and communities. It is not enough to focus on the history of *one* life when we are all products of different times, significant episodes in history and affected by what is happening with current inter-personal, employment, political and economic issues. Counselling and psychotherapy training needs to be open to addressing the real world influences on people coming to therapy and to therapeutic training courses. Unless we find ways of doing this and extend the world-in-focus of the people we meet, then we are colluding with the mono-culturally produced theories which have not taken into account differences in life experience and the place of power in the world.

In addressing anti-oppressive training, this chapter is going to cover three main issues:

- How to encourage trainees and trainers to become critical thinkers and decentre normalising and mono-cultural theory.
- How to approach our learning regarding differences in lived experience and the place of power in training and therapeutic relationships.
- How we approach talking, describing and positioning in therapeutic conversation.

It is probably clear to most trainers that there needs to be coherence between the teaching methods and the counselling practice being taught. However, we are often less mindful about the reflexive relationship between training and practice. Training is not a one-way street where trainees are taught by their institutions. That would simply reproduce an existing, unchanging culture. Trainees and tutors have a lot to teach institutional discourses and expand the range of narratives we can draw on.

This is a chapter about training relationships. The first people who come to mind might be the trainer and the trainee, but I'm including some others too. The peer training group of which the trainee is a member plays a significant part in a person's learning and wellbeing. I'm including the staff team for the course and for the institution who perform a similar role for the trainer. We are always in conversation with the authors of the papers we read, too (Montuori, 2005).

Hearing our experience described by others: time for a new way of theorising

Sometimes, people see examples of inclusive practices at work in counselling and psychotherapy training and assure themselves that as a professional community we have arrived, that we are inclusive, positive about difference and equal; indeed, that we are now a 'we'. There are several problems with this set of conclusions. First, many trainees and trainers feel they cannot comfortably be themselves in their training institutions while the discourses are dominated by mono-cultural values and practices. Second, while some courses have made good progress, many post-graduate counselling and psychotherapy training courses are still not recruiting and maintaining trainees from oppressed and marginalised groups in numbers which reflect the communities in which they are based. Furthermore, members of oppressed and marginalised groups often report not feeling part of a 'we' and hold back on sharing aspects of their identities with their peers so as to preserve parts of themselves and their relationships with peers (Simon, 2010).

The concept of 'equal opportunities' has, for the most part, been interpreted in training through recruitment. However, it is perhaps naïve to separate out admissions policies from the core theories an institution promotes. Perhaps we can afford to be more open to exploring the consequences of different theories? Theories are not truths. They are stories – products of specific times, places, cultures and agendas.

We are still experiencing the fall-out of centuries of dominant groups writing about others. These stories have at times become theories with powerful social consequences. In critiquing the colonial history of anthropology and ethnography, Kamala Visweswaran points out that, sooner or later, the subject always writes back (Visweswaran, 1994). Inaccurate stories about people, about communities, have often preceded the infliction of abuses such as exclusion, misrepresentation, withdrawal of liberties, disbelief, deprivation, violence, theft, punishment, murder, incarceration, enforced migration, pain and more. Their voices must be louder in our ears than the misinformation which has lead to injustices and atrocities against fellow human beings. We may even have a part to play in the recognition and facilitating of real life stories.

It was only in the late 1990s that several psychoanalytic training institutes agreed (under pressure) to offer training places to lesbians and gay men. By asking direct questions about their sexual experiences, prospective lesbian and gay trainees were assessed during admissions interviews for their potential to be encouraged into heterosexual relationships with the aid of their training analysis. Why did they have to experience this abuse and why were they refused admission to the academy? Because the theory taught by these institutions was based on normative models of development which theorised 'homosexuality' as an indication of unhealthy development and deviance. So while public opinion forced these institutions to change their admissions policies, their theories have to a large degree remained intact. Can we guess the experiences of lesbian and gay trainees in these institutions? I spoke to a trainee.

Trainee: Can we keep this, um, anonymous? Okay, thanks. Generally speaking everyone is very friendly and welcoming. I'm in a good group. But I can see that we all struggle when we read the stuff about 'homosexuality'. I struggle because everyone expects me to have an opinion (I'm the only gay man in the group) but I don't want to be characterised as oppositional – and that's what I would be if I spoke my mind. Well, I do speak my mind and a couple of people, straight people, in the group, also critique the theory, but I feel, um, so exposed, and the silence of others sometimes sounds like 'Who are you to be challenging Freud?' There is one person at least who thinks like that. He is quite anti-gay.

Author: How does your tutor handle that?

Trainee: Oh, she's very nice. I like her. But ... she doesn't say very much at those times. She looks reflective. Like she's thinking and processing what's going on in the group. I often check for signs to see what her position is. If she doesn't say anything, I can feel a bit of a social and theoretical freak!

Author: And after the seminar?

Trainee: Mostly, I have lunch with three or four others. But the week we did 'homosexuality' I went off by myself. Needed some space, some air, to remember who I was. Rang a friend. I didn't want to hear anyone say that they wished they had spoken up. But I felt kind of worried that if I didn't have lunch with them, then it would add to their discomfort.

Author: What did happen?

Trainee: Actually, something nice. As we were going back into the room after lunch, my friend Jane said to me, 'I think we could make better theory than this listening to people on the street.' I felt her despair and we spoke about it all on the phone later that evening.

Exercise 15.1 Where are you in this scenario?

Before you read on, take a few minutes to hear your own ideas about what you think is going on in the example above.

- Create a relational picture in which you imagine the different people in the scenario and what each of them might be feeling or thinking and how that might impact on their behaviour.
- Can you connect the issues in this example to other scenarios in your own training courses?
- Which characters do you identify with in this scenario?
- Who can you speak to about your feelings, thoughts and their impact on the choices you feel you have in that kind of situation?
- What is it that facilitates or blocks you developing new or alternative strategies?

Knowledge and know-how

Language is a cultural and social creation. It lives in communities as opposed to individuals. Through communication with others, people develop stories about themselves and about society which, at times, can act as constraints. People are recruited into dominant discourses that exist to maintain the imbalance of power in the world (Foucault, 1991 [1975]; White, 1991). The narratives available to us influence our sense of who we are in the world. Some stories carry more weight than others. Who is allowed to tell which stories or to use certain terms? What counts as *knowledge* and how does that link with what we might call *know-how*?

Therapists have been invited in to a more reflexive way of 'knowing' with the shift into postmodernism and its critique of universal truths and cover-all theories (Burr, 1995; Gergen, 1985; Leppington, 1991). We inevitably act out of our own deeply held beliefs, our cultural bias, our family's narratives and our own life experience. We are likely to choose a therapeutic approach that fits with our values and beliefs. There is a danger we can get over-attached to theory and try to make it fit across the board. Some schools of counselling and therapy have had the idea (encouraged by traditional academic ways under the influence of modernist thinking) that there is a fixed set of ideas which must be taught, learned and made easy to assess; a solid body of knowledge which will:

- guide us in how we do what we do with people; and
- tell us what we need to know about people.

The impossibility of being able to learn about everyone and every single way of working with people can push us towards making generalisations, creating overarching theories and unrealistic expectations of ourselves, our trainees, our trainers and, of course, the people coming for therapy. And to manage the impossibility of those expectations, we create theories for the exception to the rule – resistance, deviance, abnormality, psychosis, not ready for counselling, and so on – which excuse the limitations of the counsellor, supervisor or trainer and pathologise the trainee, supervisee or people coming to therapy.

When practitioners ask for training on 'how to' work with a particular group of people, they are looking for skills to apply globally to any one group of people – who may not really be the same as each other at all. Kitzinger (1987) warns us against seeing people who are different to us as the same as each other. And sometimes, people from minority groups fall into the trap of going along with that story: 'Well, you know what lesbians/black men/us oldies are like ...'

The danger of using one-size-fits-all theory is that it is expected to transcend all the varied life experiences people have, the historical, social and political influences which have contributed to making them who they are and what they bring to the conversation. It is so important to hold in mind that *it is the counsellors and the people coming for therapy who make theory.* The texts we live by need to be living texts. By living, I mean they need to have *resonance* for all parties in a training or therapeutic relationship. Theories should change and grow as much as the people with whom we are working, be it in a training or a therapeutic context. The stories we hear from people tell us how rich in resourcefulness people are. Trainees and trainers are well placed to develop and elaborate on existing theory. After all, the trainees of today are to be the custodians and elaborators of our living practices.

This can only truly occur in a culture committed to deconstructing its own ideology. 'Many teachers are disturbed by the political implications of a multicultural education because they fear losing control in a classroom where there is no one way to approach a subject – only multiple ways and multiple references' (hooks, 1994: 35). Can we afford to have 'trainees' (or worse still, members of the public) running the institution, or would institutions risk losing control over their identity? Krippendorff suggests that undoing oppression might be better undertaken by individuals:

> Undoing power, getting out of dialogical entrapments is a challenge that individuals have to create for themselves. Artists know it. Therapees come to realize it. Revolutionaries do it. (1995: 125)

Figure 15.1 shows how institutional theory can impact on community narratives. Where reflexivity is encouraged at all levels of context, changes in therapeutic narratives would as much arise out of social conversation as out of professional conversation.

hooks advocates an approach to teaching which encourages students to think critically about whatever subject matter they are presented with or come across: 'To engage in dialogue is one of the simplest ways we can begin as teachers, scholars, and critical thinkers to cross boundaries, the barriers that may or may not be

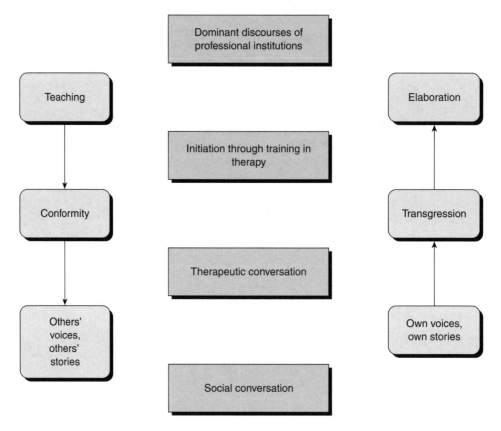

Figure 15.1 The influence of therapy in communities

erected by race, gender, class, professional standing, and a host of other differences'
(1994: 130). Freire (1972) and hooks (1994) critique the banking system of knowledge, which requires learners to hold on to knowledge until the time comes when
they need it, then they can get it out, use it and put it away again.

If we choose or are encouraged to position ourselves as the knowledgeable,
expert fixer in relation to a person's problems, then we are likely to hear the texts
of others over and above the voice of the person coming for therapy. While we can
respect the sources of the theories, we can afford to be irreverent enough to use,
change or discard theory when we have respect and usefulness to others at the
forefront of our minds. People in therapy or therapy training can be encouraged to
develop a sense of active, critical ownership of theory – not feel they are expected
to passively absorb and worship an inherited set of relics. Texts are conversational
partners, not gods.

It can be helpful to ask ourselves what knowledge about a particular social or
ethnic group of people can be useful inasmuch as you may have some awareness
of the social, historical and political influences on the culture; it might be useful to
have some idea of geography of a country or region, of religious or spiritual beliefs,
the significance and timing of festivals; policies affecting people; stories about

aspects of their life experience as understood within their own families and communities. Understanding the differences between Punjabi and Urdu may allow you to speak without discomfort and communicate a respectful attempt to know something. 'A postmodernist position allows us to know "something" without claiming to know everything', says Laurel Richardson. 'Having a partial, local, historical knowledge is still knowing' (1994: 518).

What choices do we have about how we acquire that knowledge? Do we ask people directly to tell us about their culture, their family's life experience? Do we read books – fiction and non-fiction? Do we spend a week imagining a particular person's experience of accompanying us around our world in terms of access, legibility, imagery, spoken language, sense of safety and know-how, information needed, finances, choice, being noticed, dress code and so on? And if we imagined following them into their world?

Exercise 15.2 Your own identities and life experience

With your training group or team, consider these points.

- Talk to each other about how you describe your membership of different groups in society.
- When or with whom do you feel one aspect of group membership more than another?
- What sorts of things do you feel a counsellor or psychotherapist would need to know (or unknow) about the different groups of which you are a member in order to work with you?
- What kinds of displays by a counsellor/psychotherapist of familiarity with your life experiences and group memberships would work for you or alienate you?
- What do you find helpful in orienting others to your language, terminology, dealing with their knowing and not knowing, challenging their myths and stereotypes?

We need to remember that a person's description of an experience will vary depending on the context in which the conversation is being held, depending on who is asking the questions, what is being asked, and the consequences of the conversations in and for the broader context.

Training courses cannot equip students with all the knowledge they will need, but they start off your learning and hopefully give you confidence and an excitement to want to learn more.

Professors who expect students to share confessional narratives but who are themselves unwilling to share are exercising power in a manner that could be coercive. (hooks, 1994: 21)

That means that teachers must be committed to a process of self-actualization that promotes their own well-being if they are to teach in a manner that empowers students. (hooks, 1994: 15)

Exercise 15.3 Resourcing your learning needs

With your training group, work through the following.

- Try to identify gaps in your own knowledge about groups with whom you are likely to be working.
- Which groups of people are you most likely to get to know? What gets in the way of you acquiring further knowledge for other groups?
- List the resources about difference life experiences and group memberships the course has.
- What resources can the institution, your workplace, your social life offer?
- How are the life experiences and group membership of the course and institutional staff used? When life experiences and different opinions are shared, give a detailed response of how they were greeted.
- What sort of responses might you want from talking in this group about some of your own life experiences or those of your family, group or community? How might you react if you did not get those responses?

Summary: encouraging critical thinking

- There needs to be an evolving and reflexive relationship between personal experience and theory.
- Individuals who challenge theory need visible or audible support from their peers and trainers in order to combat isolation and invite more aspects of a trainee's life experience into the course.
- Trainees who speak about aspects of their personal and social experiences are making a great contribution to the learning of others. We need to acknowledge that while they are speaking as well as afterwards so they know how what they are saying is being received.
- Trainers have a central role to play in creating a culture in a training group in which everyone feels safe to express themselves.
- Trainers need to invite trainees to be critical thinkers and recognise that learning arises as much from conversations with peers, people in therapy and others in their lives as from curriculum texts.
- Trainers can feel torn in their allegiance to the theoretical beliefs of the institution and the emergent critical thinking of trainees. Institutions can support tutors by encouraging a more fluid relationship to the development of theory and practices.
- Alliances with people who understand where you are coming from are necessary for survival until a group or institution can hear and act on what people are saying about their lived experience.

Connecting across difference

What does difference mean to us? And why does it matter? How much should we acknowledge differences in lived experience?

Trainees often ask 'Should I acknowledge to the client that my ethnic origins are different from theirs?' This can be a useful prompt for a broader conversation in the training group. On the one hand, such an intervention could be experienced by the client as clumsy or objectifying. They could be surprised at you focusing on that one aspect of themselves which they feel has little to do with what they want to focus on. On the other hand, sometimes it can help to open up differences in lived experience so we can create some space for the impact of culture on our understanding of a person's experience.

After a talk at a conference about listening out for differences in lived experiences, a group of women gathered and spoke in animated tones about their experiences on training courses. There was a strong sense of 'we', yet 'we' were speaking of quite different life experiences from each other yet we understood something of each other's experiences despite the differences.

Dualisms dominate everyday ways of speaking and thinking. Concepts such as black/white, old/young, lesbian/gay, disabled/able bodied are understood as characteristics belonging to the individual. Difference is not something which exists so much as socially constructed.

> Descriptions and explanations of the world are themselves forms of social action and have consequences. Different descriptions and explanations have different consequences. (Gergen, 1985: 268)

Sexual categorisation, for example, is seen by Foucault as an invitation to participate in self-regulation and he suggests that 'homosexuality' has been constructed as pathology in the history of psychological discourses. So should we name difference? And how should we name it? One quick answer is to ask people what terms they want to use in this setting. People may use some terms with their peer group or in their community group but not in their training group or with a therapist. Terminology does not just have different meaning, its usage may need to be earned. So how does one bring the richness of cultural stories into therapeutic conversation while at the same time recognising the particular stories of each individual, family or social circle?

Jill felt that Jacinta was feeling conflicted in telling her about an episode of abuse which had happened as a child. Jill had a hunch that Jacinta may feel conflicted as a black woman about speaking with a white woman about abuse which she had experienced in her family, in her community. Jill drew on an idea that Jacinta may not feel safe to talk about people and values important to her while Jill was an unknown quantity to her.

Exercise 15.4 How might you respond?

Which of these responses would you choose? Discuss them with someone from your group.

- You lay a hand on Jacinta's arm and say 'It's okay. I have friends who are from the Afro-Caribbean communities and who were disciplined harshly as children.'

(Continued)

(Continued)

- You ask Jacinta if she would prefer to see a counsellor who was also Afro-Caribbean.
- You tell Jacinta that sometimes people are cautious about telling a counsellor about their experiences in case the counsellor feels critical of their family or their community.
- You ask Jacinta what you could do to make the telling of her story easier.
- You choose to say nothing.
- You ask 'What might be important for me to know about you, about your family, about your cultural background?'
- You ask 'What sorts of things can I tell you about me, about my ideas that will help you to tell me about your experiences?'

Re-centring experience

The task of training institutions is to centre it own discourses while encouraging trainees to both consider and decentre them. Decentring the therapist, the theory and the institution creates a space to hear the voices of others whose experience is not mirrored by existing texts.

Therapists can learn to act as a connector, to find ways of bridging differences in lived experiences. Rather than try to fit the client into ready-made theories, therapists can listen out for new stories by trying to explore the identification of and with others. In creating opportunities for bringing in other voices identified with the client's circumstances, the therapeutic focus shifts from the personal to the social sphere. The therapeutic relationship comes into its own as a microcosm of larger communities of conversation.

These are examples of connecting questions:

- Instead of the therapist interpreting, invite the others in a similar situation to interpret: *'What would they suggest is going on for you?'*
- Instead of the counsellor reflecting back their understanding to the client, you could ask *'How do you think other members of the Polish community who have been living in London for three years might sum up the dilemma you are facing? What might they be able to guess how you are feeling?'*
- Instead of the tutor exploring the basis for the beliefs of the trainee, you could ask 'Who, in all the world, would see things the same way you do?', 'What would they make of the theory we have been looking at today?'

Here are some more examples of questions which situate the experience of the client(s) or trainee(s) against a backdrop of others with similar experience:

- What sorts of things would other older lesbian couples who understood your sense of alienation from the mainstream heterosexual communities say your strengths were as a couple?

- What would other new couples who are attempting to share the parenting of teenage children suggest is going on for the two of you at this point in time? What would they say you need to do?
- If you were writing a handbook for other dual heritage, heterosexual single women living in a mainly white rural environment, what would you be including as chapter headings?
- Do you think there are any people in the whole universe who you think would have managed this predicament well?
- If we were to ask 50 other Moslem–Jewish couples living in the UK which parenting differences they found easier to negotiate and which they found more difficult, what do you think they would say?
- What would it be like for you if you could talk to other men who had lost their parents at a young age and who also went through a break-up of their marriage later in their life and had to live apart from their children?
- What might other people who have recently moved to this country as asylum seekers be able to guess about how you are both feeling at this stage in your relationship, with one of you fulfilled in their work and the other feeling utterly deskilled?
- If you were in a training course with 20 other women trainees who were all from Northern Ireland, how would the talk be different to what happens here? What would be enabling about being in that group, and what might be restricting?

- If we could bring together all the black counselling trainees in the UK to discuss how they cope with the implicit invitation in their training to be a 'nice', non-threatening black person, what sorts of characteristics would there be in the group which you might want to carry around with you when at your course?

We believe that postgender practice must be active, in that therapists recognize themselves as mediators between the client(s) and the larger society, and as individuals who play a role in relation to social change. (Knudson-Martin and Laughlin, 2005)

Conclusion

Developing anti-oppressive practice starts with the training course – not as a module in *how-to-work-non-oppressively* but through the relationships established and modelled during the course. Training is not just about helping people connect up theory and practice; it is living the experience of listening and responding to meet people's needs without prejudice and, in so doing, ensuring inclusivity. We need to create coherence between the values found in counselling relationships and those in training relationships. It is plain good practice in which the opinions and needs of trainees and trainer are heard and responded to with respect.

Readers of this chapter have been invited to:

- collaborate with others to find ideas and theories which work for them;
- step outside of the textbooks and invent context specific practice as needed;
- put not-knowing to work – not knowing about differences need not be a hindrance;
- develop better and better reflexivity. Ask yourself 'How are these ideas connecting for people? Which stories open up possibilities and which close them down?';
- examine your own prejudices, your most taken-for-granted assumptions, your inner dialogue, and allow yourself and your theories to be cha(lle)nged in the conversation;
- turn up the volume on your own voice so others can hear your reactions when you hear things that don't fit with your experience – and expect support for this courage; and
- show support for each other's efforts to bring lived experience into a discussion of theory. Noise counts. Silence doesn't.

References

Burr, Vivien (1995) *An Introduction to Social Constructionism*. London: Routledge.

Foucault, Michel (1991[1975]) *Discipline and Punish: The birth of prison*. Harmondsworth: Penguin.

Freire, Paolo (1972) *Pedagogy of the Oppressed*. Harmondsworth: Penguin.

Gergen, Kenneth (1985) The social constructionist movement in modern psychology. *American Psychologist*, 40: 226–75.

hooks, bell (1994) *Teaching to Transgress: Education as the practice of freedom*. New York: Routledge.

Kitzinger, Celia (1987) *The Social Construction of Lesbianism*. London: Sage.

Knudson-Martin, Carmen and Laughlin, Martha J. (2005) Gender and sexual orientation in family therapy: Toward a postgender approach. *Family Relations*, 54(1). 101–15(15).

Krippendorff, Klaus (1995) Undoing power. *Critical Studies in Mass Communication*, 12(2): 101–32.

Leppington, Rozanne (1991) From constructivism to social constructionism and doing critical therapy. *Human Systems: the Journal of Systemic Consultation and Management*, 2: 79–103.

Montuori, Alfonso (2005) Literature as creative inquiry: Reframing scholarship as creative process. *Journal of Transformative Education*, 3(4): 374–93

Richardson, Laurel (1994) Writing: A method of inquiry. In *Handbook of Qualitative Research*, Denzin, Norman K. and Lincoln, Yvonna S. (eds). London: Sage.

Shotter, John and Gergen, Kenneth J. (eds) (1989) *Texts of identity*. London: Sage.

Simon, Gail (2010) Self-supervision, surveillance and transgression. *Journal of Family Therapy*, 32: 308–25.

Visweswaran, Kamala (1994) *Fictions of Feminist Ethnography*. St Paul, MN: University of Minnesota Press.

White, Michael (1991) Deconstruction and therapy. *Dulwich Centre Newsletter*, 3: 21–40.

Index

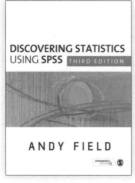
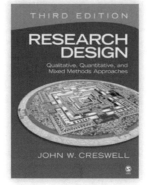

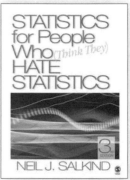

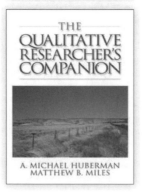